# THE QUR'AN
# AND
# THE WEST

*Kenneth Cragg*

**GEORGETOWN UNIVERSITY PRESS**
**WASHINGTON, DC**

*The Qur'an and the West*
GEORGETOWN UNIVERSITY PRESS, WASHINGTON, DC, 2006

Simultaneously published by Melisende, London, England

As of January 1, 2007, 13-digit ISBN numbers will replace the current
10-digit system
Cloth: 978-1-58901-086-4

LIBRARY OF CONGRESS CATALOGING-IN-PUBLICATION DATA
Cragg, Kenneth.
    The Qur'an and the West / Kenneth Cragg.
      p. cm.
    Includes bibliographical references and index.
    ISBN-13: 978-1-58901-086-4 (cloth : alk. paper)
    ISBN-10: 1-58901-086-8 (cloth : alk. paper)
      1. Koran—Criticism, interpretation, etc. 2. Koran—Commentaries.
3. Koran—Study and teaching—Europe.  I. Title.
BP130.4.C715 2005
297.1'226—dc22

                                                          2005027685

10 9 8 7 6 5 4 3 2 1                              2006

*Printed and bound in England*

# CONTENTS

| | | |
|---|---|---|
| | INTRODUCTION | 5 |
| 1 | A DEEP DIVIDE IN A SINGLE SITUATION | 14 |
| 2 | HUMANS WHO OCCUPY: NOT GODS WHO OWN | 27 |
| 3 | LEGITIMATE SELFHOOD | 38 |
| 4 | 'WHISPERINGS IN THE BOSOM' | 50 |
| 5 | THE VITAL POINT OF THE SECULAR | 66 |
| 6 | THE BURDENED SIGNIFICANCE OF WORDS | 78 |
| 7 | WHERE THE HEART HAS ITS REASONINGS | 94 |
| 8 | THE ONUS OF NECESSARY SHAPE, ART AND RITUAL | 107 |
| 9 | THE TABLE AND THE MEMORY | 122 |
| 10 | JOURNEYING THE DISTANCE | 139 |
| 11 | DIVINELY LIABLE POLITICS | 155 |
| 12 | OUR HUMANLY LIABLE LORD | 173 |
| | AFTERWORD | 192 |
| | GLOSSARY | 204 |
| | QURAN CITATIONS | 213 |
| | BIBLICAL REFERENCES | 217 |
| | INDEX OF THEMES | 218 |
| | INDEX OF NAMES AND TERMS | 229 |

بِسْمِ اللَّهِ الرَّحْمَٰنِ الرَّحِيمِ

الْحَمْدُ لِلَّهِ رَبِّ الْعَالَمِينَ الرَّحْمَٰنِ الرَّحِيمِ

مَالِكِ يَوْمِ الدِّينِ إِيَّاكَ نَعْبُدُ وَإِيَّاكَ

نَسْتَعِينُ اهْدِنَا الصِّرَاطَ الْمُسْتَقِيمَ

صِرَاطَ الَّذِينَ أَنْعَمْتَ عَلَيْهِمْ غَيْرِ الْمَغْضُوبِ

عَلَيْهِمْ وَلَا الضَّالِّينَ

In the Name of God, the merciful Lord of mercy.
Praise be to God, the Lord of all being,
The merciful Lord of mercy,
Master of the Day of judgement.
You alone we serve and to You alone come we for aid.
Guide us in the straight path,
The path of those whom You have blessed,
Not of those against whom there is displeasure,
Nor of those who go astray.

# INTRODUCTION

The Qur'an, as the founding and defining Scripture of Islam, makes intriguing reference to 'two Easts and two Wests'. It is alluding to the two extreme points in the changing incidence of sunrise and sunset between winter and summer.[1] Our current century might find a strange foresight in the phrase, the two hemispheres by so many factors tied into each other. The West is forcibly present everywhere by dint of its commerce, its media and its language. There is a significant Muslim presence in a diaspora far from its birth-territory.[2] 'One East and one West' has become a very antiquated formula.[3]

This single consideration should have given pause to the frequent 'Islam and the West' language in recent analysis of current affairs and the grim aftermath of September 11 2001. *Foreign Affairs* gave an odd twist to its title in publishing the forebodings of Samuel Huntington about an inevitable confrontation between two crudely cast identities.[4] The versatile

---

[1]  Surah 55.17. The context is about celebrating the sundry aspects of the natural order which should evoke responsive gratitude and wonder in the human soul. 'How can you deny them?' it is asking like any psalm. The translations vary, some with 'Lord of the two Easts/Wests', others 'the twofold East/West'. Here, is a worship alert to the horizon in careful observation. 'Lord of the sun's risings' comes in 37.5, with 70.40 noting 'the rising and setting places of the planets', while 50.39 bids Muhammad sing Allah's praise in face of hostile calumny 'before the rising and the setting of the sun'. The Arabian day gave ample occasion to know the drama of both and of Allah as 'Lord of all between'.

[2]  By one estimate no less than one quarter of all the world's Muslims are outside what their long tradition would call *Dar al-Islam*, i.e. where Islam holds political power. Their presence in the West requires them to devise ways of being 'a minority culture'—an entirely novel situation both for theory and practice.

[3]  It is sad that Rudyard Kipling's lines have been so long quite misquoted. 'O East is East and West is West and never the twain shall meet ...' The next line tells of a kinship of courage that made nonsense of the alleged divide.

[4]  In that any such inevitable, and ominous, 'clash of civilisations' was far from being 'a foreign affair'. Its alleged menace had made it a crucial domestic issue on which would hinge that all engrossing business—'the security of the American people'. The issue of *Foreign Affairs* was Vol.73, No. 3, 1993, pp. 22–49.

'and' in his formula will add or multiply, relate or confuse, at the whim of the reader. 'Life and death' is a different contrast from 'thought and idea'. There are 'ands' that inter-penetrate as well as those that antagonise. Relationships destined to do the former are not well joined by willing the latter. It is part of the hope of being 'justified by faith' that one does not foreclose it by starting from antipathy.[5] The psychic factor here would suggest the same attitude as any ripe theology. Enmities are never faced by assuming them fated or pregnant with doom.

'The Qur'an and the West' offers a better formulation of whatever odds there are and it is the purpose of these chapters to substitute it for the other, the Qur'an being the crucial text in which to encounter Islam in its own recognisances. Its contents, if duly consulted with a 'Western' mind, are apt for our education. Muslims can assess for themselves the fitness of the chosen passages, so that there is no exercise of vested interest or bias and all is subject to scrutiny. The vital ones are given in their native Arabic—not for any annoyance to non-Arabists but only because, for the Muslim, that Book and this language co-exist. The proposal is to explore their meaning as both elucidating the textual Islam and addressing what most pre-occupies the mind of the West, whether of suspicion, apprehension or the finer instincts of hope and goodwill. There is a case-making in the Qur'an (and therefore for it) well calculated to reward those instincts and to allay the apprehension, provided that it is patiently understood and realistically pursued.

Truly horrendous and catastrophic as the attack on the World Trade Center was, both for its audacity and its awesome media-relaying to the whole watching world, it was wrong to proclaim forthwith a 'war on terrorism'. The phrase adopted misread the situation. To speak of 'terrorism' is to concede that one can be 'terrorised'. To announce 'war' in answer is to take the adversary on his own showing—and to his advantage. The malignity in the perpetrator is faced on its intended terms of provocation and, to that extent, confirmed in its hostile stance.

It would have been saner to summon goodwill anywhere to a 'World Order against Criminal Conspiracy'. That would have been naming

---

[5] That New Testament phrase, source of so much fervent debate during the middle centuries, belongs even in the realm of social and political things. 'The measure we offer is the measure we are likely to receive,' whether of answering anger or a foregoing of it. It is a sort of positive *lex talionis*, of like rewarded with like, where we can hope to abate conflict by not assuming we must keep it raging. This, between persons or nations, is much more than 'the soft answer'. It runs risks for the gains of deliberate hope.

the deed for what it was and with a descriptive that did not infer in the crime a strategy in which one conceded one could be trapped. Such implied concession invited a continuance of the strategy as having, that far, already succeeded in gaining recognition—by the other party—of its depraved intent. The language of pursuing a criminal would have avoided that pitfall. There was, to be sure, much talk of 'bringing them to justice', but that is done more aptly by a powered jurisprudence than by armed belligerence. The distinction is by no means artificial, least of all if there is any viable concept of international order, as there has been for many decades. The 'war' alternative may well be proved non-winnable, given the nature of the scenario and the resources of current technology.

In the immediate trauma of bewildered anger and appal, a policy of 'A World against International Crime' would have needed the utmost control of leadership and a discipline of will perhaps impossible in an unwieldy and grief-torn democracy. Even so the soundness of its wisdom could have gained it hearing. With such an acumen, in the quieter days of the early 19th century, President John Quincy Adams had said:

> America's heart ... goes not abroad in search of monsters to destroy. Once embroiled in foreign wars of interest and intrigue, the fundamental maxims of her policy would insensibly change from liberty to force. She might become the dictatress of the world: she would no longer be the ruler of her own spirit.[6]

In those terms—as President Adams saw them—'of her own spirit', response to September 11 2001, would have meant, not, 'anti-terrorist war' but 'anti-criminal action' on two fronts, the one political and the other spiritual, a common venture in crime-policing and an effort after human sanity which took up the promise as well as the menace of religion.

The former was, in part, meant in and by the 'war' policy. Truly no 'anti-criminal action' can be taken without power. Something forcible proves inseparable from the stability of peace, long after its attainment. This means a readiness on the part of those so equipped to bring their capacity to bear on the situation which requires its potential. Yet it must also mean its closest possible bonding into international auspices so that, in its vital

---

[6]  Cited from *Connections*, London, Vol.7, No.3, 2003, p. 20., The date was Independence Day, 4 July 1821, before John Quincy Adams was elected president.

availability for these, it does not appear, or intend, to supersede them. If doing so, it risks compromising the role it has toward crime, with designs it has toward a war of self-interest. Impatience with the international order, however galling to those who afford the sanctions it needs, has to be curbed by the constraints of genuine co-operation and of shared commitment to its necessity. The procedures may be cumbersome but they are less frustrating than what follows when unilateralism overrides them—as the Iraq War has proved.[7]

The lack of a convincingly inclusive internationalism in the 'anti-crime action' will generate suspicion of ulterior political and economic motives present. From such suspicion will develop, in turn, a sense of distrust which jeopardises the theme of crime-requital and may supply a propaganda incentive for the criminality. Or, negatively, it will not exonerate the other party from charges already against it. The United States has struggled with its problem, of 'why do they hate us so?' and set up advisory commissions to explore it. In measure, September 11 had already given the clue—that 'World-Trade-Center' with that 'Pentagon' the chosen targets. How disenchanted, how reprehensible, they seemed in angry and envious eyes. 'Trade' the engrossing sinew of a money-having 'world': that 'world' having its alleged 'center' there, on both counts a triumph of pretension fit to be struck down. Why should such concentrated vested interest be so proudly equipped with the resources of a global dominance? In the tensions of cultures one has to reckon with the psychic yearning of human collectives to have 'something to hate'.[8] The grounds may be fictive and the harbouring insane, but the menace and the malignity are no less real.

Hence the need for the response that, curbing the will for reproach or despair, takes up the spiritual struggle for a sanity of mind where envy might learn its own lunacy and disown its hate. That religions, by their own inner constraints, are prone to insanities is evident enough

---

[7]  In that Iraq's borders have been made far more open to suiciding action, than they had ever been before the war, and that invasion of a Muslim territory served to stimulate a Muslim will to retaliate, thus reversing the antipathy earlier prevailing between such fighters and the 'Islam' of the Ba'ath regime. Far from countering *Al-Qa'idah*, the war only further confirmed its incentive and widened its occasions.

[8]  That was all too evident when the Russian 'evil Empire' and its 'Communism' filled the role in the Reagan era, when there was 'trading' of mutual anathemas in harshly political terms. There is something seductive both ways in the art of reciprocal demonisation.

down the centuries. Islam is no exception and by factors for which we need a discerning care is more prone than some.[9] Fanaticism and obscurantism are not healed by being merely deplored or rebuked. The anxieties they shelter have to be patiently allayed. The factors that induce them need to be resolved. There are bigotries that stem from fear—fear of guilt under a taskmaster, of treachery to an only sanctioned truth, of what may be aspired to beyond death—or devoutly found retrieved from it, of loneliness in a non-vicarious world.[10]

Such is the nature of these burdens of selfhood that they are best shouldered by the ministries that begin in and from the faith their bearers hold. On every ground both of psyche and of Scripture, this is so. What hallows and dignifies Islam is from its own sources, what weighs upon Muslims of religious stress must be relieved in their own context. Islam belongs to Muslims and Muslims to Islam whether in the joy of assets or the register of debits, if such are the terms we use. Muslims need and want to be Islamically secure and secured. The terms of their present inner crisis belong with their historic inter-possession of faith by faithful, of truth by troth. Wise relationship from outside must, therefore, learn to come within. It would be spiritual imperialism to think to serve Islam with Western wisdoms or alien prescripts.

Hence the purpose here to care about an aberrant Islam, from which the menace comes, by caring with the Islam that can and must disown the other. That there is high tension between them with the Qur'an as party to it, cannot be in doubt. There is a dimension of harsh belligerence in the Qur'an, a strong pugnacity on behalf of faith. Its being there can perhaps be explained by the situation in which Muhammad's mission was embroiled by the obduracy of his local audience. The legacy of that

---

[9] Many factors in its origins, its Scripture and its story contribute to the characteristic self-assurance of Islam. They emerge in the chapters that follow, especially 6, 7, 8 and 11. What 'seals' all prophethood, enjoys 'final revelation', fits human nature and is 'religion as Allah would have it,' has scant reason for diffidence about its warrant to prevail.

[10] 'Lonely' in that the Qur'an's portrayal of 'the Last Things' lays such stress on the solitary individual, without all mediation, no plea about collective factors inseparable from private guilt, and one's own physical members witnessing to one's condemnation. The frequent refrain of the Qur'an as to 'No burden-bearers bearing other than their own burden' seems to exclude the whole dimension of the vicarious in human life. True as 'no burden-bearing' must ever be about guilt in wrong, it can never be true about the 'bundle of life' where the guilt of crime in one party means suffering and grief in another. See discussion more fully in my *A Certain Sympathy of Scriptures*, Brighton, 2004, Chapter 8.

militancy abides but can well be offset or abandoned by considerations no less explicit in the same Qur'an. These we are set to examine, in company with contemporary Muslims who know their crisis—the crisis between the two 'minds'—for what it is.

It will be long and hard to resolve. For it bifurcates the *Sirah* as well as the Qur'an and has its symbol in the sequence of both from their Mecca to their Medina. The sense of legitimate belligerence came with the sinews that availed for it after the Hijrah. Yet that Hijrah supervened on thirteen years of powerless faith-care which might be likened to the first three centuries of New Testament Christian faith. Muhammad foreclosed these in forceful power, as if to be his own—and immediate—version as Islam's 'Constantine', and thereby seeming to abrogate the Meccan 'innocence'. Thus the pivotal decision had the sanction of his own doing and came to be embedded—as Constantine has never been—in the founding Scripture of the faith.

Conditioning all that the Hijrah validated, however, was the priority of the preached message in Mecca, for which sake alone the Medinan sequel was ventured.[11]

The issue with which historic Islam is thus left can only be contained by Muslims as an ever present crisis of options about its very enterprise, the pith and marrow of its meaning in the human scene. The belligerence will always remain as a will to dominate and Islamise the world, to pursue that in which alone its fidelity consists. It will be pointless for observers to opine that such 'is not Islam.' A duty-bound ardour will negate the negation and think itself the only obedience a Muslim can bring. To think to counter *this* Islam in terms of 'war' will make the war interminable.

The global hope has to belong with the Islam of Muslims who, with no less ardour, no less Quranic warrant, will define—and be defined by—the other Islam, the peace-held Islam that first was, and ever remains, the *raison d'être* of the whole, the Islam to which, in the Qur'an, Muhammad was rigorously bound as only 'a preached summons' to submission to Allah. Since that preached religion has survived these

---

[11] The sequel soon proved that Mecca held its honour as the place of *balagh* by the turn around of the *Qiblah* from the Jerusalem it had initially obeyed to Mecca and its Ka'bah. The whole logic of the ensuing campaign lay in its recovery. The exit from it had been no mere adventurism but a strategy on behalf of its preached significance.

fifteen centuries into a day for global order, what was once *a* rationale for recourse to armed belligerence is quite superseded. Armed partnering of faith-conviction has become incongruous. The ongoing finality to which Islam lays steady claim must know it so. A faith that holds with entrusted creaturehood and guiding prophethood can, in the present world, have no place for 'compulsions' to belief, such as armed religions seek to bring. That Allah is 'not overtaken'[12] is only proven by their repudiation in a world whose contemporary peace calls all religions to be satisfied only to persuade in their first, original, intent.

Such is the case to be drawn from the Qur'an as its axiom for the very presence of Islam now in the world. The situation of many Muslims in a diaspora where they lack explicit Islamic statehood confirms it. The chapters that follow are set to underscore it further—Chapter 5 stressing a right measure of 'the secular' and Chapter 11 arguing that this 'solely religious sanctioning of religion' means no desertion from the duties of the political order. Chapters 1 to 4 rehearse the founding themes, while 6 to 8 reflect the vital art of Scriptural exegesis and possession.

No enterprise like the present with 'the West' and with the Qur'an could neglect the expressly Christian bearings of either in relation to the other. These, fraught with so much impeding and self-frustrating controversy, are compressed into two salient territories in the Qur'an, which bring them imaginatively as well as doctrinally into the necessary focus. The final Chapter 12, in sequel to *our* divinely liable politics, takes up 'the human liability of God', as being the central themes of both Scriptures. They invite us to the worship of One for whom all our human meaning reaches, as His creaturely trustees with whom He shares that trusteeship through the ministry of prophethood, the investment in our privilege. The question presses, in the light—or the dark—of accumulated human history, whether that 'sharing' goes beyond investment in privilege into a more costly relation still and be the more divinely known through the story and the imagery of 'a man of sorrows, acquainted with grief'.[13]

We may be sure that, of late years, the Qur'an has been more urgently consulted in the West than, outside academic circles, was the case

---

[12] The phrase in Surahs 56.60 and 70.11—*ma nahnu bi-masbuqin*. Whatever the verses may mean in context, they certainly express the absolute finality of Allah and the ultimate revelation in the Qur'an. A never out-dated timeless is assured.
[13] Isaiah 53.3 and the 'Servant' in the measure of the Messianic role, which to the mind of the Qur'an as Sunnis read it, is either incomprehensible or repugnant to a right theology.

earlier. But has the access of new readers meant a readier comprehension? For the Qur'an has a way of disconcerting its beginners. There is the hurdle of its cherished Arabic and the problematic of due translation where the native feel is forfeit. The current flow of new English renderings can often confuse, though it may excite comparison. Then there is the problem of chronology and sequence. The identifying of surahs as Meccan and Medinan indicates a relevance for timing, but surahs may sometimes be composite astride that radical divide, while their actual order defies the chronological principle. The new reader, like any Arabist, does well to begin with what, in the West, would be the end of the book. For the earliest passages in Muhammad's mission, being highly poetic and ecstatic, now comprise the surahs with which the Qur'an closes. It is no bad plan to read inwards from Surah 114 and reach Surah 2, via a still non-chronological sequence, into the more protracted legal language of institutional formation. The narrative of his *Sirah* will be latent everywhere, as are the Qur'an's own perceptions of history, Biblical and pagan.

Aside from such areas of the cohesion of the Qur'an, there are the problematics of style, so that Muhammad's preaching, renewed as it had to be through long and tense years, entailed much re-iteration of its essential themes. Moreover the 'piecemeal' pattern (17.106) of its receiving 'on his heart' (see Chapter 7 within) made for a kind of 'spiral movement' forward quite unlike a Socratic 'dialogue' or the disquisitions of an Aquinas.[14] The alert reader, however, can with patience find this situation yielding its proper fascination. That may serve to check a sense of confused impatience to which frustrated readers have succumbed, either in haste or dismay.

In present context, as in no way academic but seriously relational in minding current history, the vital thing is to appreciate the decisive concern of Quranic theism with the stature of our humanity exercising 'a divine right of kings' (or queens) whereby we are only safely and sanely ourselves as 'dominion'-conscious both ways, neither self-preening gods,

---

[14] The 'dialogue' in the Qur'an—if seen to be compatible with the classic thesis about *wahy* or 'inspiration' in Muhammad—is with the hostile charges the Quraish made against him. These left no occasion for the *tadabbur* that was his hope and plea. The suqs of Mecca and the terrain around Yathrib were no Socratic garden. The Qur'an reader has to inhabit that original scene in the will to comprehend.

nor hapless puppets, but accountable divinely for the time of our mortality and the cosmic 'sacrament' of our creaturely 'privilege'.[15] The Qur'an and the West rightly read each other in those terms once—as a poet said in another context—you have 'walked the length of your mind.'[16]

---

[15] 'Privilege' in the strict sense of *privilegium*—a special advantage uniquely granted and enjoyed, a dispensation to possess a status and fulfil the role it bestows. We understand theism truly when we perceive the truth of our own humanism. See below Chapter 5. 'While 'sacrament' is not a word congenial to Islam, its meaning as 'minding all as holy' is there in the concept of 'signs' enabling, the human 'caliphate'.

[16] Philip Larkin, *Collected Poems*, London, 2003, p. 177, 'Continuing to Live'. His meaning seems to be life's quest for 'necessities' proves ill-rewarding and deters further venturing. It seems possible to use the term here, away from his weary private sense, to see the need for 'minding the length' our thinking has to 'walk' with present world 'necessities' and 'trace them home'.

# Chapter 1
# A DEEP DIVIDE IN A SINGLE SITUATION

A mirror faced a mirror: ire and hate
Opposite ire and hate: the multiplied,
The complex charge rejected, intricate,
From side to sullen side ...[1]

The poem is about Ireland early last century but might well echo some passions of some versions of the now familiar formula: 'Islam and the West'. The deep divide is there, though only malign thinking makes it blindly and fatally so, seeing that warped and garbled images have been its shaping. Soberly, the mutual indictments might be intelligently disarmed. Sharpening the formula to 'the Qur'an and the West' gives us better hope of doing so. For the Qur'an has much that could bring a better discretion to Muslim assessments of the West, and also a strong potential to disabuse Islam of venomous misreadings of it. That hope has to enthuse and control all the chapters that follow.

Yet, meanwhile, the facing mirrors have their mutual grimaces. There was fierce anger alike in the deed and the symbol of that fateful day in September 2001. There has been anger in the reaction of a proud and wounded nation, conscious of the power it brings to confrontation. 'Security' has been its insistent pre-occupation, with fears about 'weapons of mass destruction' wielded in roguish hands, and a responding decision to assert the right of 'pre-emptive action' in any direction where that roguery is suspect. The yearning for 'security *from*' feeds upon its own fears as if to make its satisfaction ever more elusive.[2] Meanwhile 'security *in*'

---

[1]  Alice G Meynell, *The Poems of*, London, 1940, p. 169. She is writing of Ireland and the long-running 'troubles'.

[2]  George W Bush would do well to recall the theme of his presidential predecessor, F D Roosevelt: 'There is nothing to fear but fear itself.' Certainly apprehensions can fuel themselves.

turns upon feasible perception of a single world and diversities humanly co-existing.

There is a crucial passage in the very earliest part of the Qur'an—one that breathes a constant yearning that recurs throughout—to which we do well here to turn. It is about 'security', 'security' linked with doubt, that 'modern crown of thorns',[3] and with suspicion, of which there was often occasion in the time of the Qur'an and Muhammad's situation.[4] So it is apposite to look at how the Qur'an handles 'insecurity', by what recourses it solves it and in what context.

First, however, there is need to note an intriguing point about the grammar of Arabic. Grammar and theology have often been compared as disciplines which keep all their regulations in their own power, to which users must defer.[5] Arabic requires that its most honoured word, Allah can never be 'possessed', that is, 'governed' by something else as in Paul's Greek *Ho Theos tes hupomones,* or *Ho Theos tes elpidos,* or Peter's *Ho Theos tou Kuriou humon Iesou Christou,* 'God of patience,' 'God of hope,' 'God of our Lord Jesus Christ'.[6] God, Arabists say, is never thus 'in construct' with another. For to belong this way is to be somehow less than uninhibitedly Allah, as 'over all things Almighty'. To speak, then, of 'the God of love' one must call up another word *ilah* and say: *Ilah al-mahabbah. Ilah* is the common noun, which is pluralised in *Alihat* (as Allah never can be), and occurs in the confession of faith *La ilaha illa Allah,* 'there is no deity except Allah', that *la* of absolute negation.

Hence, if one wants as a Muslim to say: 'The God of all humankind', *Allah al-nas* being forbidden, one must say: *Ilah al-nas,* which is precisely what Surah 114 does:

---

[3] T E Lawrence: Introduction to C M Doughty, *Travels in Arabia Deserta*, London, 1923 ed., pp. xx-xxiii.

[4] *Zann* against Muhammad was frequent on the part of the sceptical Quraish resisting what they saw as his 'pretensions'. Witness the exchanges: 'They are saying ... so Say thou ...' concerning their charges of 'alien factors',' rhyming', madness and disturbing trade and tradition. Later in armed encounter or occasions of feigned 'adherence', there was 'suspicion' of hypocrisy and altercation. *Zann* anywhere is 'great wrong', witness the accent on *ikhlas,* 'sincerity'.

[5] For example, John Henry Newman's *Grammar of Assent.* There is a sense in which syntax is its own law though language is also malleable in the hands of users. The analogy with 'faiths' is obvious either way

[6] Romans 15.5 and 15.13, 1 Peter 1.3.

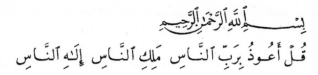

'I seek refuge with the God of humankind', 'of men', of what Marx and Engels called 'the masses', i.e. 'folk in their endless multiplicity'. 'Seeking refuge', known as *ta'widh* in Islam, is a very frequent religious theme and echoes through Buddhism, the Hebrew Psalter and Christian hymnary. It will always have 'with' or 'in' or 'from' as its prepositions, the first a sure place or haven or bastion, the third an enemy, real or perceived.

In the case of Surah 114 (and of 113 also) the 'from' meaning was virtually 'other humans' and their wiles. Its study belongs to Chapter 4 below. Here our concern is only 'with' or 'in'. The surahs' answer, so germane to our circumstance of mind, is 'in and with' the sovereignty of God, under-writing the common human-ness of all mankind. The Arabic verb that takes one preposition for an English two ('with/in') *'adha/ ya'udhu bi* is rich in meaning, if we recall the Biblical 'cities of refuge' for 'fugitives', if we realise the measure in which all people and their cultures are 'fugitive', all of us 'doomed to broken off careers'.[7] The verb means to 'have recourse to for protection', to 'rely upon under danger' and—in that context—to 'entrust oneself to'. Surah 98 has the puzzling injunction to 'seek refuge from Satan when reciting the Qur'an, and elsewhere (7.200) in respect of 'slander' (40.56) vis-à-vis disputings, and (41.36) about those 'whisperings' that concern us in Chapter 4. Some seven times the root comes in the singular: 'I seek refuge' in such situations as Mary's at the Annunciation (19.18), Noah's (11.47), Muhammad's (23.97 and 98) and by the inclusive 'refuge-seekers'—as the surahs themselves are called—113 and 114. There is good reason to apply such *ta'widh* to our contemporary fears and anxieties, so many of which derive from a like capacity of ours for 'ghostly fears and fantasies', if only in suspicions, fears and enmities.

---

[7] Robert Frost, *Collected Poems*, New York, 1964, p. 475, in 'The Lesson for Today'. The meaning of *ta'widh* as reflected in Muslim prayer manuals is best researched in C E Padwick, *Muslim Devotions*, London, 1961, pp. 83–93. Chap. 6.

What is intriguing about Surah 114 is that it places *Ilah al-nas* as the third in a 'trinity' of descriptives by which Allah is also *Rabb al-nas* and *Malik al-nas*, the Lord and King of humankind. We seem to be meant to read and know these capacities on the part of Allah as the solidarity of humanity in such inclusive care.[8]

For all Semitic faith, there has ever been something reciprocal between what we believe about God and what we understand about man, as creature and addressee. Here the emphasis on the divine triad of relation being with us in humankind argues plainly that His unity is the guarantor of *al-nas*, i.e. all of us in an undiscriminating plural. Such is the 'single situation' we are in, as this chapter's heading tells. Allah is 'the One ... in whom we have being and have to do.' Right theology and right humanism belong together. While we must allow a 'beyondness' about His transcendence we can never glimpse or grasp, it will not—in transcending—contradict what the relationality of *Ilah al-nas* for ever denotes. That is the descriptive in which we seek 'security'.

For *al-nas* here means that diversity which, for example, the Biblical John of Patmos feels he must include as voices in his 'Hallelujahs'— 'all peoples, tongues, nations, tribes ...' Surah 114's triple use of the one noun *Ilah* 'annexed' (as grammars say) to the one repeated *al-nas*, brings us all—and none uniquely—under the governance and jurisdiction of Allah as One.

The word *al-nas* derives from the root *anisa*, meaning to 'be friendly, or congenial' or 'mutually gentle' (cf. the English 'kin' and 'kind'). Some 'kindly' bonding of humanity would seem then to follow from God's being their 'Lord and King'. Yet religions have so far contrived to have it otherwise. Our destiny as 'God-possessing' in the sense of *Ilah al-nas* has hardly availed to ensure our one-ness.[9] On the contrary, faiths have so

---

8   The possibility of Christian influence has often been mooted. Archaeology has unearthed inscriptions in this triple form, one used in Egypt in 62 BC by Ptolemy XIII. The Greek *kurios* as applied alike to God and to Jesus, in Christology, was a large factor in the doctrine of the Trinity, as 'exploring' (never contravening) the Unity of God. It transpired, not from abstruse reasoning in some Socratic garden, but to help express experience actually undergone. There is much—as it were—'incarnational' and 'proceeding ...' about God's being 'Carer' and 'King' of humanity. See further, Chapter 9.

9   If 'possessing'—though denied by Arabic grammar—has to be conceded by Muslim worship where 'having no other god' means 'having' the One, as when the psalmist cried: 'Whom have I in heaven but Thee' (73.25). There is no doubt that *Ilah* thrice here in Surah 114 is Allah, only that grammar, not theology, disapproves it. 'There is no God but Thou' is also the cry of the Qur'an (21.87).

fondly bound themselves to empires or nations, exclusifying their several humankinds with Yahwehs, Zeus-es, Theoi, *alihat*, their sundry patrons. From several angles, ethnic, climatic, historical, cultural and linguistic, nations are mandatory.[10] Now, however, it is clear that the 'refuge' they all need, i.e. from one another, in the contemporary world is in transcending themselves politically and morally. The quest for 'security' is at length and at last the quest for world community.

The tragedy of the 'Islam and the West' formula is that it suggests a hemispheric 'block', an uneasy and dubious 'coalition' dominated in every effective sense by one over-weening party,[11] facing what is, thereby, falsely identified as a Muslim 'block' when it posits a contentious reading of 'Islam', its *Jihad* and its *dhikr* of Allah.[12] Hence the concern here to move right away from it by dint of 'the Qur'an and us humans' as the surest way of deliverance from a complete *non sequitur* in the soul of either.

That contentious reading has come to the fore precisely where and when it could be least valid on every count of current global reality and sounder perspectives of the Qur'an. Perhaps the USA has fallen into a snare. The 'War on Terror' language was a mistake from the start, as if concerting an ambush by pre-announcing it. What the proclamation might more wisely have sounded was 'A Quest for World Community in

---

[10] A satisfactory definition of 'a nation' is hard to come by. Perhaps 'any people believing themselves to be one' is as good as any. The Qur'an, in many places, certainly agrees that the factors making for diversity of peoples are Allah-meant and Allah-ordained—and, therefore, divergent cultures all within the doctrine of creation and of creaturehood in it (Chaps. 2 and 3 to follow). The argument also is that *Ilah al-nas*, 'God the people's Lord' makes the same point. Islam is now *de facto* in and among 'united nations', with approximately one quarter of all its 'muslims' outside any Islamic realm or statehood.

[11] The descriptive is not hostile, but obtains as long as the USA wants and maintains that sort of posture. Happily, it is one that is disqualified by the long US tradition once ably commended and exemplified by the late Adlai Stevenson and earlier by George Washington's plea for 'no inveterate hatreds' (as well as no 'passionate attachments') in its foreign relations, or Abraham Lincoln's 'with malice toward none' at Gettysburg, despite the intense domestic divide of that Civil War. *Both* parties in 'the Islam and the West' formula are in crisis about themselves and the world waits for their sanity.

[12] Namely that of a single 'Islam' (see note 13 below) as the only Allah-given realm, i.e. *Dar al-Islam* (in which 'nations' plural are invalid) to be forever inimical to *Dar al-Harb* which it must subdue. Did this 'us and them' syndrome begin with the Biblical 'chosen people' faith as to special covenant, making for 'us Hebrews' and 'those Gentiles'? If so, it was in spite of the fact that the three things making for covenant, i.e. ancestry, land and entry on it (tribe, territory and story), were the common ingredients of all identities. Amos (9.7) knew that Yahweh, being *Ilah al-nas*, gave all folk their exodus and their entries—and their 'forefathers'.

concert with Islam', if 'Islam' was being obliquely recognised as the 'evil' in a confrontation. For all the gestures that were made about 'not against Islam' the actual policy alienated, and by implication excluded 'other' Muslims than those it had in 'war-sights'. Thus it contrived—against it own deepest interests—to obscure the essential crisis enveloping *all* Muslims and doing little to help resolve it.

The Usama bin Laden philosophy demands to speak only of one Islam—its own. It repudiates all 'internationalism' which it decries as no more than American guile and intrigue. He preaches the one 'nation'—the *Ummah*[13]—of Islam, excoriates the capture of Baghdad as once 'our caliphal capital', and exploits Iraqi Ba'athism as the new, unwonted ally of his own *Jihad*.[14] Only a 'coalition's' ill-judgement in the invasion gave him the occasion.

Thus the strategy of 'the West'—if we do not discriminate inside that category—has failed to identify or set forward what was its supreme duty, namely the inner self-definition of Islam in coming through the crisis which Usama bin Laden sets for it. While it is one that only Muslims can resolve, it is well to realise how deeply it is there and that Western attitudes have a part in either accentuating its dangers or aiding its decision. It has also embarrassed relations with the West's own Muslim populations which clearly have a pioneer role to play in how that crisis is concluded, prolonged and complex as the process must be. It is complicated by Western impatience or impercipience of its nature, that a caring and careful attention to the Qur'an could educate and amend.

---

[13] Like Sayyid Qutb before him, Bin Laden admits only the one *Ummah*, of all Islam. So does 'Black Islam' in its 'the nation of Islam'. This is a more insistent concept than that of any 'Christendom' in 'Constantinian' forms through long centuries. It is its new lease of life now in *Al-Qa'idah* that flouts the finality of Islam, as never admitting of current globalism. Insofar as the long Caliphate was the legal symbol of one Islam, it never effectively so operated and after abolition in 1924 has not been renewed. Muslims have been in schism from the outset, stemming from issues around the Prophet's own family. There was a 'mosque of discord' erected in Medina during his own sojourn there.

[14] Until 2003 there was little in common between Saddam Husain as Muslim and *Al-Qa'idah* as Muslim, nor in the origins and story of the Ba'ath Party. Bin Laden also saw Iraq under Saddam as a tool of American interests when he invaded Iran (and its Muslims) yet bids his followers redress that ruler's overthrow by insurgency against those interests in 2004. Bin Laden is simply exploiting the front the US has opened for him across Iraqi borders, now widely porous, which under Saddam were closed to him, at least on the present scale.

Muslims addressing their own vocation need to be enlisted, but only on their own principles, not as if recruited for Western interests. There has been much Western vested interest, political, diplomatic, academic, in nexus with Islam.[15] Its potential to be enlisted, not in the West's cause, but in humanity's and their own, is not in doubt, as these chapters are set to argue. It has to repudiate the *Dar al-Harb* concept about a world which will not be won until it is subdued, as if 'the political kingdom' was the vital pre-requisite of 'having' Islam. That concept has often been mitigated, in response to fact and reality.[16] It now needs to be abandoned for good and all, disowning its universal threat and global conspiracy of hate in surrender to the quest for a community of nations. Far from being a world now fit for the formula (whether Islamic or 'Western') 'Only safe under our hegemony and submissive to our surveillance', its only hope of 'security' is in *Ilah al-nas* whose will to human community must be also ours because of His.

What this might mean can be discerned by thinking on the other two 'constructs' with *ilah* in Surah 114, on Allah as *Rabb al-nas* and *Malik al-nas*, Lord and King. The two terms, coupled with *al-nas*, mean a presiding sovereignty of God in the creation's association with humankind in all areas of that 'summons-to-be'. For it is *Al-Rabb* who is behind all its physical processes, in nature and nurture and *Malik al-nas* whose will must be politically discerned and 'fulfilled'. Was *Malik al-nas*, for example, ever compatible with any *Ahl al-Dhimmah* notion when some of *al-nas* were only 'under God' because Islam took off from them all political responsibility for themselves, as if Allah were only *Malik al-muslimin*?

If people—and peoples—are duly under God in unilateral terms that make them all equally liable, might this not validate the separate

---

[15] A state's 'foreign policies' and thence its 'diplomacy' will always be with a mind for 'the national interest', if with hope that 'interest' may be enlightened. The now famous Samuel Huntington 'encounter' thesis seemed to argue that 'interest' and 'encounter' could not disengage. Academic Islamics in the West have sometimes been duly suspect when government financed, with some more than academic 'interest' in the findings. Edward Said's now famous *Orientalism*, 1970, New York, brought a distorting animus into its portrayal of 'bias' and 'self-mirroring', and did scant justice to the massive contribution of Western scholarship to Islam in the 20th century.

[16] As when, in the middle centuries, the Papacy claimed jurisdiction and concepts like *Dar al-sulh* were used in compromise of rivalry in *de jure* matters, for better *de facto* trade or travel or practical 'tolerance' of the other. See, for example, James Muldoon, *Popes, Lawyers and Infidels*, Liverpool, 1970. 'Capitulations' concessionary to Europeans in the Ottoman empire in the 19th century amended the traditional *Harbi* stance against them.

nationhood *Al-Qa'idah* would disown, and legitimate 'nations', like Nigeria and Egypt, with dual (or more) religious communities and require viable minority status for all citizenry, however small or diverse? *Ilah al-nas* clearly connotes more than *Dar al-Islam* traditionally admits. Accepting so is part of the present crisis, helped as the admission may be by any *Dar al-Gharb* ('Realm in the West') adequately demonstrating the way—which is a significant part of *her* crisis.[17]

Intriguing use was made of *Malik al-nas*, in right reading, in the 20th-century advocacy of the Iranian thinker, 'Ali Shari'ati (1933-1977). He sensed that Muhammad himself had been, as it were, a 'populist', the core of whose prophetic mission was to galvanise his people into true possession of themselves. Translating *Ilah al-nas* as 'God of the masses', he pioneered what might be called a 'laicisation' in Islam, having the people throw off the tyranny of the *'ulama'*, the *mujtahids* and the monopoly they claimed over the interpretation of the Qur'an and the Sunnah. He saw in their foreclosing of a shared *Ijtihad* a major factor in the atrophy of Muslim initiative in response to the radically changing world.[18] More of this issue around religious aspects of academic freedom belongs to Chapter 6. Similar demands for 'the role of the laity' against whatever in religious authority, in 'clerisy', makes them only 'laic', are familiar in religious history elsewhere but Islam has a uniquely difficult experience of them.[19] Should not ordinary mortals monitor their own faith?[20]

---

[17] Insofar as vigilant measures against subversive conspiracies, real or feared or assumed, cast doubt on minority loyalty and brought psychic and social pressure on resident, loyal Muslims as, anyway, suspect also.

[18] Among Sunni Muslims, the concept of *Ijtihad* or 'enterprise' in potential change in Shari'ah, with a view to arousing an *Ijma'*, or 'consensus' that would go along with it, had long been in place. The 'turbaned ones' sought to 'close'—as the phrase went—the 'door' to it on the ground that all such necessary 'initiative' had been taken, thus to exclude the non-experts from 'reserved' territory. The struggle has been to 're-open' that 'door'. The principle stems from a hallowed Tradition that Muhammad's people 'would never converge ('agree') on an error.'

[19] Compare 16th/17th century struggles, long persisting, to lift the clerical monopoly on interpretation of Biblical Scriptures in Europe. The issue of 'laity' among Muslims is more acute because of the disparity—between Bible and Qur'an—in the very nature of the text as 'God's Word'.

[20] For Bibliography on 'Ali Shari'ati see, e.g. *On the Sociology of Islam*, trans. Hamid Algar, Berkeley, 1979, and a comparative view in my *The Pen and the Faith*, London, 1985, pp.72-90. For all his boldness, he was pitted against a rugged and entrenched establishment.

Shari'ati's logic mounted other arguments too. Acutely alert to the writings of such as Franz Fanon and Albert Camus, he sought in lectures and pamphlets to stir a mind for social justice, with his emphasis squarely or the Meccan *balagh* or 'mission-as-message' to which Muhammad was initially confined. Shari'ati wrote:

> His mission consists only in conveying the message ... For it is the people themselves who are responsible ... His mission being completed men are free to choose.[21]

His bold reading of Islam, critical of Western culture yet alert to a right vocation of Islam, tried to meet a darkly adverse Iranian situation. What, though, of the implications for 'democracy', that supposed panacea the USA hopes to export and implant, with its blessing, on the Arab East? What of any 'God of the electorate', in universal suffrage, as 'the masses' somehow in authority?

It is a vexing problem. How is a sane, durable, political enlistment of 'the masses' to be achieved? America shows how far its processes can be suborned by wealth and money, by lobbies and powered interests, by media manipulation and even sure reading of what the 'levers' tell. *Demos*, too, must be reasonably educated, reliably informed by a free press and sufficiently income-blessed to be un-bribe-able. Gullibility, waywardness, vagary, are all too likely among those 'masses'. Yet, in the rich and serious meanings we await in Chapters 2 and 3, God is *Ilah al-nas*. The Qur'an has an ideology of 'counsel among themselves' for its Muslims but its translation in electoral terms is inconclusive.[22] The *Rabb* word in Surah

---

The issue was neatly captured by John Dryden in 'The Hind and the Panther' (Part 2, lines 385–88):
> 'The sense is intricate, 'Tis only clear
> What vowels and what consonants are there.
> Therefore 'tis plain its meaning must be tryd
> Before some judge appointed. to decide.'

[21] *Op. cit.*, note 20, p. 48. See also his *Marxism and Other Western Fallacies, An Islamic Critique*, trans. R Campbell, Berkeley , 1980, p. 113.

[22] See the analysis of 'Caliphate' after its abolition in 1924 by the Egyptian scholar 'Ali 'Abd al-Raziq, *Islam wa Usul al-Hukm*, Cairo, 1925, in which this Azharite lawyer found there was no Quranic warrant for it. His case was much vilified at the time but has been vigorously sustained since, and e.g. recently by Muhammad Husain al-'Ashmawi in *Al-Khilafah al-Islamiyyah*, Cairo, 1992, and *Al-Islam al-Siyasi*, Cairo, 1992. On *shura* see 42.38 where *amr* ('way', or 'custom') could be claimed for democratic suffrage but may only imply tribal habit.

114 and everywhere in its very wide Quranic incidence responds to the human as *'abd*, or 'servant', as being thus Allah's 'subject'. How does that fit the democratic ideal of 'government by the people' when 'subject-status before God' is so fair an actual or potential autocracy of politics and/or religion?

Sundry other passages of Allah as 'King' leave ever open how this 'Kingship' moves to its exercise through human means to have its duly divine incidence in history and society.[23] Of one thing we may be sure, namely that there never was, nor could, be 'theocracy' as the unmediated rule of God, immune from all human part—though some have appropriated the term, if only for what they themselves have contrived in Allah's Name.

Perhaps the nearest the Qur'an has to the hope of 'theocracy' comes in the repeated dual command: 'Obey God and obey the Apostle,' when, during the Medinan *Sirah*, Allah and Muhammad are thus conjoined in rule. The injunction to Muslims is re-inforced in such passages as:

> 'It is no right of a believer, man or woman, to retain any opinion of theirs in any matter in which God and His Apostle have ruled by decree. Whoever goes counter to God and his Apostle is in grievous error.' (Surah 33.36)

or:

> 'Believers! in what has to do with God and His Apostle, usurp no private authority for yourselves' (49.1)

> 'Whoever repudiates God and His Messenger there is awaiting the Fire of *Jahannam*, the eternal abiding place.' (72.23)

Yet there must be serious doubt whether this near identical allegiance and obedience to Allah and the Apostle can extend the sole sovereignty of the One[24] into identity with the governance of later Islam.

---

[23] See Surahs 24.116 and 59.23; 'Exalted be God, the King, the True,' the second adding seven other divine titles. See further note 24.

[24] Numerous passages affirm *Al-Mulk li-Llah*, 'Sovereignty is God's', from 2.107 to 85.9, while 3.26 speaks of 'Allah as the Sovereign of the sovereignty'. It cryptically adds: 'you bestow sovereignty on whom You will and from whom You will withdraw it.' This divine

There are two good reasons. One must be that this linking of rulership belonged strictly with the task of the Prophet, as such and during his *Sirah*. That role did not—and could not—abide inside any succession, being as faith held, for ever finalised in Muhammad. No political Caliphate inherited the prophetic mantle. Thus, if a 'theocratic governing' was the Prophet's right in Allah's Name, the title to it passed with his death, being un-inheritable by every count of Islamic doctrine. The emergence of the Caliphate under Abu Bakr was a pragmatic answer to an obvious need. The theory came later.

A second has to be that the theme of political power-exercise only came at all for the briefer Medinan period and had been firmly excluded throughout the defining Meccan years when only the ever prior preaching task was given him.[25] Even when Surah 64.12 brings the absolute obedience and the 'word-bearing' together there is a crucial caveat.

> 'Obey God and obey the Messenger, but if you turn aside Our Apostle has but one duty—the bringing of the clear word.'

Moreover, the juridical status of the Caliphate has long been in doubt, and no success has attended efforts—abandoned in the nineteen-thirties—to renew it. The only 'caliphs' of which the Qur'an knows are *al-nas*, us mortal humans, God's *khulafa'* (pl. of *khalifah*, 'viceroys') as we must study in the chapter that follows. Are those right then who, with 'Ali Shari'ati and others, argue that in our contemporary society in its urgent need for inter-human commonweal, Islam needs to identify itself explicitly with its Meccan norm? That is, be legitimate only in its religious sense, disqualifying its long political instinct and theory of an exclusive political dominance of the world? In such identity of Muhammad with his precious *balagh*, what belongs with *hisab*, or 'reckoning', is where the Qur'an always requires it to be, with God alone. Could the reckoning of Islam with the world, or of the world with Islam, be in surer, safer hands?

---

*Mulk* excludes all partnering in it and, in many verses, is linked with final judgement. These meanings of 'King of humankind', however, do not indicate how it obtains through human means in a duly divine incidence in history.

[25] Muhammad's mandate to *balagh* alone is repeated in Surahs 5.99, 13-40, 24.53, 29.18, 36.17 and 42.48.

This would, could, mean no Muslim abdication from the obvious role of the political order in the pursuit of the common good. There is no sane immunity for religious faith from the business of power in and among *al-nas*. How, though, is *Ilah al-nas* truly among them in their political role? The answer, by the lights of Mecca, must be that of private or 'citizen' conscience that has legitimated and established a pattern of regime, which has its people enjoy that right and itself enjoys having it so.

For *Malik al-nas* is one with *Rabb al-nas* and *Rabb* is mutual with *'abd* who is not only 'servant' but 'worshipper'. Religious faith, then, has to inform politics by the quality of the God-perception it brings to its means and ends, i.e., honesty, justice, compassion, liberty of mind, equality of persons, and a set antagonism for all that violates these elements. Faiths are soundly 'political', insofar as they bring these to the vision and the ventures of the structures they approve collectively and serve personally. Only such citizen-conscience and citizen-integrity allow politics to be the art of worship in true awareness of *Ilah al-nas*. For that naming of Him can have no other satisfaction. We resume this theme in Chapter 11.

This conclusion and its gentle prescript for a contemporary Islam, being the claim of its Meccan priority, has surely to be sustained by intelligent reference to where humankind now is, i.e. the 'single situation' of this century. Have not science and technology irreversibly 'unified' the globe in material terms of mutual 'knowability' across all frontiers, whether or not religious faiths have yet conceded how far it is so? The 'deep divide' implicit in that elusive word 'and' belongs with a humanity that is more and more 'global', less and less reciprocally immune as for long it formerly was, by ignorance, distance, poverty, oceans and mountain ranges, even forests and fogs. That versatile 'and' compares and contrasts, adds and multiplies, links and separates. What can we usefully mean by 'Islam and the West' even when we narrow it into 'the Qur'an and the West'? That we 'multiply'—tensions arguments, prejudices, fears and charges—is not in doubt. We certainly also 'contrast'—as some do maliciously only to embarrass how to do so soundly.

What, without doubt, the 'and' can certainly mean here is that, even if faiths will not, time and actuality inter-engage us. There is a long, and global, indictment of Western politics and Western culture, an indictment in which perhaps Islam is more strident but which the patience of Africa and the instincts of Asia honourably share—and must share, as long as human environments are imperilled by consumerisms far away that will not curb either their appetites or their profits, to diminish the peril. It must be so, as long as sugar-beet subsidies in one continent make sugar-beet growers unemployed in another, or some two-thirds reduction in the price of raw coffee by the buying power of one hemisphere denies fair prosperity to the growers in another. The calls of Bin Laden to a Muslim *Jihad* have acute cultural self-obsessions of their own[26] but that should not exempt his tirades from due audition in the conscience of the West. Venom has to be heard in the very excesses which feed its irrational substance. For passions speak no less for the futility of their argument. Even a hater's 'quarrel' pleads an un-hating hearing.

Apart from imbalance between practioners in gain and loss, development indulged or denied, there is the political and cultural arrogance that some Muslims are minded to see as 'walking proudly in the earth'.[27] To posit 'Islam and the West' as if to some fated encounter in brazen assumption of advantage in the odds, is to register no obligation to the sane salvation of both parties. That is a hope—and a possibility—which, with due discretion, a patient and perceptive West could perhaps make good by the positives of its own scholarship, and a service to academic freedom.

Catalogues of debts and duties are invidious and can never be complete. Other aspects will emerge in chapters following and the fields they aim to cover, under the scrutiny of salient Quranic verses. Choice of these is not random but monitored by the desire to be comprehending of the Qur'an's own 'unison' round the divine and the human, the reality of *Ilah al-nas*, and the meaning of that 'construct'.

How, then, does the Qur'an characterise and equip our humanity for our divinely meant significance?

---

[26] Though finding refuge in the high mountains of Asia, he deplores what he sees as the perverse Arab custody of the twin shrines of Mecca and Medina, the sacred *Haramain*. These, however, belong by Pilgrimage to the whole *Ummah* (for which he argues) by the sheer right (rite) of Pilgrimage thither. His bitterness against Jewry and Israel tells an Arabism that leads him to miss the sober, moral case the issue needs.

[27] Surah 17.37. 'Walk not proudfully in the earth. You cannot cleave the earth, nor match the mountains in stature.' Strutting (Texas-style?) has no place in politics or culture in the eyes of *Ilah al-nas*, equally their Lord and so holding them all equal.

# Chapter 2
## HUMANS WHO OCCUPY:
## NOT GODS WHO OWN

It is there, all unsuspected, in Robert Frost's poem 'The Gift Outright', a sort of epitome of 'the Qur'an and the West', if we will forget what he forgets and recognise his theme as central to the Islamic Scripture. The poet vividly celebrates the sense of things to be possessed and their capacity to be the very making of those answering the call they hear in them. 'Realising' is his word—'realising westward' through the slow discovery

> '… that it was ourselves
> We were withholding from our land of living,
> And forthwith found salvation in surrender.
> Such as we were, we gave ourselves outright
> To the land …
> Such as she was, such as she would become.'

The lines are eloquent about 'the West' in what they ignore: apt about the Qur'an's theme of what is reciprocal between place and people, land and life, tenancy and time.[1]

'Still unstoried, artless, unenhanced' he thinks the  territory that, thus, was 'ours in Massachusetts and Virginia'. The image given of 'the West' is the more telling being so self-preoccupied in its *superbia*. 'Amerindians' it might come to learn were there ahead of them, but only to be named by a hybrid word, half foreign, like (Rhodesia) half by sailors' error. There is much about this 'West'—at least as far as represented here—told in the America of colonial European origins. 'She was our land,' Frost is bland to write 'before we were her people.'

---

[1] *Complete Poems of Robert Frost*, New York, 1964, p. 467. If we only think of continental vacancy, the poem has a moving warrant with its theme of 'ex-English', once inhibited by a gone connection, forever now 'realising westward',  possessing themselves in the act of answering a land's enlarging invitation.

Yet whatever the incongruity of the incoming tenancy and its blind injustice, such—to return to the Qur'an—was and is the way of inhabitant with habitat, of either with the other in their mutual reality. The precedent is there in Surah 11.61 where a very minor prophet Salih tells the tribe called Thamud:

'My people! Worship God. You have no other God but He.
He brought you into being from the earth and established you
as colonists there. Therefore, seek his forgiveness and return to
Him in repentance. For my Lord is near and ready to answer.'

Here an early 'messenger' speaking as a 'brother' to his kin, perhaps on the terrain of those cave-hewing, cave-dwelling folk, the Nabateans, breathes the primal humanism of the Qur'an, the theme of Frost's poem in a different idiom, the ancient mystery of being a people by belonging with place they can populate. The verbs in the Arabic tell of a 'fashioning' of humans from the earth and thence their tenure into tenancy.

وَإِلَىٰ ثَمُودَ أَخَاهُمْ صَٰلِحًا قَالَ يَٰقَوْمِ

ٱعْبُدُواْ ٱللَّهَ مَا لَكُم مِّنْ إِلَٰهٍ غَيْرُهُۥ هُوَ أَنشَأَكُم مِّنَ

ٱلْأَرْضِ وَٱسْتَعْمَرَكُمْ فِيهَا فَٱسْتَغْفِرُوهُ ثُمَّ تُوبُوٓاْ إِلَيْهِ

إِنَّ رَبِّى قَرِيبٌ مُّجِيبٌ

The second verb *ista'marakum* yields to current Arabic the hated term *Isti'mar*, 'imperialism', exactly the charge much of the non-Western world has—with long and loaded memory—to levy against the West. For Salih, however, it meant simply our human delegacy over the earth as occupiers with a livelihood, as trustees with a privilege, or—as Christian terms would say—dwellers in a sacramental order minded for a consecration by steady awareness of its meaning.

This perception both of our mortality and our cumulative competence as a divine/human situation is the central theme of Bible and Qur'an alike.[2] Islam, for its own interior reasons, finds the word

---

[2]   It is brought together in *A Certain Sympathy of Scriptures, Biblical and Quranic*, Brighton, 2004, with relevant texts from both sources and review of other writing.

'sacrament' unfamiliar. Yet the meaning it has of 'minding for sacred' belongs squarely with the repeated insistence of the Qur'an on the cosmos of our habitation as a realm of 'signs', *ayat*. Just as these arrest the scientist and invite investigation in empirical terms, leading to 'mastery', so they also summon the soul to glad recognition of mystery as inducing to gratitude. We perceive a bestowal *to* us of what will enable culture and civilization *for* us.

It is a situation implicit with a meantness to which our humankind is the clue. The *imperium* which both Scriptures would have us identify stands in what stays mysteriously neutral and 'secular', only in order that it might be known and handled as potential and 'religious'. Its 'secularity' must be studied in a later Chapter 5. To explain and—as far as language may—enforce that human role is the mission of the 'messengers'. There would be no point in these mentors unless they were addressing custodians with an option on whom the benison or blight will turn. Prophets have no mission to puppets. Only out of our dignity have they an errand to fulfil.[3]

In contrast to the political colonialism which only usurps and violates what does not truly belong, God's making us colonials of His creation dignifies and liberates. So much else in the Qur'an confirms Surah 11.61 concerning our delegacy as Allah's *khulafa'*. The caliphate announced in Surah 2.30 is one with the 'dominion' granted in Genesis. The words *khaliqah* and *khalifah* differ only in one consonantal point, as index to the identity between them. Our being creaturely means our being also competent and managerial in a world where the shape of things responds to our intelligent discourse with it, alike in pure and applied science and in religious awe and thankfulness.

When in Surah 2.30, the angels protested against Allah's purpose to delegate this 'caliphate' to us humans, as ones who would 'corrupt and shed blood', He over-ruled their demur and summoned them to prostrate to the creature in a salute to his vocation. If they perceived a dark risk in what was ensuing, they were made to know that He was undertaking it, and making His creation a realm of 'signs', of a 'significance' they could take in mortal hand. In so taking it, as responsive to their capacity as its

---

[3] Should we not wonder, in this context, at how the mandate (according to Genesis, since Noah and the deluge) has never been withdrawn, despite the long human cost to the creation—and the Creator—of the dark content of our history? Allah 'does not weary of mankind.'

custodians they operated 'secularly', in the right sense of the word, namely that they co-operated with the 'laws' or 'patterns' present for their handling in the natural, intelligible, world. Those given features of that world, thus divinely 'meant' for such human management and sober exploitation, were never outside Allah's realm as ever 'somewhere' from which He could be ousted or excluded. Rather it was precisely a realm which His design had charged humankind to undertake on His behalf as His trustees.

This situation is clearly proven such by two facts. One is that sending of His prophets to teach us how to make it so and sustain in the doing of His will by steady exhortation and example. The other is how plainly the natural order waits on our moral response. It does so by not discriminating between 'believers' and *mulhidin* in its working, or between religions or sects or their *manasik* in its neutral quality.[4] Male and female procreate in intercourse, irrespective of their faith adherence. Planes fly, as aeronautics have them, negligent of the faith-ties of pilots or passengers. The medicine and surgery of hospitals are indifferent—in respect of their efficacy—to where, or if, the patients worship. It is just this neutrality of the natural order that makes any ethics possible. It is the 'secular' order of the natural world, not as ever outside Allah's sovereignty but set by Him under our sub-dominion, wherein to 'live and move and have our being' in His Name and for His sake.

To be sure, the reach of our human competence inside the natural order is not limitless. There are, mercifully if enigmatically, many areas of vagary and mystery, the unpredictables in nature which are reserved from us and retained from us in enigma. Even so, that reach of competence, stretching now into space exploration and reading of the ocean depths, is ever enlarging, thanks to all that has been cumulative through long generations, wherein is a Quranic theme for another text and place.[5] It

---

4  *Manasik* (sing. *mansak*) are the rituals or liturgies by which faiths identify and express themselves. They are a theme of prayer (to be shown them) in Surah 2.27 and of recollection (as against mere asking) in 2.200. 'Devotions' is one translation. Surah 22.34 says that every people has been given the valid forms of invocation, while 22.67 validates diversity of such hallowed rituals and forbids dispute around them. We should unite on 'summoning to the Lord', however dispute-laden that may be.

5  Namely the theme of 'forwarding' to the future, due in Chapter 3, as applying to individual life 'towards eternity'. It would also seem to apply to the seriousness of history as containing the ongoing productivity (of devices and means) from a long and tireless past. We are in a different situation from when travel was ever only at pedestrian pace and when it is jet-propelled. A bow in hand with arrows is less horrific than the finger on a nuclear button. 'History' has to matter for 'religion'.

is, therefore, all the more urgent for us to have and keep in mind this true meaning of 'the secular', and realise that we only submit to our transcendent Lord by receiving duly and reverently from His hands the colonist's tenancy and trust His very sovereignty has granted.

There is another re–iterated text in the Qur'an which firmly underwrites this truth of a natural order yielded into a responsive/responsible human cognisance, namely the particle *la 'alla* with its plural added pronouns *kum* and *hum* (rarely *ka* as singular) 'you' and 'they'. It occurs more than a hundred times with a telling variety of verbs, *la 'allakum ta'qilun*, 'perhaps you will use your wits,' *la 'allahum yatafakkarun*, 'perhaps they will bring their minds to bear,' i.e. on the phenomena before their eyes.

To be sure, there are occasions when the appeal in *la 'alla* is a plea for audience for the spoken Qur'an. But that in itself is significant. For the same word *ayah*, 'sign', is applied both to a verse of the Book and some instance of divine 'mercy-in-address' to us humans via external nature. In that sense, the visible world and the audible word have the same summons to a human realisation of this related reality of nature and meaning, and both for active cognisance. Witness in the same sense the constant invocation of dawn and sunset, of the night sky or the sun and the landscape, and all else visible and tangible to our senses. This feature is especially notable in the early Meccan period of ardent preaching prior to the strife beyond the Hijrah.[6]

It is clear from the sheer force of the logic in *la 'alla* and its sustained recurrence that the dignity and liability of our *Isti 'mar* are central to Quranic reading of the human condition. Such attentive cognisance of the natural order and its amenability to mind and hand are at the heart of all the rich meanings of the Arabic root and its ample derivatives.[7] *'Amara* means 'to live', 'to live long', 'to thrive', 'to prosper', 'to be inhabited, peopled or populated' (of lands), 'to build', and so 'to let be' in all the true forms of the entrusted incidence of 'being'. *'Umr*

---

[6] They are brought together in *Readings in the Qur'an*, London, 1988, pp. 86–92, entitled: 'God and His Praise'. They make doxology the prior theme of theology. One might recall how Thomas Hardy wanted to be remembered after his demise as 'One who noticed such things.' *Collected Poems*, London, 1932, p. 521, 'Afterwards', 'When the present has latched its postern behind my tremulous stay.'

[7] It is capable of all three medial vowels and fills nine columns of Edward Lane's classic dictionary.

is 'life in its duration'; *'imarah* 'building' or 'structure'; *'umran* 'prosperous habitation' or 'civilisation'; *mi'mar* 'a builder' or 'mason'; *musta'marah* 'a colony' or 'settlement'.

Thus the term gathers together the sequence in history of the familiar triad—nature, through nurture to culture. The comprehensiveness of its derivatives make the verbal root an epitome of the whole argument of the Qur'an, concerning global human tenancy. When in Surah 3.33 we find *Al 'Imran*, 'the family of *'Imran*' (the father of Mary, for whom the Surah is named) 'preferred' with 'the family of Abraham' above all others, perhaps a bold play on the name might think us all belonging to that 'family' as allowed 'to thrive' in, from, with and through the nature of this earth in the *'umran* we call 'civilisation'.

The nurture, mediating between nature and culture, means that procreation—perpetuating creation's own sequences—belongs in the Qur'an as the most 'sign-laden' of all our human powers. Despite every index in the social image of Islam of a heavy male supremacy, the essential partnership of male/female sexuality as being among 'the signs of God' is laid down in Surah 30.31:

> 'He has created *azwaj* for you from among yourselves that
> you might live in joy with them and He planted love and
> tenderness between you, wherein surely there are signs for
> thoughtful folk.'

The *azwaj* word is almost neutral (cf. 'spouses') meaning 'mates' or identities that 'counterpart', rather than 'He created wives for you ...' that would indicate an inferiority. If sexuality 'signifies'—as being among God's *ayat* here insists—then marriage, for the Qur'an, might be more than the 'contract' which it readily finds 'divorceable' and approach a 'troth' that might stay. Either way, we are a far cry from the verdict that 'to live in love and peace ... is an impossible ideal and unnatural.'[8]

Such sacramental mutuality might be read in the query of Surah 4.21, asking how parties could take back a dowry 'when you have lain

---

8    The verdict of Camille Paglia, *Sexual Personae: Art and Decadence from Nefertiti to Emily Dickinson*,
     New Haven, 1990, p. 18, adding that it is 'one of the outstanding contradictions Christianity
     has imposed on its followers.' In her context 'sex is all and all is sex.' Aspects will recur later.

with each other and entered into a firm covenant with your wives?' The equal creaturehood of 'male and female' is clear in 49.13:

> 'Humanity! Truly We have created you male and female and made you to be nations and tribes in order that you may know each other.'

It would seem that only a sound reading of sexuality is any ground for ever speaking of 'the family of nations'.

There is another significant query in Surah 56.58 about intercourse itself, as a (potential) procreation firmly in the setting of Allah's creation. It asks—perhaps in relation to what we cannot visually detect in emission but more deeply: 'Do you realise what you are transacting?' as participating in what God has allowed to be creative.[9] There is also a discernible reference to copulation when Surah 2.187 says that 'husbands and wives are a *libas* for each other.' The word is used elsewhere for 'the night a covering' (78.10) and, in 16.112, as 'the utmost degree of' (e.g. hunger or ardour). Given the sense of privacy, intimacy—maybe modesty— what here is between limbs and bodies might 'tell' what is between soul and mind, exploring the 'sign' order in the physical.

Whether the exegesis holds for all, there is no doubt that a creation designing human sexuality as the order of its continuity entirely confirms how inclusively 'colonists' we humans were meant to be. For the art of such mutual *libas* involves the parties in the tasks of parenthood. The Qur'an has much to say about the inter-liability of parents to children and of offspring to parents. It has also a keen solicitude for the wellbeing and protection of orphans.[10] Does the orphan condition of Muhammad belong here? Or the sadness in the note that he had no surviving male heir?[11] The long—and in infancy total—dependence of the human young

---

[9] The verb *a fa ra'iytum* plays on the double meaning of actual 'seeing' and 'comprehending': what the eye cannot detect the spirit must realise. The same verb of question comes in the same Surah, at 63.68 and 71, in relation to 'land we till,' 'water we drink' and 'fire we kindle,' the four cardinal elements in pursuance of our colonial status, its dignities and duties.

[10] In Surah 4.3 the permission of plural marriage turns on 'doing justly by orphans', perhaps taking 'war-widows' into an existing household, though still with the proviso that you 'think you can do them justice'—when fear one may not enjoins monogamy. That proviso has been much invoked as a 'virtual prohibition' depending on what 'equality' is meant. The vicissitudes of exegesis belong with Chapters 6 and 7.

[11] One of only four mentions of the personal name in the Qur'an laments this fact (33.40).

makes parenthood among the most strenuous and painstaking aspects of our 'colonisation'.

Seeing that 'being' and 'doing' are so far synonymous in the art of living, and seeing that parenthood is so vital a part in our creaturely trust, Salih's plea to his 'people' sounds for us all. More personal aspects of our sexuality belong in the chapter following, while Salih's note about 'seeking forgiveness' points to Chapter 4. Meanwhile, there is another pointed passage in Surah 2.138, which—for all the puzzlement it arouses—may best be taken in this present context of 'being' and 'doing' in the constant inter-play of 'who' we are and 'where', of folk and farm, of land and human 'lord', and all the potential between place and people. It turns on the initially strange theme of 'God's baptism'. Surah 2.138 reads:

صِبْغَةَ ٱللَّهِ وَمَنْ أَحْسَنُ مِنَ ٱللَّهِ صِبْغَةً وَنَحْنُ لَهُ عَٰبِدُونَ

Depending on how we read the noun *sibghah*, the English might—if enigmatically—be 'the baptism of God who is better than God at baptising?' The question is rhetorical and the noun, in the accusative, has no 'possessing' verb, nor does Islam have any rite of baptism. The context has to do with Muhammad's affirming his claim to prophethood as a true 'heir of Abraham', which Jews and Christians belie, holding Abraham as exclusively theirs. That would seem to suggest that 'Allah's baptising', being 'better', means rather his divine authenticating of Muhammad's *Ummah* or *Millah*. *Sibghah* would seem to be a 'community-marker'.[12]

The following verses imply some continuing tension or debate and anyway: 'All worship belongs to Him (Allah). God is our Lord and your Lord. Do you want arguments about Him. We have our deeds and

---

[12] For a more detailed study of the passage and the different translations, see *The Muslim World Quarterly*, Vol. xlvi, No. 3, July, 1958, 179–133. Obviously there cannot be a subjective genitive. *Sabagha*, the root verb, is used of 'altering' a thing radically while its essentials abide, i.e. hair turning white, fire glowing in coals, of a coat dyed or cleaned. Some medieval exegetes refer to 'receiving' from Allah His 'religion', in line with the idea told in Surah 30.30 around *fitrah* as meaning both 'human nature' and the 'religion' apt for it. The old English exegete, George Sale, thinks that 'God's baptism' means that 'the signs' of this 'religion' 'appear in the person who professes it, as the signs of water appear in the clothes of him who is baptised.' Given the 'immersion' idea, may we not well—as here—apply it to 'who we must be, thanks to where we are'?

you have yours.' By the time of Surah 2, Islam has reached a robust self-assurance about legitimacy and about the communal expression it gives to it.[13] Abraham is not to be monopolised and, anyway 'Who knows best, you or Allah?' (2.140).

'Baptism', then, rather that 'dipping', or 'colouring', or 'soaking', as the verb might mean (in its association with dyers and laundries) seems a sounder translation then these more mundane ones. However, since 'peoples'—for the Qur'an and in its theme of liable 'colonisations'[14]—are 'let be' into creaturehood on an entrusted earth, the 'baptism' Allah is 'best at' is precisely this His enterprise with the custodianship of and in humankind. The rhetoric underlines all we have been studying thus far. The 'trust' is not only granted to us as Allah's 'caliphs' (2.30f), it is guided and disciplined by prophets and by all that *islam* signifies. Can we not read God's *sibghah* as just this 'mutuality' between the way we relate to 'earth' and 'earth' to us, reading 'earth' as the whole mystery of 'land' as the raw material of everything economic and social, the domain of all 'harvests'—edible and technological alike—the realm of all identities because it is the ground of all identification? We might, perhaps, even invoke the saying of Jesus about 'the baptism I am baptised with' (Luke 12.50) far below its once for all Messianic meaning, and know ourselves in a positive destiny to divine ends. Emerging from the act of sexuality we just studied of procreation within creation, we were not prior-consulted. Nor did we consent to be here—until we had to do in the very business of breathing. That 'breathing', in its long or short progress into 'dying', initiated us into the 'being/doing' order whether read or not as a 'caliphate'. For it was such, in any event and the better handled in being recognised for what it was. All genetic imprinting apart, it carries the features of its parenting and enters on a heritage. In a strange way, this 'no option' situation around nativity persists as a 'no option' situation in the incidence of life. We may consult with ourselves about many 'options',

---

[13] It was by this time that the *Qiblah* had been changed away from Jerusalem towards Mecca, that—as far as we can tell—the feast of Ramadan begins to be instituted and the daily *Salat* as fivefold and the collective mutuality of *Zakat*. Muslims become much more firmly distinguished from Semitic heritage, and mutually so—as is evident in Medinan Surahs.

[14] The Qur'an is clear about all as included in this land-love category, in distinction from the special 'covenantalism' of the Hebrew tradition, for whom 'Only one land and only they on it' could be authentic. Was that the legacy of an earlier nomadism? Anyway, as we have seen already, the triad of 'land, tribe and history' that underlay it is universal. 'Zion' has many imitators.

but not about the 'whether' of existence itself. At all events, in the poetical idiom of Gerard Manley Hopkins:

> 'Generations have trod, have trod, have trod;
> And all is seared with trade; bleared, smeared with toil;
> And wears man's smudge and shares man's smell.'[15]

We could say that the Qur'an has captured this earth-having human situation in the force of the divine question in Surah 7.172, addressed by God to assembly, en masse, of all human generations: 'Am I not your Lord?'—to which they have all replied: 'It is so, we bear witness, all doubt away.'[16]

The Qur'an, then, has for 'the West' this 'minding of a meaning', as its central witness, whether we think with Robert Frost in Chapter 1, of his American 'west' as the ever beckoning frontier or of that 'West' as fair analogy for the temper of 'the West' at large, the hemisphere that thinks it calls the tune for everywhere. 'O God, we are not gods' is its only sanely human cry. The force of the humility that disclaims all wild pretension needs the affirmation Islam commends, namely that 'there is none but He.' The formula: 'In the Name of God' is no mere invocation. It is the principle or watchword by which we rightly know ourselves the humans we are.

---

[15] Gerard Manley Hopkins, *The Poems*, ed. W H Gardner and N H MacKenzie, 4th. ed., Oxford, 1970, p. 66, 'God's Grandeur'.

[16] For a more incisive study of this crucial text see my *Am I Not Your Lord? Human Meaning in Divine Question*, London, 2002. Coming from 'the Almighty', and as a negative question, it awaits a 'Yes' answer but with a strange divine inference. Surah 7.172 envisages all humankind of every generation as a single audience to which the question is put. Thus the 'pledging' that acknowledges divine Lordship is, like the Noahid covenant, ecumenical and, unlike that of Sinai, belongs with all. No generation, in later time, can plead its being 'led astray' by ancestors. Also it pre-dates—if the mythical may—all revealed Scriptures that purport to teach and discipline the Yes answer.

So may there be a certain wry humour in the query: 'Who could be a more admirable *(hasan)* baptiser than Allah?—given Islam's dislike of 'priestly' auspices of the sacraments in Christianity? Adam is named (or with *bani Adam*) more than twenty times in the Qur'an but nowhere was he named 'Adam' by Allah. Could it be that his 'baptism' was precisely in his being taught 'the names' (2.31), i.e. of things in the world in general? For such 'knowing the names' is the clue to all science and society (cf. Genesis 2.19-20). See the chapter following.

There are the more intimate personal realms of creaturehood than these of collective earth-dwelling. They await the chapter following. Chapter 5 takes up sundry features of the 'secular' all the foregoing entails.

## Chapter 3
# LEGITIMATE SELFHOOD

$$\text{يَـٰٓأَيُّهَا ٱلَّذِينَ ءَامَنُوا۟ عَلَيْكُمْ أَنفُسَكُمْ}$$

To think and write of 'legitimate selfhood' is to concede that there is also the illegitimate sort. Right selfhood, therefore, has to be duly discerned—wherein lies the whole business of religions in a long and differently concluded debate about any feasible distinction between 'selfhood' and 'selfishness'. For either could be comprehended inside the same 'egoism'.[1] In the bleaker mind of Asian Buddhism the two are always one, so that to speak of 'self-responsibility' can only be of something due—at length—to be foregone into the ocean of non-being and, meanwhile, have the amending form of 'the Eightfold Path' with its highly moral care for a 'rightness' of being in mind, conduct and compassion.[2] In any ultimate sense, selfhood is an illusion from which to be delivered by surrender into the 'non-being' the illusion has concealed. In the 'meanwhile' a right selfhood wills to refrain as far as in it lies from the pursuit of its own self-interest.[3]

---

[1] Seeing that the word itself and egocentric as a descriptive have a double sense that often confuses us. 'Egoism' is the truth of us in the sense that we are physically and consciously in a selfhood that is ineluctable, each the 'I/me' who is. In that way all are 'ego-centric' in an inevitable individuation. But we may well be also, in a moral sense of being—even ruthlessly—'for ourselves', acquisitive, aggressive and callously bent on our interest. That will be what we do with our individuation, our verdict against what quite contrastedly, we could do with it. The first 'egoism' is merely the place for the decision which will determine the second where 'innocence' first awaits a character. Issues will be long and equivocal.

[2] We have to beware of talking about 'extinction' as if we had not realised that there was no 'self' to 'extinguish'. 'The Eightfold Path' has a deeply moral passion about our 'other' egoism (note 1) but on the basis of a direly Asian view about any 'innocence' of the second.

[3] How being can be and not be, or 'pass' as both 'happening' and 'being unhappened', or why what 'matters' (with passion) as 'the Path' should not also 'matter' as a different clue to selfhood

Deep paradoxes attach to this religious stance.[3] Here the point in noting their verdict, and its moral strategy is simply to have the contrast in clear focus. For the Qur'an has a quite robust confidence in the legitimacy of being human and with the world in a caring trust, a trust which takes in its 'signs', appreciates its potential to our hand and holds it for a theatre of the divine praise from our hearts. Beyond all the undiscerning or puzzled reception the West has dismissively entertained for the Islamic Scripture, this its 'humanism' surely deserves due reckoning. Can Muslims translate its practice for us in the quality of their possession of its mind? For that must be the vital factor in any ministry of texts to others, any kindling of outsiders to their content.

The Qur'an's measures of legitimate selfhood begin with the Arabic phrase already quoted from Surah 5.105: 'O you who believe! On you are your own souls.' The preposition *'ala* always has this sense of 'liability', as in 24.61 where there is exoneration from 'blame' in listed things. There are many other verses about what is 'to' *(ila)* our souls, or 'of' them *('an)*. There is no mistaking the force of 5.105 about selfhood being an inherent responsibility. For because it addresses and is addressed by an intelligible world, lives and moves and has being from that mental habitation, it is answerable to it. Their world leaves humankind answerable for it. There is behind all—and ourselves with it—this enabling *kun fayakun*: 'Be! and be it is.'

Whether the ever acquisitive but thereby often the more jaded West can heed this re-assuring theme from a source whose own self-imaging it has in such apprehension or disdain may be far to think. Yet two facts are plain which in a curious way unite the parties. One is that the Qur'an has this ring in its bell, however muffled or muted; the other is that 'selfhood' is in such question or distortion, in the Western world. It follows that the Qur'an's 'humanism' can only be tuned for Western heed, if the Islam of Muslims now will let itself take in the factors which have for long occasioned in Western literature this 'loss of the self' to which the doubters of significance so often point.

The two demands belong together and the Qur'an brings them so by the antithesis it sees in the full reach of its antonyms *shukr* and *kufr*, our attitudes of 'gratitude' and 'gross negation'. If, as argued in Chapter 1, God

---

than the one on which the Path relies. But paradoxes should not be pressed, as if to embarrass. For all faiths incur them differently and need tolerance about them.

is *Ilah al-nas*, 'the God of humankind', and if, as to be argued in Chapter 12, he is 'our Humanly Liable Lord', and if, further, as due in Chapter 5, we have to be gently 'secular' if ever to be 'sacred', then 'legitimate selfhood' must find a true worship. The worship will know and love its source as the sure ground of its entire legitimacy as found in the other. We are authentic in our self-possession only by our God-devotion. To be sceptical of the one is to be withholding from the other.

So much we may read in Solomon's words in Surah 27.40 or Luqman's in 31.12 (both celebrated for wisdom) sensing that God 'tests' them, whether they would 'give thanks' or whether they would 'grossly disbelieve'. *Ashkur* and *akfir* (1st person, present tense verbs) need to be fully plumbed. 'Thanks' is no formal or perfunctory gesture, but the deep ability to cry: 'This is from the bounty of my Lord' (Surah 27.40). *Kufr*, likewise is not some trite or flippant agnosticism, but rather an ugly disavowal of grace. By the repeated antithesis between *shukr* and *kufr*, the Qur'an teaches that to be in sullen negation of God is to be dumbly sceptical of one's own meaning as human. 'Gratitude to' God is much deeper faith than bare 'credence in', more reflective, more heartfelt. 'Thanks' (to God) in 31.12 is the very health of the soul, while *kufr*, in giving the lie to God, belies the self also[4] (27.40). Surah 59.19 puts the point tersely in saying: 'Those who forgot God ... God caused them to forget themselves.' 'The-God-we-ignore' in the very nature of *kufr* is far different from John Keats' theme of 'negative capability', as a capacity to be in doubts and fears without demanding relief. It is the studied disallowance of any 'somewhere' where 'doubts and fears' might be resolved, or what the Qur'an calls the deliberate 'exclusion of God'.[5] We need the 'trust' we place in God for the art of being entrusted with ourselves. A right humanism lives with a right theology.

---

[4]  There is an impressive frequency about the Qur'an's allusion to gratitude, and its role as a prime characteristic of 'faith'. It belongs with awareness of natural phenomena, the cognisance of 'signs' (7.28), the attitude to parents (46.14) and safe-keeping in danger. There are all occasions when the Qur'an deplores the prevalence of 'thanklessness'—'Most of them give no thanks!' (2.243, 6.63, 10.22, 27.73, 34, 19, 39.66 and 40.61.

[5]  While 'doubt' must seem to be ruled out for minds akin to the Qur'an (cf. Surah 2.2 *la raiba fihi*—'nothing doubtful in it')—as Chapter 6 must note there is ample room for personal decision about text and text-meaning.

The more corporate and collective aspects of our human 'caliphate' passed at the end of Chapter 2 into those that are private and personal within our selfhoods. The transition means that the liabilities of politics and societies become the stresses and verdicts in individual souls. Tumult and confusion in the one spell tension and yearning in the other. What possible bearing can the Quranic theme of 'caliphate' have on 'the loss of self-significance' in the Western scene? Might Muslims in the custody of their own Qur'an ever be able to mediate it in a global dialogue with contemporary malaise? If so, in what would it consist? How convincing might it be? Would there ever be a mind bias-free to take it in?

Such are the imponderables that await any spiritual relation between 'the Qur'an and the West'. At least, there would need to be some full Islamic measure of the sundry inroads of dubiety and loss of intellectual nerve in the Western soul. They have been many and dire. They are not to be discounted by ample evidences of political arrogance and of material prowess. Rather these are part of the same equation.

There has been the forfeiture of confidence in the sanity of language since the conjecturings of Michel Foucault and of the linguistic analysts. We no longer inhabit a Socratic garden where open and genuine conversing might convey the parties to a satisfying consensus of their minds. Rather we are parties to 'the game of words' which—like all games—is self-enclosed in its own 'construct' and that 'construct' liable only to itself as no more than self-contrived and self-proposed. Do 'games' need to justify themselves outside the ambit they themselves provide?

If language is quite disabled from converse with transcendence, transcendence is also discountable in the sheer pragmatic competence of the scientific mind, evermore yielding the fruit of dis-inventible technologies. Reliance on these, to the point of habitual assumption, means a steady *de facto* recession of the impulse to worship, the point of prayer, or the humility of wonder. Yet there is no genuine logic why this should be so, seeing that sciences are themselves 'caliphal' enterprises, creatures also of 'imagination' and dependent on the same 'neutrality' of the natural order which was always, via ethics, the threshold of religion.[6]

---

[6] The point is further developed in Chapter 5. While science is much more than empirical testing, the products its techniques yield for society still have that 'neutral quality' which belongs to the physical order out of which their inventive contrivance came.

Reliance on techniques is scant warrant for a foregoing of humility. But on the popular level, and with the atrophy of wonder, due gratitude easily erodes.

Further again, the mood towards irreligion—or away from faith-practice in any exacting sense—is kindled for many in the West by dismay or despair at the image presented by the history of religions and their current reputation. Islam is not least liable for agnostic discounting of its spiritual capacities as these are deduced within the prejudice they invite. The degree to which religions can be their own worst enemy is seldom well realised inside their bastions of tradition and *taqlid*—the term with which alert Muslims reproach a self-indulgent authoritarianism which fails to reckon with the salutary challenge of the 'secular'.

The resulting loss of 'purchase' a faith-system undergoes on this drift into indifference should not be obscured by the many evidences of aggressive attitudes from within. Indeed, the two features belong together, in that popular negligence gives rise to a certain panic, fearing for the future. Strongly assertive accents of what is loosely called 'fundamentalism', are often an index to unease prompting the vehemence instead of the self-searching that might better serve a right persistence of belief. No faith-system is exempt from this phenomenon, letting its alarm about a changing world take the disserving form of unthinking authority. Islam, however, is the more prone to a rigorous mind-set by its distinctive sense alike of Scripture and Tradition, despite the patterns of lively intellectualism it has brought to other realms through its finest centuries.

Yet another area of disquiet, apart from language, doubt, indifference and anxiety, characterising East and West alike but bearing on Muslims by a different time-scale, are the faith-corrosives present in the mass-media. They combine with all else but diffuse the other factors more widely. Society is exposed to those solvents of mental focus and spiritual conscience in which Salman Rushdie excelled as—to use his term—'hybridisation', the merging and confusing of once stable identities. The 'hybrid' tends to be the 'trivial'. The media culture, on every hand, tends towards a society that wills and expects to be entertained and that, for the most part, visually. Hence, a certain forfeiture of the power of sustained attention and the capacity to be seriously discursive, whether the theme be political, religious or societal.

It can readily follow that boredom intervenes or the kind of apathy that can only be consoled by larger doses of unreality, whether administered by drugs or novels or soap-operas that diminish a lively personal zeal for existence, as ever a heartening pursuit of meaning.

As the major seed-bed of this social pattern, the Western world has powerfully affected the Muslim scene, evoking either the radical rejection of its menace in intensified dogma and discipline or a variety of emulations, avid or reluctant, What seems to emerge is whether our very lives are not somehow 'a constant evasion of ourselves'?[7] as those who are for ever 'extemporising time'. In this regard, it is illuminating to turn away from the pundits of faith and listen to the poets and novelists, among whom there is an evident cross-stimulus of kindred lendings and borrowings that are the stock-in-trade of literatures across the world. The debt, for example, of 20th-century Arabic to T S Eliot is familiar to many who know how his post-First World War sense of lostness echoed in the poetry on Palestinian tragedy of his translator, Tawfiq Sayigh.[8] There are unspoken kinships everywhere, surely unconcerted and coming only by a contagion of forfeited meaning, as in the Egyptian, Salah 'Abd al-Sabur's 'This is the age of boredom ... the age of lost truth ...', and Philip Larkin's 'This empty street ... the present ... a time unrecommended by event.'[9] Najib Mahfuz acknowledges his debt to Marcel Proust and Franz Kafka, as fellow purveyors of the same bewildering fascination of time and the times for the private self of a man.[10]

What does the believer do when voices around him proclaim that belief is dead and that its sentence of death is, somehow, pronounced by life itself? Is our only stance to be sardonic and await a future with an absence of conviction?

> Always too eager for the future, we
> Pick up bad habits of expectancy.
> Something is always approaching, every day
> *Till then*, we say.[11]

---

[7]  T S Eliot, *The Use of Poetry and the Use of Tradition*, London, 1933, p. 155.

[8]  Sayigh (1923-1971) translated 'The Four Quartets', and has numerous echoes of Eliot's themes and phrases in his *Thalathun Qasidah*, Beirut, 1954.,

[9]  They were contemporaries, 'Abd al-Sabur (1931-1981), Larkin (1922-1985). The former is quoted from his *Aqulu Lakum*, Beirut, 1965, the latter from his *Collected Poems*, ed, Anthony Thwaites, London, 1988, p. 65, 'Triple Time'.

[10]  See discussion in Rasheed al-Enany, *Naguib Mahfuz: The Pursuit of Meaning*, London, 1993, p. 18. He is the only writer in Arabic, thus far, to be a Nobel Laureate in literature.

[11]  Philip Larkin, *Collected Poems*, note 9, p. 50, 'Next Please'.

Can the Qur'an's solid message of our *khilafah* retrieve this situation, whether for those of its own culture whom it enervates or its victims—if such we hold them to be—in the West?

The question is complicated because of an emphasis the Qur'an has which broods on precisely this same theme of the future's presence in our consciousness day by day. It consists in its concept of 'forwarding' ahead the cumulus of deeds which will shape our 'reckoning' at the end. We do not merely have 'habits of expectancy': we have 'tallies of actuality', adding towards a verdict that takes stock of them to determine our *masir*, our destiny.

For the devout, this perception could bring a certain awe and character into our living, but otherwise it could be overtaken by the very vacuity it ought to banish utterly. It thinks a future that already relies on the significance of a present, and will not save the still dubious about themselves *per se*.

There is—and incidentally—a puzzling angle on this 'forwarding' in the current practice of 'suicide bombings' in the assertive culture of some Muslims. For it throws into one a single, grim inclusive self-'forwarding' and its strange verdict on the significance of life, namely a sort of self-oblation. It is, of course, selfishly interested in the assumed rewards of martyrdom and employs the cunning calculus of surprise which it has, like old Samson in Gaza, at the supreme cost to itself.[12] It does not stay to ask about some 'living sacrifice' in the costly, patient cause of reconciling love, where an unsparing investment of the self would more worthily belong.

Is there by some grim and twisted logic, a clue here? Time, which is the setting of the ennui of 'lost selfhood', is inexorable anyway. Whether we see it so or not, its content is cumulative. That, in itself, argues 'A mercy in his means' as Dylan Thomas wrote of 'being green and dying', i.e. young and mortal in a sequence. Hence 'end' awaiting, means 'end' attending, enlisting the two senses of the word. The suicide bomber precipitates the end in the horror of 'the means'. Thus the living we can escape in sequence, we can embrace in purpose, and 'sing in our chains like the sea',[13] if so it be. Since mortal time will not exempt from its course,

---

[12] It is often forgotten that Samson (the Book of Judges) was among the first (?) to adapt suicide as a means of mass destruction. Sadly Gaza has produced many emulators since.

[13] Dylan Thomas, *Collected Poems 1934-1952*, London, 1952, 'Fern Hill,' pp. 150-51. That 'time' spells 'means' because it makes 'occasions' from youth to age is clearly akin—in its own glad idiom—to the Quranic theme of 'forwarding' into a future that is being thus 'determined'.

all 'living in' must be some sort of 'living for', and this will be true even if we drastically conclude with a last verdict about life. Thus the inevitably cumulative must defer to 'purpose' in the very business of 'lasting', even if we foreclose it for ourselves. We have no option about what started the 'lasting': we do have about what engages it. Quitting or merely enduring exercise that option. Time as duration is the occasion for time as destiny. So much the Qur'an's 'forwarding' assigns it, but with the commendation of a 'caliphate', 'a given liability-in-privilege', as 'the mercy of its means'. It is thus wiser to accept a purpose of vocation, rather than, as otherwise we must, propose one to ourselves. Then as significantly 'meant' here, the corrosive 'losings of our selfhood' would give way to the legitimated kind, namely loving self-expenditure.

Thanks to time, life does not leave us any option to deny existence, presenting us—as it does—with a sequence of occasions of it. The suicide bomber only confirms these by closing them more drastically. When, in 1994, the Cuban regime officially denounced suicide as 'a non revolutionary position' it caught the point exactly. It meant that existence was 'programmed' from which the suicide absconded, leaving the living task undone and, indeed, besmirched. A Cuban ideology apart, does not a Biblical, Quranic understanding of our 'caliphal' status as humans confront us with a time of life and a life with time, meant for 'a fulfilling position' on our part *ad majorem Dei gloriam*? That could dispel all ennui, boredom, apathy or disgust, in the vindication of unselfish selfhood. Time being ours, should there be despair at its invitation to be a self? In an oddly perceptive way, in negative terms, Charles Dickens had his David Copperfield reflect sadly on 'what might have been' 'only to arrive at the conclusion that it could never be.'[14] Thus if lapse of time closes 'roads not taken', the thrust of time seals the ones that were. To refrain from the options of existence is only to invite its futility, with the boredom self-caused.[15] The Qur'an's 'To God is our becoming' is only a verdict about destiny in being a policy about life—a policy within our power to will.[16]

---

[14] Charles Dickens, *David Copperfield*.

[15] It would seem fair to wonder whether 'boredom' is the fruit of wilful neglect of its own remedy. This is not to discount sundry factors of job-tedium, excessive routine or harsh perpetuation of circumstance. Does some frustration of 'the pursuit of happiness' theory have to decline into 'the cult of misery'?

[16] The term *Wa ila-Allah al-masir* as in Surah 35.18, or with the pronoun 'Thee' occurs several times, *masir* deriving from the verb 'to become'. It has in view the final judgement but only as that climaxes the mortal sequences.

Scepticism here cannot be all embracing, because it is itself a grimly adopted policy. We find the same logic we are tracing in the implications of 'time', if we pass to discourse upon 'meaning'. Just as the one demands a policy, so the other implies 'significance' even in its alleged absence. If it matters about doubt and despair, as to the bewildered it plainly does, is there not 'meaning' in that search for it is urgent? Time only allows *some* options to be ignored, not all, so meaning belongs where the seeking of it pains, or troubles, or darkly occupies the mind.

Do not the bored or the agnostic alike have the solution in their own power—in their power to perceive and receive existence as a gift, 'thanking whatever gods there be,' but more sanely the only Lord there is?[17]

Since, as argued in the previous chapter, our human sexuality is a large dimension of a 'caliphal' understanding of the-privilege-to-be which we enjoy, in that procreation helps to renew creation, it follows that its trivialisation is so dire a feature of some aspects of Western culture. It takes the form of excessive exposure of the physical in sexuality at the expense of self-forfeiture in the spiritual. Marketing and advertising use the female form to cruel excess, whether in the name of fashion, or beauty-culture, or crude publicity, or the profit motive. There is a cult of gross indulgence and a de-valuing of ideals of modesty, reticence and honest admiration. The cheapening of the sexual mystery recurs in films and the media and in literature of the likes of John Updike's *Couples* and Vladimir Nabokov's *Lolita*,[18] paralleled in a host of others.

The more public aspects of the onus, noted in Chapter 2, become more intense in the private sphere of selfhood here in mind. There are few areas between Islam and the West more liable to mutual denigration. Broadly, for the Muslim mind, the female is seductive for the male as thereby, in measure, predatory or prone to provocation. The Qur'an has sundry guidance about a non-flaunting of female charms and rigorous limits about mutual access outside a narrow family circle. It has a marked distrust of male restraint in the presence of female proximity, while, as

---

[17] Facts have a way of defying those who deny their existence. So, given a 'caliphal' autonomy, the mind has to be an instrument of 'intention', not only of 'acceptance' but also of 'resistance', in that there are wrongs to oppose, as well as meanings to salute. 'The set of the soul' is the crucial vocation, recognised, served and—as far as may be—loved.

[18] 'Where marital behaviour, not to say adult discipline, were grossly travestied in the will of the novelist to indulge both the pen and the reader in a cynical exercise of wanton-ness.

earlier argued, it has a firm place for legal marriage, as a contract, and a strong prohibition of adultery. Its guiding precept on sexual love is 'love and tenderness' as a potential 'sign' or 'sacrament'.

It is, therefore, provocative to most Muslims to be subject to Western style sexual mores, given how well-nigh irresistible is their intrusion into the Muslim scene through the penetrative power of the internet, the film and the insidious forms of infiltration almost impossible to prevent, unless by the most rigorous repudiation of such media themselves, recourse to which only accentuates the mutual estrangement. It follows that the adoption of the head-scarf, if not the harsher forms of veiling, seems to many Muslim women a necessary safeguard against the menace and a token of their due modesty, their will to be soberly Islamic. That perceived necessity militates against measures of genuine liberation and makes a sharp dilemma for the feminist movement. Is there to be no 'middle way' to full female personhood, seeing that the 'caliphate' knows no crippling discrimination between the sexes?[19]

Those in the West who care about such full personhood for Muslim women against oppression and for womanhood in the West against exploitation in current terms have a duty to relate the two travesties wisely, with patience for the one, disavowal of the other. The clue and the motive have to be drawn from the clear potential of the Qur'an for the hallowing, either way, of the trust of sex and of that sex in trust, from where-ever the violations come. This has an obvious bearing on current inter-Christian debate within the Western Churches and its sharp implications for inter-faith concerns.[20]

All in all, do we look, as the suicide does, to death for what life cannot give, or do we distort life, as the profligate does, for what we think

---

[19] The 'deputy in the earth' of Surah 2.30f. may need a masculine pronoun—as Allah also does—but the words *khaliqah* and *khalifah* are feminine in form. There is no doubting that the 'creature-custodian' is other than a dignity of both sexes, their being so clearly inter-dependent in its discharge, alike in pregnancy, parenthood, nurture, family and society. Campaigning feminists in Egypt, Iran or Morocco and elsewhere, have to decide whether to argue the case from what avails for it in the Qur'an (e.g, 'sign of love and tenderness' for the perceptive) or whether to conclude that other passages are too dubious or adverse and opt for a quite non-Quranic case-making, which—in some quarters—would be far less compelling..

[20] The American Episcopal Church concluded in 2003 that the disquiet in African and Asian Churches about their innovation on 'homosexuality' was either 'primitive' or negligible. They did great disservice to the principle of ecumenical consensus they ignored, despite the urgent—and now continuing—call for patient reflection.

makes up its lacks? Truly sensed, time awaits more than 'temporising' with it, either way. It calls for the self-legitimation it affords but in terms of due surrender to the privilege it must be seen to yield. Such is the Quranic vocation to the 'caliphate', the delegacy we have from God to be on 'self-behalf' only as on 'God-behalf'.

How duly this delegacy role chimes with the dimensions of the present global scene, its ecological crisis and its political urgency! How decisively it dignifies each selfhood, as never exempt, as always relevant! How in its bearings, it evokes an inter-human mutuality across all frontiers—as, otherwise, frontiers they must be. In such 'dominion' the self, without ceasing to be private, becomes a social factor. The world loses a parasite and gains a benison. Our birth being unconsenting is all the more reason for consenting to life.

As the Qur'an became more involved in the emergence of communal structure and developed distinctive 'Pillars' in prayer, fast and alms, it also developed the theme of *niyyah*, or 'intention'. One should be focused at prayer, intent—not casual—in the payment of *Zakat*, explicit in the making of pilgrimage.[21] Hence the formula: *nawwaytu-l-Salat*, I intend the prayer-rite,' said as a kind of 'preface' at the outset.

The usage can be invoked more broadly for all our 'on-behalf-of-God' situation, so that we might say: *nawwaytu al-hayat*, 'I have intended life' being the self I am.

This 'will to be' in such defining terms leads clearly into 'the point of the secular', which is here deferred to Chapter 5. It also raises deep issues about the form and reach of divine bearing on our 'will-to-be', in what divine responsiveness or 'salvation' might be, as only 'education' that guides or also as 'grace' that co-operates. Here Islam differs sharply from Christianity over the nature of 'wrong and sin', as deeply implicit in all selfhood and its 'legitimacy'.[22] Here it is fair to say that Christianity

---

[21] Surah 4.43 decries prayer in 'polluted' state and 7.31 enjoins decorum in dress and demeanour in the mosque. Since the body is itself a mosque, the ritual ablutions make the same point of 'intention' and reinforce it. 107.5 reproaches 'the heedless at their prayers'.

[22] The point is made in more philosophical terms by F H Bradley, *Ethical Studies*, Oxford, 1876. 'How can the human–divine ideal ever be my will?' he asks. He replies that it never can be 'as the will of a private self'. 'To that self you must die, and by faith be made one with that ideal ... Resolve to give up your will, as the mere will of this or that man, ... and put your entire will into the will of the divine. That must be your true self ... You must hold to both with thought and will and all other you must renounce', p. 325. The point of this distinction bears heavily on the ensuing chapter. See the whole discussion, pp. 275–342.

demands more and assumes less, in ways we must measure in Chapters 9 and 10. More immediately they pre-occupy the chapter that follows here, as crucial for either and all things else.

'Our caliphate' is fraught with menace. That was foreseen. It is under-written by the liability of God. We may not elude its privilege by arguing that no such writ is ours as some Muslims have been liable to do on the ground that Allah's sovereignty left no genuinely sharing option to us. Birds on the wings of flight do not flout, nor do they displace, the writ of gravity. They defer to it by their very shape. They would not, could not, fly if they were weightless.[23] So it is with us humans in the realm of the divine. The terms *islam* and Islam, so often rendered in English by 'submission' or 'surrender', call not to a slavery but to a vocation. They bid to an informed conformity that waits on a willed intention. They have the shape and summons of the transcendent only in being also the sanction in a human decision. They are what the Qur'an holds all humans were fitted for, but only by the option of their own souls. The guidance of that option being the whole strategy of prophethood, prophethood too disclosed how crisis-fraught the issue would be. For the crisis transpired 'in the bosoms of men', where alone its writ could come.

---

[23] While the Qur'an nowhere uses this analogy directly 'birds on wings of flight' figure in its praise of Allah's 'signs' in the natural order and the human art of their celebration (Surah 24.41).

## Chapter 4
# 'WHISPERINGS IN THE BOSOM'

The words of the last Surah in the Qur'an (114.4-5) about 'the whispering insinuator who whispers in the human bosom' could well align at once with the words of the French poet and novelist, Charles Baudelaire, taken much to heart by T S Eliot:

'La vraie civilization ... est dans la diminution des traces du péché original.'[1]

The 'ravages' he might have said of 'original sin'—a theme in Christianity sharply repudiated by traditional Islam but only on the basis of a deep misapprehension of its meaning. For what it has essentially in view is deeply present in this 'whisperer' in the Qur'an who beguiles the hearts, the choices, the motives and so, in turn, the deeds of humankind.

بِسْمِ ٱللَّهِ ٱلرَّحْمَٰنِ ٱلرَّحِيمِ

قُلْ أَعُوذُ ... مِن شَرِّ ٱلْوَسْوَاسِ ٱلْخَنَّاسِ ٱلَّذِى يُوَسْوِسُ فِى صُدُورِ ٱلنَّاسِ

The Arabic verb, as the English, uses sound to echo sense as well as state it. You suspect the mischief before you apprehend its drift. For it conspires with things within you, ready for its promptings and apt for its cunning. The Qur'an has a fondness for the word *sudur*, the 'rib-cages', of 'breast-boxes' of us humans. 'Hearts', *qulub*, is another word, somewhat synonymous (see Chapter 7) as with *sudur* the house of the emotions and the motives, or what the Hebrew psalmist summoned in his song (103.1) as

---

[1]  Quoted in T S Eliot, *Selected Essays*, London, 1965, p. 381.

'all that is within me'.[2] Quranic 'bosoms' can be 'straitened' or 'confined' as well as 'opened'.[3] They could approve John Keats' 'the purity of the heart's affections', but know also how prone to 'impurities' they can become. For they are governed by the verb *sharaha* used also for the 'exegesis' of a text, so that they are 'read' and 'sifted' for the contents that may be less or more than they seem.[4] The idea of 'bosoms' being truly read, unlike what they enjoy from repute or 'public opinion', brings us very close to the wiles of the 'insinuator' who knows how to beguile, distort or dupe.

But who is this 'master-mischief-maker' who 'whispers'? The Qur'an uses the doer-noun, from the same verb but describes 'him', as *al-waswas al-khannas*. The epithet is intensive and comes to connote 'the Devil', from the root meaning 'to shrink', 'recoil', maybe at the mention of God, *al-khannas* is 'furtive', 'sly', 'a surreptitious loiterer with evil intent'. Or, playing on words, we might say 'a lier/liar in wait'.

The inter-association the passage makes of 'humans and jinns' as his prey is puzzling throughout the Qur'an, for a more science-minded time like our own.[5] The 'puzzles' of life itself were more dire and daunting in that 7th century Arabia where the 'inexplicable' and the 'mad' could readily be linked, where erratic behaviour or abnormal doings seemed that folk were—as the word might be—'besides themselves', i.e. goaded or driven or duped by some 'other' than themselves who had usurped their selfhood and were 'so to madness near allied'. The old commentators had other musings about the jinns but the derivative *majnun* means, precisely, 'one estranged from his senses'. Certainly the machinations of *al-khannas* for present reading of Surah 114 have squarely to do with the moral realm, with 'the desires and intents of the heart'.

There are two reasons why bosoms within us are a sort of minefield, a territory in need of watchfulness and of urgent inward negotiation and disciplined care. What is 'original' about sin in the intended

---

[2] He was hardly referring to a good digestion. *Sudur* occurs more than thirty times, with or without possessive pronouns.
[3] See Surah 6.125. Cf. 94.1 about Muhammad.
[4] Surah 39.22 tells of a man's bosom being 'interpreted' into Islam *(islam)* as the very benefaction to him, on the part of God. A 'narrowed' bosom in Surah 11.12 would be one that had forsaken the message given him to teach.
[5] It would be possible to re-visit that world by recourse to the camp-fires and oases nights in C M Doughty, *Travels in Arabia Deserta*, 1881, new ed. 1923. See my *The Tragic in Islam*, London, 2004, Chapter 3.

sense of a much misconstrued term has nothing to do with heredity *per se*, nor ours by heredity from the parental generation responsible for our birth, save that it was they who ushered us into the situation in which each of us is 'original'.

The first reason has to do with our selfhood as implicit, the second with something in the very nature of law. We are all inalienably 'ego-centric'—not, as noted earlier, in the sense of ethically always self-serving and self-promoting, but as being, by the very fabric of personhood, self-aware. We each look out from two private eyes. Our toothache, if we have it, is inalienably our own. We exist in un-shareable identity. We cannot, physically or mentally, 'be' another person.

As noted at the end of Chapter 3, this 'individuation', being thus 'self-possessed', becomes the place of many options, the core of many choices, the arena of perpetual decisions. Thanks to its inalienable self-awareness, these are liable to be—by instinct—'self-pre-occupied' and 'self-serving', at least unless we discover the nature of society, of debt and dependence, and our needfulness of others. Relatedness and love register their call to us for a certain self-expenditure, a giving of the self beyond the taking instinct, a certain self-dispossession on behalf of relationship, but happening only on the part of the self-possession that is its only 'place for such grace'. We need the self to be unselfish. In the utmost such unselfishness (so Christian faith will say)[6] we will never be 'unselfed'. The ego-centric will be crucial to the non-ego-centric, the way we are as individuated being central to the sort we may be morally.

This critical situation is, of course, 'original' to our very existence. It will always be at issue, though discipline, or habituation to love, or lively compassion, may train the 'right' self to stay such.

Precisely because we are persons in a 'caliphal' liability, by being such we contain or retain an innate self-assertion, a selfish wilfulness in moral terms as, maybe, aggressive, sulky, resentful, ambitious, envious, combative. The world around—its tensions, its economics, its passions

---

[6] It is here that Biblical and Quranic faiths differ so sharply over selfhood from the Hindu and Buddhist faiths of Asia, at least in the more radical forms of the Theravada tradition.. There, somehow, the unselfish self is held impossible, seeing that selfhood is inherently self-assertive. The empirical self has to be at length foregone in a 'forfeiture' of its 'illusion' into 'oneness' with a totality of being, its 'apartness' from which is its privation. Hence—on this view—the long training towards—not 'extinction' (since there is no 'real' to extinguish) but 'absorption'.

and its lures—will readily instigate these attitudes, or connive with their pursuit. These pages must examine more closely what these are, whence they derive and where they lead. For they are the theatre in which *al-waswas al-khannas* secretes himself to 'whisper in the human bosom' as where desires and motives dwell.

Clearly, this is where all law belongs, as monitor and guide. Thus, ethics and religion would always need to embrace and enjoin 'law and tradition' in their tribute to the human situation as, essentially, a realm of selfhoods. Law constitutes the 'tether' but has to deal with the human instinct to want to be rid of it. An illusion of would-be 'lawlessness' is present in the very need of law, in that being 'irked' by regulation is 'original' to these 'bosoms'. If a 'caliphate' was bestowed upon us, why should we not indulge it, take it as the freedom it confers but without restraints to curb us? All experience indicates that there is about law, about injunctions, negative or positive, what evokes their own defiance. To be commanded, is to ask: Why? To be forbidden is to enquire: Why not? Such is the 'originality' of sin and wrong.

The Qur'an, of course, is well aware of this situation. Indeed, one might say that, in the foresight of Allah, it exists because of it. Its major emphasis is on law and guidance, the setting of 'bounds' and the discipline by which they might be made to hold.[7] By the would-be wilful, law is seen as restrictive, even—when we are perverse—provocative and thus, in turn, somehow self-frustrated in itself, so that, in the setting of disobedience, it can only become punitive and then never be redemptive. Broken law does not regain what obtained before its violation. It has to concede offence and requite it.

In this situation the Qur'an places its firm hope in our human nature becoming amenable to law and exhortation, to reminder, to the awe of reward and dire retribution, and all these re-enforced by the discipline of habituation and of solidarity, as these are seen to avail in the 'Five Pillars' that uphold them, namely Prayer, the Fast, Pilgrimage, Almsgiving and the Witness that informs these. The 'Last Day' will have the verdict-bringing word.

---

[7]  The point has often been made that the Qur'an is more about 'man and his behaviour' that about 'Allah and his nature'. It has also that *Jahiliyyah*, or 'state of wilful ignorance' confronting Muhammad's mission, which had to be dispelled. There is even the concept of a *marad* or 'disease' as a factor in human non-submission.

This the law's dilemma is no less prominent—but differently—in the New Testament, alike in the teaching of Jesus and that of the Apostles. Paul in Romans aligns law with the very consciousness of sin. It convicts only too well as proven by its very failure. Because of it, we know the more how wrong our offendings are. But the Christian faith is less confident than Islam concerning the 'rescue' or the 'solution' available to law with its devices of reminder, of plea and of requital. These we urgently need and would be in worse case without them, as if under no indictment. Wrong must be perceived, less in terms of what we did *qua* deeds, more in terms of who we are *qua* character.[8]

This deeper diagnosis of human wrong than the ways of law can answer means in turn that we must have a larger expectation, from God,[9] from God as the source of all being, the Giver of our 'caliphate' inside which the whole quandary arises. That 'more' divinely answering this 'more' humanly, i.e. some equation between wrong and grace, must come in Chapters 9 and 10,

However the two faiths engage now with this disparity, we return to the 'whisperer' and these 'bosoms' of ours.[10] He at once goes for this dilemma of law and exploits it, by insinuation that the 'caliphate' is duping us because it has a 'tether'. What it gives, it contrives to take away. It is, therefore, suspect. It must be read under the terms of *zann*, the Qur'an's term for 'suspicion'. If not fraudulent, it is malign. 'Has God said ...?' is his doubt-casting ploy in Genesis. God is somehow 'jealous' of His own creature, this human to whom He has commanded His

---

[8] That distinction emerges very clearly in the teaching of Jesus, for whom personhood and its desires were always deeper than actual actions 'published' concerning them. There may always be inward evils which never manifest themselves in terms identifiable or indictable by laws. Paul, who knew how to examine himself in these radical terms, cried—not: 'O wretched the things that I do!' but 'O wretched man that I am' (Romans 7.24).

[9] In the sense that God's liability as being the law's 'ordainer', must pass (in the light of its violations on our part) into the law's 'repairer' which must mean more than retribution. The very fidelity of God to the intention behind law warrants what the psalmist meant by his *Expectans expectavi* (Psalm 40.1). He anticipates redemption as God's 'consistency' with Himself.

[10] Guile only functions because it senses there is already an ally within us to which it may appeal, a fallibility of character for which its suggestions are already congenial. This sense of things, tellingly explored for example in T S Eliot's drama about Archbishop Becket or Albert Camus' study in *The Fall* of his 'judge penitent' is what is meant by 'original sin', i.e. what is there within, not yet acted but already pondered. The verb *waswasa* has this double sense. It does not have to shout for a hearing.

angels to do—in some sense—that *sujud* we are bidden bring to Him.
We must imagine some kind of 'regret' on His part that He ever gave
'being to beings' as in creation He did. Have we humans been taken in
by a fraudster?

Are there not similar moods of ultimate scepticism in Western
atheism also about the God we must more than deny? He is the God we
must spurn. We renounce the very goodness of existence, denounce the
fraudster we let ourselves trust. Believing in belief is a confidence trick
we now see through.

Or, in some Western moods, perhaps it is we ourselves who are
'fraudsters', 'the more deceived' by a projection of our own. Do we posit
a 'presiding Lordship' to assuage our anxieties or safeguard our ventures,
like the poet with his poetry 'shoring up his ruins'? The world, to be sure,
is bewildering and it is re-assuring to believe that we were intended and,
thereby, qualified to 'intend' our living as those whom Surah 5.105 had
told: 'Your souls are your own.'

Radical misgivings recoil upon themselves. Either way,
decision is ours to make and we have made it positively in Chapter
3. It is in trusting that we are entrusted. The 'whisperings' about a
'suspect' world can be dispelled by courage. The timidity belongs
with those who heed them.

The wiles of this *al-khannas*, however, have ample other ruses
when thwarted by the human will to lively faith. Indeed, the irony is that
believing religion affords him major opportunity. The reason is not far
to seek. Its 'intention' to be confident exposes it to dangerous pride. Its
toughness of will may provoke it to hardness of heart. Assurance is slow to
realise that its sanctuaries may likely harbour its hypocrisies. Baudelaire was
modest in asking only for a 'diminution' of 'original sin' in any 'securing of
civilization'. With his keen register of 'sentimental education', like many
of his time, he knew the fallibility of religious disciplines.

'Nothing,' it has been observed, 'is easier to counterfeit than
devotion.' The Qur'an has its own alertness to the *munafiqun*, those
'dissemblers' who in the closing verses of Surah 49 came to Muhammad,
thinking they were 'doing him a favour'. This kind of hidden menace to
*ikhlas*, or 'sincerity' is the more likely when sanctions of outward success
attend the course of religious structures and it is seen to be 'advantageous'
to belong. While there is no virtue exempt from its own peculiar
'whisperer' advising satisfaction or self-esteem in its wake, religion by

its own nature is the most prone of all, because it gives to the ethical a dimension of obligatory sanction it holds to be divine. Therefore, in its reckonings, the good and the bad alike, the grace and the guilt, acquire an aura from a height of heaven.

So it follows that there is no panacea that need not be 'seen through' and no 'answer' that may not beg another question. How right it was that the second Epistle of Peter (which worried the early Church 'canonisers' as to its warrant to be 'sacred') had the advisory sequence:

> 'And hereunto give all diligence: in your faith minister virtue, and in virtue knowledge, and in knowledge temperance, and in temperance patience, in patience godliness, in godliness, brotherly kindness, and in brotherly kindness love.'[11]

Will not the last need to go back and begin again with faith, each needing its due attendant guardian? Will the circularity suffice itself? Or must we go with the cynic and say that 'integrity is no more than belief in its own propaganda'? Yet sincerity is eminently desirable in this all-confusing world. Thus faith resembles biography as an art which puts the artist on trial, inasmuch as 'life' and 'reputation' should not be subject to wanton trespass. Art should be allowed a proper reverence. How much more the living of a life, as a theme of proper awe, lest we should be living it in a kind of perjury? Does putting witnesses 'on oath' in courts of law imply that when we are not 'on oath' we are free to deceive? Should not an onus that safeguards honesty be current everywhere, no less than in the haunts of ordered justice? What needs exacting on oath pays scant tribute to what is urgent everywhere.

This 'something more' that oath-taking, oath-swearing, ensures (there being no perjury) obtaining everywhere is the essential business of religion—had by reference to what is recognised as ultimate, faith as the final 'court of appeal'. Small wonder, then, that it should be ever alert for a capacity to be deceived, with watchful safeguards not to be.

Thus, just as there are no panaceas in politics, so there have to be no illusions in ethics. All is susceptible to 'the whisperer' against truth, the conniver with self-esteems. Faiths become their own worst enemy by

---

[11] 2 Peter 1.5-7. It is almost as if the reservations they had about its inclusion chimed with these multiple cautions about life and faith.

preening themselves on how well they befriend their cause. Even guilt can become a theme of boast. Thus the self-accusing C S Lewis:

> 'I never had a selfless thought since I was born,
> I am mercenary, self-seeking through and through,
> I want God, you, all friends, to serve my turn ...'[12]

Paul, according to 1 Timothy 1.15—'sinners of whom I am chief'—had given Lewis a precedent to follow, perhaps with stronger reason in the light of his former zeal to persecute. Of course, no one 'ever had a selfless thought' but, thanks to that constituted selfhood, we have to distinguish the egoism of existence from the egoism of cupidity. As for that second egoism, should the sense of guilt concerning it serve further as its instrument? So the 'whisperer in the bosom'. Let guilt itself confer some eminence. Such, as Emily Dickinson phrased it, are 'the cellars of the soul', the undergrowth through which me tread.[13]

All 'de-construction' apart as a philosophy of language, there is always in religion this 'wry-construction' to which our souls are liable. Consider the parable Luke has Jesus tell (18.9-14) about 'two men in the Temple', with the publican deploring his wrong-doing as he 'stood afar off' in a self-disclaimer of holiness, whereas the Pharisee, observing him, feels profusely re-assured about his own 'righteousness' and begins to list its evidences. The necessary lesson: 'To resemble the publican' can borrow the very words of wrong-mindedness to say: 'I thank God I am not as this Pharisee.'[14] Or, perhaps, 'Look at me, beating my breast as one who knows how wrong he is!' while such ostentatious penitence is in sorry betrayal of itself.

Religious faiths are where the sinister impulses can so readily thrive, precisely because of how crucial are the things with which they must deal, as one walking in the sun is bound to cast a shadow.[15] There would

---

[12] C S Lewis, *Collected Poems*, ed. Walter Hooper, London, 1964, p. 123.

[13] Emily Dickinson, *The Poems of* ..., ed. Thomas H Johnson, Poem 1225, Vol. 3, p. 853, Harvard, 1954.

[14] Luke 18.9-14. The Pharisees, in part because of too adverse conclusions from this passage, have needed some vindication in 20th-century scholarship. All that this one said was true. It was not any lying that was indicted but his high consequent self-esteem and will to despise the publican and disown how 'his sort' could ever repent.

[15] In another poem, C S Lewis uses this same analogy—
> 'She who never since her birth
> Looked out of her desires and saw the earth

seem to be two factors at work, especially when their structures of liturgy and system and authority play their necessary role. The one is a certain brand of fear: the other is the reproach of 'rivalry'—the deep fretfulness about 'the other'.[16] 'Heresy', for example, is a source of fear—fear lest the truth be at stake to deviation that defies 'proper' authority. Institutions of faith acquire a status in themselves which then becomes essential to the very being of the God in whose Name they exist. His stake in them is seen as crucial to His own reality. To phrase it so seems fantastic, yet it happens as a corollary of the doctrinal trusteeship where, we believe, it has pleased God to locate His meaning. Hence the sure warrant to equate the writ of heaven with the writ on earth. The 'whisperer' whispers that the care for orthodoxy is paramount. This daunts the will that knows how 'love must cast out fear,' how faith must let its Lord be the only Master and itself only the servant—lest that very service hide a temptation to the contrary.

So the integrity of faith has to mean a steady vigilance against itself, lest the way it is for itself should disqualify it. Here the necessary modesty is hard to come by. Asserting its formal creed, observing its pattern of ritual and maintaining its organs of authority become its instinct, inclusively of one another and, too often, with a disinclination ever to assess them anew, lest some danger these frames have kept at bay should start to threaten. A Church, an *Ummah*, will persuade itself its mission to humankind is so vested in itself that to sustain the assertion of itself becomes that mission *per se*. It is then liable to sharpen the rigidity of its own character and contrive stronger sanction on its own status. This self-counsel is the more instinctive, if the faith is sinewed by a monopoly of political power. Bigotry and obscurantism then ensue. An element of bitterness enters the arena if 'rivalries with truth' induce a state of war.

A dark example of mutual malediction came in the setting of the tragic 'cursing' of either by the other, both before and after the tragedy of

---

Unshadowed by herself.'
*Loc. cit.*, note 12, p. 86.

[16] Cf. Robert Browning's plea—'Christmas Eve & Easter Day', *Poetical Works*, Oxford, 1905, p. 407, Para.xix.

'A value for religion's self
A carelessness about the sects of it.
Let me enjoy my own convictions,
Nor watch my neighbour's faith with fretfulness.'

Karbala'. The thrust of Husain's fateful expedition against the Umayyad Caliphate owed something—for it was long held back by hesitation and, the Shi'ah say, a deep forbearance—to the mandatory cursing of 'Ali in the Sunni mosques. After the tragedy, it became emotionally no less mandatory in the Shi'ah mosques to cry 'the curse' on the power in Damascus. For verbal vituperation, if not itself availing as a enmity, could at least sustain it.

There are endless examples of comparably grim resentments inside the annals of Christendom, no less than its hostility externally vis-à-vis 'competing' faiths. William Tyndale's urge to make an English Bible accessible to all and 'truth in the vernacular', was bitterly opposed and cruelly harried by the 'saintly' Thomas More. The scholar–translator held that the text could—and should—be intelligible to common folk beyond the concealing veil of Latin. The scholar–chancellor held that it could only be well cognised via the interpreting authority of 'Mother Church'. The one saw a clergy themselves too ignorant to teach and whom his labours would equip. Was not society on the crest of a new exhilaration with the media of printing? The other saw a sacrosanct religion in no way to be risked with the vagaries of vulgar souls, who alone could be informed by truth's custodians. Was not the new culture of printing/reading, anyway a likely menace of which the Church must stay vigilant? What divided them was taken by the powered side to violence. For the other party it spelled suffering, exile, imprisonment and death.

On all sides, examples of such enmities and of the passions they arouse litter the centuries. They also give occasion to another 'whispering' temptation in that they provide an alibi, or an exoneration, for the 'right' party, a ground to slant the charge sheet elsewhere, away from itself and on to the other. Consider the long impulse in 'anti-Semitism' to pillory Jewishness as the party to blame. Or consider the self-justification of many Zionists to absolve themselves from blame by citing anti-Semitic prejudice in any reproach on their behaviour towards the equally 'patriotic' aspirations of Palestinians. Those issues are undoubtedly heavily political but a religious animus enables them.

A prophet of the calibre of the herdsman Amos, in the supreme days of Hebrew prophethood, underlined this menace by in fact invoking it as a tactic to disown it. His 'book' begins with diatribes against Damascus, Gaza, Tyre, Ammon, Edom, Moab, the traditional 'bogeys' of his people, but only to turn the tables abruptly and lay like imprecations (2.4.f.) on his own people. This capacity for an inclusive—and so domestic—sense of wrong was the supreme glory of such prophethood. So far was self-accusation taken, that the likes of Jeremiah were seen as 'traitors' to their nation in the very act of being its most candid friends.

It is evident enough that the Qur'an gives heavy place to a reproach of non-Islam. It believed it had good reason for being harsh with the Quraish and condignly assertive against their *Jahiliyyah*, their stubborn rejection of its *balagh*. Yet in its own Meccan prescript, its will to be uncompromisingly heard stayed strictly vocal only. Its Medinan story passed to an appeal to the other sanctions of armed conflict and then the 'alibi' of the physical argument afforded no pardoning of the enmity.[17] Such struggle supposes, if it does not excite, the assumption that evil is all in the other party. There is no surer exoneration in the psyche, if not in the conscience. Absolvingly, the necessity is understood as being 'for truth's sake'. We avoid recruiting an insincere adherence, if we refrain from acquiring one by imposition or by threat. It is in its being otherwise defenceless that faith is truly commended.

Yet such defencelessness must take non-evasive form. There have been age-long examples, in the Semitic world as in the Asian, for faith to opt out of this hard dilemma by a pure quietism, a cult of asceticism and the will to self-abnegation. Some of the problems here come better in Chapter 11 and 'Divinely Liable Politics'. For the present concern we have to note that 'escape' is not escape and that the cunning 'whisperer' finds a way into the hermitage.

This is not to argue that all we need is a steady activism—an activism that leaves no space for recollection or perspective, that excludes all depth of meditation. Yet, wherever we resort to abandon or subdue our egoism (moral), do we not thither take our egoism (existential)? The more hermit-like and isolated our discipline, the more intimate we are with pride. It seems clear that active self-expenditure is the surest form of self-transcendence. Paul, for example, in his active mission, argues a sort of 'not-but-and' situation, in which 'negation of ourselves' makes 'ourselves' germane again but only as 'your servants for Jesus' sake'.[18] Only the positive

---

[17] When war ensues its claims over-ride the mutual 'tolerance' that purely discursive or 'witnessing' relationship might still admit, prefer or require, depending on their spiritual quality—the quality war will come to exclude altogether.

[18] 2 Corinthians 4.5. Abnegation, taken into vocation, becomes again recruitment only *qua* 'servant'.

of purpose dictated the negative of self as being, needed again unselfishly. It has often been remarked that all who have a high sense of vocation are markedly egoist, yet with an egoism of a surrendered kind.

That there are dangers here is not to be denied—dangers needing the caveats, the correction, of the monastic about which, as we saw, the Qur'an is ambivalent, while remaining suspicious. So we see how there may be a self-indulgence in asceticism or a reluctance for life in the option for the cloister. We cannot be excused from selfhood. Our only option after birth was about receiving it. Hence the open question of 'original sin'. Whither, and how far, will our egoism reach? For 'reach', in some measure and in some direction, it surely will. Rudyard Kipling's poem about Napoleon can ask:

'How far from S. Helena is a little child at play?'

and capture the whole 'originality' of that biography.[19]

Martyrs, too, are not exempt. T S Eliot's drama explained how darkly Becket's willing encounter with death heard loud 'whispers' of post-mortal glory and of posthumous victory over his humiliated king, and generations of pilgrims flocking to his bejewelled shrine. Thus he could criminally 'do the right thing for the wrong reason' and be guilty even in his vindication.

Nothing comparable may have attended Samson's victorious demise, but with scores of dead and dying Philistines John Milton in *Samson Agonistes* salutes nothing but 'what may quiet us in a death so noble.'The *al-khannas* is surely guileful.

Nor does he leave Muslim suiciding martyrs immune. For they forfeit life itself, not Samson-like, with 'what may quiet them,' but with what may requite them eternally and exult their families with high prestige. They die self-assured of Allah's promise, both absolved and crowned.

Suicide forecloses forever what might be done living on through living years, which—given youthfulness—could well be many. So what

---

[19] Rudyard Kipling,'A St. Helena Lullaby', *Choice of Songs from* …, ed.T S Eliot, London,1925, p. 260. In the light of Napoleon's disastrous 'retreat' from Moscow, with his army perishing in the Russian snows, Kipling goes on to ask:'How far is St. Helena from the Beresima ice?', p. 261.

our wills 'originate' passes judgement against things otherwise potential. Wilful martyrs—as opposed to the victim ones—terminate their 'caliphate', which amounts to despising it.

These are difficult areas, for all their close bearing on religious faith. Either way, the deviousness of evil in the very context of the good, is plain enough—so plain that even vigilance against it can be overtaken by it. 'The whisperer in the bosoms of men' is resourceful in his wiles and wily with his resources. Honesty has to acknowledge the sheer resourcefulness of sin and its many occasions with religion. There is this seemingly endless regression in the practice and pursuit of evil. Greed uses more money to serve larger greed, and malleable money will lend itself to the congenial occupation. Calumny will invite retort in the same vein. One lie will require another to cover it. Humility may foster its own latent pride. Motives distort the drift of argument and bad reason drives out good. The worthy passion in enthusiasm may degrade itself into a fanatic's blindness and truth become the hapless victim of its own zeal. There is no end to these machinations and religions, as their supposed monitor, are beset and harassed by them all.

It is the panorama of these features that many intelligent Muslims see written large across Western culture, while hopefully seeing their own society exempt because it has—in their view—a sharper religio-ethical discipline by its more authoritarian legal patterns and its reception of 'revelation'. That attitude can be reinforced by the perception of danger in the Western ethos and its irresistible export on to them.

Can it somehow be wrong to think to be estimable by and in society? Yet can it ever be right? It is the main charge against religious faith of such ethicists as Iris Murdoch that it will never resolve this regression of evil, since it always somehow plays into its hands by the very nature of its answer.[20] Religion never eliminates the subtle entanglements of self-

---

[20] Her point, as tersely expressed by one of her characters, is 'We cannot be good, unless we are good for nothing'—not, of course, as 'useless, lacking all skills', but with a goodness that neither wants nor possesses incentives that would compromise its integrity. Many incentives are in the hand of religion to bestow, but only falsely, such as reward, threat, comfort, grace, salvation. With these in view, she argues, there is always a 'returning surreptitiously to the self with consolations ...' There is no 'disciplined overcoming of the self.' *The Sovereignty of Good*, London, 1970, pp. 91 and 95. Christian faith would respond that the only steady self-transcendence is in self-investment in what is itself 'unself-seeking', i.e. 'the Kingdom of God'. Only when thus employed is selfhood cancelled and still fulfilled—not one without the other.

approval or finds devices that might end them. Yet, without faith, does the ethical fare any better?[21]

For the ethical realm, left to its own intellectual lights and its inner moral stamina, is still the same, fickle, frail human thing, prone to the self-deceit of self-esteem. In secular terms, it believes itself all the wiser and the cleaner for opting out altogether from religious norms or revelatory constraints, those the theisms—and Islam most imperiously—impose. Faith-people need to acknowledge that such irreligious 'humanism' has a telling case to mount against the evil dimension in the religions. For it is registering within them the very wiles of the Qur'an's *al-khannas*. There is, however, no escaping him by noting his successes with the devout and the religious. He succeeds comparably well with the Voltaires, the Benthams, the David Humes, of this world. To dispense magisterially with the readiness of God to belong in law and love with our humanity, or merely to do so cynically, is no prescript for honest self-possession, as Nietzsche came tragically to learn.

But if that 'whisperer' avails himself so well by means of the pitfalls of religion, the dark recesses of sanctuaries and pieties, he has no less ripe occasions in the corridors of political power.

It has been hard already in this chapter to separate the two realms which Medinan Islam so firmly amalgamated. But there is point here in thinking of 'the whisperer and power' aside from any formal or avowed nexus with religion. For when, as in 'secular' statehood, there is a deliberate concern to separate the two realms, that pattern will be in no way exempt from the criticism faith must have for it. Nor—as we have just seen—will its 'political ethics' be answerable only to its own counsels.

We are familiar enough with the dictum that 'power corrupts and that absolute power corrupts absolutely.'[22] Its exercise is likely to further its own self-interest, especially that of its continuity. Things political

---

[21] That might remain conjecture but, if its values truly 'govern' it, are we not back at a certain theism in values worthy to preside? The Qur'an must come sharply under any Murdoch-style reproof, in view of its steady invocation of judgement and its pledging of reward. Also there is—by her lights—its emphasis on discrimination between the good in having faith and the bad in harbouring unbelief. Thus, in the prayer of the *Bismillah*: 'Be Thou to us the Guide of the straight path, the path of those who enjoy Thy favour, not of those on whom Thine anger lies or who deviate.'

[22] Lord Acton (1834-1902) in a letter written to the Bishop of London. See *Life of Mandell Creighton*, London, Vol .1, p. 372.

can so readily take all else into their sphere, religion most of all as a tool to wield.[23] Power-wielders like Napoleon thought that religious faith was a useful factor in keeping the masses quiescent. Karl Marx, differently, had the same idea. Since the 19th century some in Islam have been anxious lest the Western cult of sociology, as a science of human behaviour, relegated religion—as advertising does female sexuality—to the mere level of a utility for a purpose, thus eliminating any divine warrant in faith, any deep claim from its ethical demand.[24] Power systems can well be intrigued by this kind of thinking and recruit it for their own ends. Indeed, what sociology might yield by way of means of control becomes in turn a new power-structure itself which, like the atomic bomb, the political order proper may come to covet, first as an ally and then as a weapon.[25]

Thus the *khannas* of Surah 114 has a very contemporary arena. One might have supposed that Islam, as the most urgent of religions for the untrammelled, never alienated sovereignty of Allah, would have avoided so far to enthrone the political order in its post-Hijrah expression, when the political realm *per se* carries within itself this explicit danger. Or perhaps that very situation required that only one 'political'—its own— could be exempt, or that the danger made monopoly mandatory.

As we may see in the chapter following, perhaps there may be a different theological truth in 'secular' statehood, in line with the caliphate of all human creaturehood in the dignity of common creation. For there, in such detachment of political power from any single faith-aegis in dominate control, all and sundry faith-wise or faith-absent would be enjoying their civic role as part of their private 'dominion'. Such a liberty, however, would leave precarious the sole magistracy of the true religion.

Such is the open issue about power either way, whether in Islam's Medinan order, or the contrasted secularity. There is no less an open matter

---

[23] Such a pattern of thought could never have been present in the 7th-century Arabian situation Muhammad faced. Had it been, the deep religious identity Islam possesses might have shrunk from its inevitable compromise in the military-political. If the religious is to be itself as inherently persuasive, it cannot also be coercive.

[24] This matter became the deep concern of the Palestinian thinker, Isma'il al-Faruqi (1921-1986). See *Islamization of Knowledge*, Herndon, 1982, and 'Isma'il al-Faruqi in the Field of Dialogue' in ed. Y Y and W Z Haddad, *Christian Muslim Encounters*, Gainsville, 1995, pp. 399-410.

[25] See the final section of Najib Mahfuz, *Awlad Haratina*, Beirut, 1965 where politicians compete covetously for possession—and monopoly—of the newly discovered power of the atomic bomb. (Also Chapter 12, note 21.)

about how the 'whisperer with cunning' will make his canny way with either. For neither will be exempt from his wiles. The immunity which power and faith in inter-bonding may think to find will be illusory. Must we not conclude that faith in God is more truly at grips with politics at an intimate distance from political power itself?[26] We have return to the issue in Chapter 11.

We have to stay well wary of this cunning 'whisperer' and meanwhile take up other issues faiths have about their business with their Scriptures in Chapters 6 to 8 before returning to him in the explicit Christian context of Chapters 9 and 10.

For to be alert to the 'insinuating whisperer' within is no more, no other, than what Christianity has always known as 'the originality of sin'. It suggests that Islam and the West should suspect and abjure idle recrimination against each other. Mutual demonising is only to be 'the more deceived'. Either could be more discerning about the other, were it more critical with itself.

---

[26] The paradox may be permitted. The 'distance' will be faith's reservations about the effect of close linkage on its own meaning and integrity. The 'intimacy' will be its urgent moral concern about justice and incorruptibility in power's exercise.

## Chapter 5
# THE VITAL POINT OF THE SECULAR

The term 'secular' denotes what is familiar enough and eminently congenial to the Western mind, while remaining troublingly opaque and even reprehensible to what is assumed to be the mind of the Qur'an. For the latter all things exist under divine decree, by divine will and to foreordained ends and destinies. It is, therefore, near blasphemy to conceive—still more to presume to contrive—anything outside His all including realm.

'The secular' and 'secularity' do not 'go' into the Qur'an's own language, its hallowed Arabic and can only be had by circumlocution that has hard work to avoid imprecision. Yet, in the Western trend towards irreligion with an instinct for 'only us', 'only here', and 'only now' by which it stays in often deliberate absence from transcendence, 'secularity' is all. A patience in the clarification of this tiresome and painful confusion is a prime necessity of realms we are trying in these pages to bring together, with a heavy onus on Qur'an reading and Western minding alike.

The needed clues are already there in the 'dominion'/*khilafah* explored in Chapters 2 and 3. To study their logic further in the interest of dispelling this sorry blindness to which either is prone about the other, we make perhaps random option for two passages. They are the more telling for making the case we need without debating the hinterlands of freedom, fatalism, or omnipotence.

أَيَحْسَبُ ٱلْإِنسَٰنُ أَن يُتْرَكَ سُدًى   أَلَمْ يَكُ نُطْفَةً مِّن مَّنِيٍّ يُمْنَىٰ

فَأَقْبَلُوٓا۟ إِلَيْهِ يَزِفُّونَ   قَالَ   أَتَعْبُدُونَ مَا تَنْحِتُونَ   وَٱللَّهُ خَلَقَكُمْ وَمَا تَعْمَلُونَ

'Does man think that he is all on his own, untethered? deriving
as he does from the mere fluid of intercourse?
(Surah 75.36–37)

'When the people came running up he said: "Are you
worshipping what your own hands have fashioned, when it is
God who has created you and that handiwork of yours?"'
(Surah 37.94–96)

In the first passage the phrase *yutraka sudan* draws analogy from
an untethered camel or donkey, free to wander off as, in animal terms,
unaccountable, a pointless creature. As Lane's *Lexicon* notes: '... left to
himself, uncontrolled, neither commanded nor forbidden,' that is, an entity
in a witless, wayless, pointless world. The imagery might, initially, seem to
play right into the hands of a familiar Muslim impression of a thoroughly
regimented human entity, tightly tethered to a moral order, beyond his
own conscience to discern and with a given destiny inexorably assigned to
him. There are verses in the Qur'an that might sustain that view. Western
prejudice has made much of them in controversy.

However, inside the very tether metaphor itself—and far more
cogent in the human case—is the meant-for-a-purpose element in the
tethered state, holding a future promise out of a given past, an existing
for which there is a role in a scheme. Were the untethered state absolute
we would, in Hebraic idiom, have the scapegoat banished to doom in
a wilderness. The metaphor avails to draw out of an animal analogy the
profound truth of man with a meaning and a meaning for man, a wanted
not an abandoned creature cancelled by negligence.

We see here 'the point of the secular' in our 'not on the loose'
situation as thus held for a meaning. However,—and by the same token—
he (the man) could wish himself 'left so'. He would prefer a tetherless
condition, were it not the forfeiture of meaning. As long as he 'minds the
meaning' he must agree the tether. For the tether is its sign and the sign
the experience.

Has not the verse then captured the very nature of our human
scene, as a crisis of self-acceptance that has no escape into some optionless condition but must always consent 'to-be-in-meaning', as one held
for it? For 'the secular' is just this open verdict around something we
may not evade but have to consent to fulfil. Our sense of being 'liable'
is real enough, but real within us also is our urge to think, and have, it

otherwise. The 'secular' belongs inside that state of things. Experience is the critical—critical—material of our own will or unwill. Things in trust with us we set at risk from us.

To see it so tallies with all we learned earlier about our 'caliphate'. It certainly belongs with all those sinister 'whisperings' breathing in the previous chapter. It tells a sense of the 'human as liable' which any intelligent humanism could also underwrite without necessarily tracing it to God. It confirms a whole Semitic faith in the onus of personhood as humans know it, at once optionless and option-laden.[1]

That paradox is under-scored by the pathos in the 75.37 verse: 'deriving as he does from the mere fluid of intercourse,'—so fraught a creaturehood from so frail and fleeting, yet so momentous, an origin.[2] The Qur'an deploys here its frequent alertness to the mystery of human wombs, embryos and intercourse in procreation, there in the founding Surah 96. Sperm has a strange fascination as the whence of all whithers. Its point in Surah 75 is surely to base our 'serious being' on a kind of 'even thus' around its origin.[3] We who never willed to be are willed to be by parenthood. The tethers begin in who and where those parents were, yet convey us to where in adulthood we must respect them as our own. The hazard of birth sobers and shapes the decisions of existence. These are our secular estate. Biography must seek its sanctity.

In its different way, Surah 37.94–96 re-enforces the logic of the other. It tells of Abraham, a model 'Muslim' iconoclast who comes to his people to remonstrate with them about their idols. As if coining an argument for a later Isaiah, he would have them know that when they fashion wood into an idol it was God who gave the forest where they hewed it. Thus He had made both it and their handiwork in the fashion

---

[1] In that 'the self-to-be' has no consulting role in his/her genesis but is nevertheless ushered into what must be willed, undergone, undertaken, where even to quit is an option taken. How much poetry and literature, East and West, muses on this central theme in all pregnancy! What, for example, of the infant, Thomas Hardy, left aside by a midwife as a non-survivor, yet surviving eloquently to ruminate on the human condition. Surah 75.39 goes on to note again the Qur'an's steady theme as to 'male and female'.

[2] The translation here varies. Arberry has: 'Was he not a sperm-drop spilled?' and Pickthall: 'Was he not a drop of fluid that gushed forth?' The one here tries to capture the literal 'origination' better. The Qur'an registers throughout a deep if frank wonderment about what the West vulgarly dubs 'sex'.

[3] The hint on the fortuitous is also on the precarious and the yet unknown, how bizarrely we 'have our entrances.'

either gave the other—and had 'made' them as well![4] 'The point of the secular' here turns on the double sense of the words 'made' or 'fashioned', in that what had been created—and feasible for human use—was the raw material of the product humanly 'made'.

It follows that the 'secular' is precisely this manageable, available, accessible world, being handled into the 'product' to enter into the 'commerce' of society, whether that of trade, or justice, or politics, or culture, or education. All of these, in turn, convey into 'the ethical', and on that 'ethical' turns whether or not it consecrates at our, or others' hands, into what 'hallows' it as duly under God. It was Allah's already. Creation made it occasion, by human use and verdict, for becoming *also* a thing morally 'according to His will'—and that because of us. We transact what the West esteems as 'enterprise', pursuing 'dominion'. It only 'signifies' for the divine praise when we know and possess it 'in God's Name'.

The conceptual—and psychic?—problem for the Muslim mind around this secular theme has always been the meaning of Allah's 'omnipotence', as all-disposing, all-decreeing, all controlling. Indeed, there are aspects of the Qur'an that so insist and Surah 37.96 has been wrongly read in that very sense,[5] by translating: 'Allah has created you and all you do,' i.e. 'your every deed' as not out of your 'freedom' but by God's imposed necessity.[6] *Ma ta'mulun* is not 'what you do' but 'what you manufacture,' in the context about Abraham deriding idol-carving carpenters. The very context banishes the fatalists.

Moreover, the meaning of the Qur'an's proper insistence on divine sovereignty cannot mean negation of the human 'caliphate'. It was

---

[4]   In the sound sense of a mistreated word we can only 'exploit', i.e. develop, utilise and so fulfil, by dint of what is 'to hand' for us. All farming, all engineering, all culture, all civilization are this way—a 'being' that is material availing for 'being more', in arts and sciences across all mortal time.

[5]   It could well have figured in Chapter 6 below as an example of wayward exegesis, culpably neglecting the context. In Daud Rahbar nearly half a century ago there was a pioneer study on contextual exegesis and the distortions had in defying it. See *God of Justice, A Study of the Ethical Doctrine of the Qur'an*, Leiden, 1960.

[6]   It was, no doubt, crucial for Muhammad—in his setting of plural worship—to stress divine sovereignty. Sundry deities mean that phenomena are plurally attributed here and there and, emphatically, 'God is not God unless God alone.' The human role, however, has to be acknowledged by the Qur'an's own doctrine as valid and real inside God's authority as what it does not compromise and, in lowly caliphal part, fulfils unless we be perverse.

Allah's explicit will (2.30 *et al.*) that the creature should be the tenant-trustee. His sovereignty wills and includes the human subject-mastery. It must be clear, therefore, that we could never have the God-fearing, the 'sacred', the hallowed, were not this 'secular' the place where it could happen—but does not if we will otherwise. And the open question is always there.

The point is re-enforced in that Abraham's local carpenters were manufacturing idols, whom then—as finished articles—they 'worshipped'. Doing so, made them 'secular', not now in the open option but in the heinous sense. How apposite 'manufacturing for idolatry' is to the contemporary West! Industry in the sheer pursuit of gain; advertisement making 'commodity' ever more 'the bias of this world'; money trading immorally to money's increase; accumulated wealth callous about accentuating poverty. The 'secular' present in its neutrality becomes the 'secular' 'on the loose'.

We have to keep that double meaning in mind.[7] The physical/material realm awaits its ethical 'right' or suffers its ethical wrong. Our 'caliphate' decides. The very codes, warnings, and injunctions of Islam[8] cannot rule out the second unless they rule in a mind for the first. Or, in terms of a constant Quranic refrain, humankind may live and act *min duni-Llahi*, 'to the exclusion of God', the God who is effectively 'excluded' or disallowed as God, by the *mushrikin* in the practice of idolatry, the heedless who violate God's order by 'what they manufacture.' That Allah can 'suffer' exclusion in the human realm is surely the ultimate evidence of the secular in the utmost form of its 'miscarriage'. Yet it could not tragically 'miscarry' in that way, unless it were the place and time where it might be bent on the good.

There has been pioneer thought among Muslims, in this regard, about the meaning of the term *islam* (without the capital letter, as usage

---

[7] Since this 'secular'-like clay on the wheel of the human potter is awaiting the 'shape' only the potter will give. Clay's malleability may suggest how—thanks to the 'yieldingness' of the (normal) natural order—that order is amenable to our skills and wills and thus affords occasion (as we crudely say) for 'what we make of it.' The analogy gains here from the fact that, Biblically, it was used of what God does with humans via circumstance. However, given our gift, by Him, of 'dominion', the two belong together. For the Qur'an's Abraham in parallel with Isaiah, see Isaiah 44.9-17. Cf. Psalm 115.4-8.

[8] As, for example, its 'edition' of the Biblical Decalogue, with further points, in Surah 17.22-39, beginning and ending with a singular worship of the One, and including a generous but discerning hand in giving (29) and the prohibition of infanticide (31).

foreign to Arabic) for the structured institution Islam It suggests that, in its quality, everything is muslim, in that things behave according to their 'law', whether inanimate mineral, or animate creatures, or humankind. Only the third is volitional, since the other two 'obey' by their chemistry or their genes or their instinct. Only intelligent consciousness weighs, debates, assesses and decides—to conform or to rebel, to 'be' or not to 'be'.

Our being thus volitional requires the secular as its arena. We are back with the reality of our 'caliphate' where 'what we do with what there is' is always at stake as to good or ill, praise or blame, grace or guilt. We humans can only be volitional because all else, from stones to stars, is 'law-abiding' that we might be 'law-acceding'.[9]

The case for 'the point of the secular' is sufficiently made. There is no Quranic ground for denouncing it in the interest of preserving an omnipotence, seen as somehow compromised unless we are its victims. Allah is indeed 'almighty over all things' and truly 'omnicompetent', and proven so by the very thing we shrink from recognising in ourselves as entrusted by His magnanimity. Soundly understood, the whole Quranic scheme of creaturehood as ours, of prophethoods coming our way with prescripts for our guidance and reminders for our negligence, conveys us to the truth of ourselves and commands us by it. We inhabit the secular in order to dwell with the sacred.

In its own Muslim terms this vocation might be seen as akin, in part, to the call to 'virtues' in the Buddhist Path, the appeal to 'right mindedness' and 'right discerning' and 'right willing'. Or what of kinship with the intriguing Christian turn of phrase about 'all good works prepared for us to walk in'?[10]—not, in context, 'walking into factories' or into 'the Stock Exchange', but in the sense where 'works' are 'deeds' not gadgets, loves and not machines.

We have an illuminating angle on this care with the secular if we consider the insights of the ascetic or the hermit, as these belong in all traditions. For it is possible, perhaps praiseworthy, to greet the secular

---

[9]  Unless 'abiding' implies conscious perception. Humans certainly have to 'accede' to what law would enjoin upon them. Even the primal: 'Establish no other worship' is defied in the committing of *shirk*.

[10]  *The Book of Common Prayer*, second post-Communion Prayer.

realm with a firm renunciation. Sufism, in some of its forms[11] has contrived to do so in 'the household of Islam' and with impressive reading of the Qur'an as warrant for it. Yet in measure, the tactic only leaves the business of things material to others who, without the ascetic, must care for the traffic of society and the onus of ongoing history. For 'works', as the English liturgy speaks of them, are ineluctable. They demand to be undertaken. They are a presence which disallows an absence. Or, in Karl Marx's dictum: 'To be in the world is to be at the world.' Response to living there has to be, even if it is only that of dis-intention. Time will not have a stop. The calendar is relentless in this secular sense and history takes all of us with it in its momentum, whether we are in its stream or in its cloisters. How well Robert Frost captured this sense of a 'secular-historical' in his lines on 'The Mayflower':

> 'No ship of all that under sail or steam
> Have gathered people to us more and more
> But Pilgrim-manned the *Mayflower* in a dream
> Has been her anxious convoy into shore.'[12]

Recluses may share, but differently, while activism has the ventures where only futures happen. And 'the point of the secular' is precisely 'happenings', their motive, their engagement and their fruit.[13]

The West, least of all the American West, has not looked to Islam to educate its activism. If now, we are seeking to relate the two, the drift of this chapter, thus far, has been to persuade Islam—from its own

---

[11] Many Sufi orders in Islam's middle centuries-were also active guilds of workers in crafts who were trading in the suqs and met in their *zawiyas*, often weekly in the evening before the Friday Prayer-rite. Islamic mysticism appealed to the example of Muhammad himself, or it argued that the doctrine of *Tawhid* was not meant as only *about* Allah as One, but the human quest for the 'unitive state' with Him, in the 'passing away' of the empirical self by absorption into 'the One'. There are many Quranic passages that might be read and claimed in that sense. While 'monasticism' (or its 'monks and priests') comes in for praise in 5.82, it is reproved as an 'invention' in 57.27.

[12] Robert Frost, *Complete Poems*, New York, 1958, p. 333, entitled 'Immigrants'.

[13] It is notable how commendable seems an ascetic disavowal of the instinct to acquire, to need, and to possess, yet also how escapist from the toils and hope of the world as a sphere for participation. Cf. Bede Griffiths, *Return to the Centre*, Arizona, 2003 ed., pp.2-3. 'India has a way of reducing human needs to a minimum ...There is no need of any furniture—people go by a stream to relieve themselves ... the renunciation of "I" and "mine".' How far must 'detachment' from a self mean exemption from one's world in not belonging with its humans?

Qur'an—to rethink its long misconception of the secular, as not really allowable because Allah is omnipotent, with no realm not immediately subject to His single will. Turning the parties round, we need to ask what positive business Islam might have with the West beyond critique of it?

That it has threatening business is all too apparent from bitter alarums and aggressions in the brutal and elusive shape of current technologies in bombs and subterfuge.

With these so heinous, negative and cursedly pre-occupying, does any Qur'an case-making as here attempted deserve any credence? Its point about our human quarrel with 'the tether' is perhaps the clue. For it captures the situation Western ways exhibit all too harshly. Let us take the foregoing analysis of the necessarily secular nature of sciences in that their processes, in the giveness of nature, are neutral with us humans and thus allowing our 'dominion'. There is, however, a moral and spiritual 'tether' to them. This our human perversity chafes at and, so bent, moves to a total 'secularisation' that lives in self-absorption. 'Dominion' is then only downward, indulging in mere mastery and its intoxicating range and lure.

Comparably, a defiantly secular impulse is present in all politics, as liable to be self-absorbing and self-serving in the exercise of power, disdaining to be 'tethered' by spiritual constraints, be its form either autocratic or democratic.[14] We have to say 'necessarily' in the realm of science and its techniques, 'inherently' of the sphere of politics, because both flow alike from 'dominion' given and pursued. 'Untethered' their point is forfeit.[15]

When, in this way, sciences and politics pursue their mandate in self-wandering ways, to the perverting of their liberties in nature and society, the moral, spiritual order is also violated and a total 'secularisation' ensues. The 'dominion' which was ever only 'given' as 'entrusted', is then grabbed in its feasible material and physical sphere, to be betrayed in its

---

[14] For what the West does not always realise is that 'democracy' is no panacea, as if somehow immune from the hazards of human nature and, not least in the USA, eminently manipulable by vested interest, lobbies, media interpretation and voting irregularities. Often the process, albeit with the admirable principle 'One person one vote', may well not produce the persons with qualities of integrity most fitted for office.

[15] The natural order does not yield to us the sciences in any deference to our religious allegiance. Its 'neutrality' means that with it, we are all 'secularists'. The faith element comes with how we utilise and employ its 'wealths' and 'means'.

moral and spiritual realms as no longer a 'dominion' for a servant's exercise. Man the master is subject no longer.

As in the New Testament parable of 'husbandmen in a vineyard' and also in the Qur'an's sense of Allah as *Al-Ghaib*,[16] there is and has ever been a certain 'absence' about God. It is just the 'dominion granting' form of His presence, though Christians and Muslims know the nature of that paradox in distinctive ways.

Three decades ago, the American Islamicist, Marshall Hodgson, both stated and mis-stated the difference between the two theologies. Digressing briefly to him furthers this vital point in the secular. He wrote:

> For Christians, being based in revelation means being in response to redemptive love, through the presence of a divine-human life and the sacramental life of which that is the source. For Muslims, being based on revelation means being in response to total moral challenge … in an explicit divine message handed on through a loyal human community.

He insists that, the contrast being so complete, the two 'exclude one another categorically.'[17] Could they?—given one God and the unifying category of 'revelation'? 'Revelation' either way is about what remains 'beyond' yet means relevance our way. There is 'moral challenge' in 'redemptive love', just as there is need for 'redemptive love' around the workings of 'total moral challenge'.

Coming back to what *must* be relatively secular, as a trust, *may* be made utterly 'secularised' by that trust's betrayal, we see that the two faiths differ, not about 'absence' and 'presence', but about whether the ultimate clue to either is a will that legislates and presides, or that presides, shares and suffers. On that clue must turn how we read the 'absence' and how we

---

[16] Used almost fifty times in the Qur'an as denoting the 'hidden' aspect of divine transcendence—though 81.24 about Muhammad's revelatory experience, says.'He is not one to keep jealously to himself the transcendent mystery.'Yet even what can be told is wrapped in a 'beyondness'. *Al-Ghaib* is also 'the realm unseen on the far side of death' of which 72.26 notes: 'He (Allah) knows that realm unseen of His and to none does He disclose it except to apostles of His choosing.' Surah 64.18 says: 'The knower of the unseen, He is ever mighty and wise.'

[17] Marshall G S Hodgson, *Rethinking World History: Essays on Europe, Islam and World History*, ed. E Burke iii, Cambridge, 1993, p. 80. The words omitted … read 'as it is confronted' which might more happily have been 'as it is known.'

respond to the 'presence'. For 'dominion'—as our experience of both—is how we must be sacredly 'secular' in order never to be fatally 'secularised', such being the neutrality of nature and the liability of politics, where for both our *khilafah* reigns.

Before tracing 'the West' by this analysis, it is urgent to notice that when we do not have the wisdom to be authentically, but will the 'exclusion of God', some of us can arrive at an intense religious absolute, as if in retaliation. Such is the dark feature of a contemporary Islam. It is as if humans had to rescue Allah from his own magnanimity with us. There are also menacing Christian forms of the same reaction. It is no proper part of ours to be somehow fearing for God's sovereignty and, in that very zeal, mistaking its quality. Surah 2.30f has Allah ruling out all fears for the 'safety' of his 'venture'—using Hodgson's word—into the grant of human 'dominion', all misgivings about how it might miscarry. There was a clear warning to Muhammad that he was not 'liable' as a 'warden/warder' might be concerning people to whom he was sent as a *rasul*.[18]

The tragedy is that these usurpers of 'the rights of God' think they are defending and ensuring them. Yet they do not shun or despise the techniques that only a 'secular' prowess down the centuries, whether in Islamic or in Western hands, has contrived to afford them. On the contrary, they avail themselves avidly of munitions and the internet, of aircraft and the media, of all the skillings in killing a global scene affords. They are 'secular' in the protection of the God who had left these means to a truer discretion, as the due tribute both to the trust He placed in them and to His own glory.

There is clearly 'a zeal for God that is not according to knowledge.' Its vehemence is, in part, due to a traumatic sense of being defied, invaded, provoked by what it must resist, as if in counter defiance, invasion and provocation. Somehow by such lights as it brings from its 'givens', its West, being essentially inimical, must be under its retaliation. That instinct finds warrant in a long tradition of *jihad* which, for them, is not to be re-minted as any inner struggle with the self as a

---

[18] Surah 6.107: 'We have not appointed you to be a guardian *(hafizan)* over them, nor to exercise any responsibility over them *(wakilan,* i.e., 'one put in charge of'). Surah 10.100 asks Muhammad 'Would you compel men to believe?' with the clear implication that he neither could nor should. Surah 76.24 bids 'wait in patience' as under the Lord's command. Even messengers are 'tethered' in truth-service.

discipline of personal righteousness. Or it goes that way inward only as an impulse to the self-abnegation of suicide as the ultimate dimension of what God, so usurped in His own prerogative of appointing one's dying, is assumed to demand.[19]

In a strange sort of way, how 'secular' the likes of *Al-Qa'idah* are in that, usurping Allah's cause as their own, they do not 'let Allah be God' in His own Quranic terms of being so via a truly 'hallowing' human submission inside the 'caliphate' of His all-governing writ. They think themselves 'on the loose' under no restraints of moral 'tether', the *hudud* God obliged conscience to place on inter-human dealings. Or they thought they could rescind these in their own religious mind. They have cruelly 'secularised' Islam itself, as a 'cause' breaking all laws.

Confronted so blatantly, it is fair to ask again whether the language of 'the War on Terror' was the right response? What reciprocally transpired has certainly embroiled the West in an intense quarrel with Islam, but only with a false segment of it. Yet the form of the response, for all its busy disavowals of itself as any such quarrel, did in fact read the situation as calling for punitive retaliation, in terms of a 'War' which—as such—it could never win. Perhaps *in situ* no other human reaction could have given public satisfaction. Could there have been announced instead a 'Campaign-for Peace between Cultures and the Faiths that Inform them'? That would have distinguished between the sort of Islam it had indeed to resist and a larger Islam capable of sharing the 'Campaign', and—more—being vital to it as the most potent factor against the other sort. Instead the single 'War on Terror' only partially identified its task and made any success the more problematic by neglecting the major part of it. The major part lay in identifying and enlisting all that could participate. As it was—and as otherwise it remains—'the War' focused on 'the Terror' is in danger of seeing 'the Terror' as its only business—business liable to be seen in hemispheric terms as what '*we* are against' uniquely.[20] 'Tethered' wisely to reality, we would need to see it and pursue it in more inclusive terms than 'war' as 'ours' and 'terror' as 'theirs'.

---

[19] Our dying, its place and time and cause are understood to be in God's disposing care, as was our receiving of life, and as will be our post-mortem 'bringing back to life'. Thus the suicide pre-empts Allah's will, seeing himself perversely as its own agent, by arrogating to himself the decisions of God. This—it could be argued—is a very 'untethered', 'secular' version of 'martyrdom' to be distinguished from that only suffered at another's hand.

[20] 'Uniquely' not as being without potential allies, but as engaging primarily as 'anti-terrorist' in concept and strategy.

All those sinister 'whisperings in the bosom' studied in the preceding chapter had their heyday in the grim build-up to September 11 2001. There have been many in the aftermath. The hope here argued of both seeing and engaging Islam and Muslims in some 'tethering' together with the West in the quest for inter-cultures duly in an inter-peace, turns in part on certain matters around their own internal possession of their Scripture and its right readership. These are the task of Chapters 6.and 7, before we reach the more explicitly Christian issues always crucial in Muslim/Western concern.

Perhaps, meanwhile, we glimpse the whole 'point of the secular' if we draw an analogy from the art of words. 'When I experience anything,' wrote the poet, Dylan Thomas, 'I experience it as a thing and a word at the same time.'[21] How keenly he savoured the inter-penetration of the two. His language could celebrate vision by capturing some double image, even a paradox, within the single word, so that the 'thing' was enriched in the telling.[22] This impulse in the poetic mind around word and thing suggests the quality of all material experience, told in the Qur'an as a 'sign-bearing' order and in Christian perception as 'sacramental'. What is present to us for our handling is trusted with us for our hallowing. Our technique-affording sciences are the material of our God-serving vocation. We do not 'experience' the secular without being confronted by the sacred. To ignore the double quality is to be 'secular' indeed but only by a treason to 'the beautiful and terrible worth of the earth'.[23]

---

[21] See E W Tedlock, *Dylan Thomas: The Legend and the Poet*, London, 1960, p. 54.

[22] Hence his innumerable, sometimes bewildering, usages, as in 'the force that through the green fuse drives the flower' about growth in the spring, or 'this monumental argument of the hewn voice', as a figure of speech alike about the meaning of personhood and the 'sculptor' 'craft' of words. See *Collected Poems*, 1934-1952, London, 1971, pp. 8 (poem named by that line) and 81—'After the Funeral'.

[23] See John Ackerman, *Dylan Thomas: His Life and Work*, London, 1964, p. x.

# Chapter 6
# THE BURDENED SIGNIFICANCE
## OF WORDS

Though from different motives, religious faith and modern culture share an uneasy relationship with words. The issue in the one case is an unwillingness to use them in the currency of holy things lest these are ill-served by their compromise. In the other context, there is either a vulgar pursuit of headline brevity which cheapens meaning, or there is a philosophic doubt of word validity as such.

This language situation has long been the burden for custodians of belief. The great Hebrew prophets used the 'burden' word not only for the weight their task laid upon them, but for any transaction with its import.[1] Old Asian faiths tend to exclude language altogether, though words are needed to explain the case for silence. The Buddha will 'speak' through the sign of an enigmatic smile, since only so may his meaning be disclosed. The Western scepticism about trusting what is verbal is of a different order. It stems from a suspicion that instead of conveying meaning, words are somehow taking it into a captivity in which language conditioned the truth of it. What William Wordsworth long years earlier had called 'circumscription' 20th-century logical positivism identified in words as a sort of pretension, things with a worth of their own coining, the value of which was not otherwise available.[2] Does not the very word 'text' come from 'to weave', as in 'textile'? Words thus wove their own

---

[1]  It meant the cost of vocation, as supremely, with Jeremiah, but also, concurrently and reciprocally, the message it conveyed. There is a similar usage when, in Surah 73.5, Muhammad is told: 'We will cast upon you *qawlan thaqilan*—'word of weight" i.e. a heavy task with a heavy text. See *The Weight in the Word*, Brighton and Portland, 1999.

[2]  He was exploring what might be called an 'inter-texture' between thought and language, the degree to which they only 'happen' in and by each other. He wrote of 'the concerns of religion ... being far too weighty for the mind to support without ... resting a great part of the burthen upon words and symbols.' 'The Infinite Being' had to 'accommodate Himself to a finite capacity'. *Prose Works*, Vol. 3, p. 65. It was in this way that he saw

fabric in the frame of their own grammars and to these meaning and intention were hostage.

It would be important for religious faith that there should be rescue from this alleged situation because spiritual anxiety is of a different order. One might dismiss abstract philosophical subtleties and invoke a pragmatic confidence to 'call a spade a spade' but there remained the haunting question about whether and how well one could speak of 'God' or know, without blame or blemish, how one understood or meant the word. What, in actual comprehension, could be meant by 'revelation' or some 'word of God', or 'divine speech' in hand as 'His Book'? There was not only the sharp Kantian dilemma of how language could credibly relate to what lay beyond the range of the sense experience from which he said the mind alone drew its knowledge. And what of that 'mind itself' as the place and the agent of the ordering of sense experience—the mind that could not think other than its own thinking or know how it might think, if only rid of itself as imposing the norm?

Faith might will to transcend or ignore these scruples and plead its own confidence in the given-ness of its Scriptured truth. Indeed, it might say that only in doing so had it known and received them—'a Book in which there is nothing dubious.'[3] Yet what if that Book itself—not to say the external world it was faith's duty to address and persuade—required it to have its contents under earnest *tadabbur* or 'reflection' so that its received authority was purposely enlisting a deliberate and painstaking consent?[4] Would it suffice for a faith's integrity to consist only in bare assertion? Was not Islam from the outset banishing *Jahiliyyah*—'ignorance'? What if uneasy or wilful 'ignorance' remained when it had purported to do so?

---

poetical language as itself 'incarnational', in that 'words give the Word a fixed home,' and the truth of things

'... through the turnings intricate of verse
Present themselves as objects recognised.'

*The Prelude*, Book v, concluding lines.

[3] Surah 2.2: *la raiba fihi* with the following words—'a guidance to the God-fearing'. Does the verse mean that the Qur'an is utterly authentic in its meaning for all such, or that—all such readers apart—it is indubitable, as is a geometric design?

[4] The point is made elsewhere in the context of our 'caliphate' and in Chapter 7. Its *ayat* need incisive reckoning with their content no less than the *ayat* of nature, to which the Qur'an repeatedly appeals.

To be sure, the duties of a faith to and with itself are more than intellectual. Faith has dealing in and with the heart no less than with the mind. Language is performative as well as informative. It moves as well as tells. The 'heart' dimension in the Qur'an is due in the chapter following. The concern of this one is with the problematics of faith–language and the text of words in what they weave for the intelligence, so that their poetry in the will is honest with their truth.

It is evident on many counts that Islam is the most textual, the most confidently verbal, of all religions. Its own mystics apart, it is farthest of all from those instincts for silence at home in the Asian world. Its Qur'an has a quite different thesis about what its language achieves than does the New Testament, where the ultimate 'Word' is the incarnate Lord and the text derivative in being 'sufficiently' descriptive of Him.[5] Thus the Bible is about what is more ultimate than its verbal–ness, namely event and history in which 'revelation' is housed and whence it becomes interpretation. This is still more true of the Gospels and Letters of Christian event-history. These are the 'de-scribing' of what, antecedent to them, is a sort of poesis as, in the end, all religious language, however literal, strives to be.[6]

Nowhere, then, is the reliance on language *per se* more emphatic than in Islam's sense of its Qur'an. Its Scripture is a realm of sound as well as sense. It must be voiced in recital as well as cherished in calligraphy. It is meant for the ear no less than the eye. Its exegesis begins with its parsing. Theme and sentence co-exist. It is the utmost in textuality, so that the excellence of its Arabic is central to its truth–credential. It was mediated into its earthly incidence as transmitted from *Umm al-Kitab* present eternally with Allah. Its faithful reception has long necessitated faith as to the total 'illiteracy' of Muhammad as its recipient in Meccan and Medinan time and place.

This Islamic sense of what a revealed Scripture exists to be must mean an obvious disputing of what we are calling the awkward necessity of words. What 'awkwardness', given the entire satisfactoriness

---

[5]  'The Word' for the New Testament is 'that we have seen and heard and handled' (1 John 1.1) —'the Word made flesh', Jesus in the full event of his Christhood, to which the writings give us access. 'Sufficient'—to be distinguished from 'infallible'—is the Anglican confidence. Trusting it, we will still need discernment but it will not fail us.

[6]  To break the word this way as of language 'setting down' its theme in the terms by which the writing 'takes it up.' Meaning has its expression by what gives it 'word' and 'form', but the authorship is receiving not inventing.

of an immortal Arabic? But something at least latent in that confidence is present and needs to be explored—which is the purpose of this chapter. A verse which has always been crucial for *tafsir* is aware of its presence. It comes in Surah 3.7.

$$هُوَ ٱلَّذِىٓ أَنزَلَ عَلَيْكَ ٱلْكِتَٰبَ مِنْهُ ءَايَٰتٌ مُّحْكَمَٰتٌ$$
$$هُنَّ أُمُّ ٱلْكِتَٰبِ وَأُخَرُ مُتَشَٰبِهَٰتٌ ۖ فَأَمَّا ٱلَّذِينَ فِى قُلُوبِهِمْ$$
$$زَيْغٌ فَيَتَّبِعُونَ مَا تَشَٰبَهَ مِنْهُ ٱبْتِغَآءَ ٱلْفِتْنَةِ وَٱبْتِغَآءَ تَأْوِيلِهِۦ$$
$$وَمَا يَعْلَمُ تَأْوِيلَهُۥٓ إِلَّا ٱللَّهُ وَٱلرَّٰسِخُونَ فِى ٱلْعِلْمِ يَقُولُونَ ءَامَنَّا$$
$$بِهِۦ كُلٌّ مِّنْ عِندِ رَبِّنَا وَمَا يَذَّكَّرُ إِلَّآ أُو۟لُوا۟ ٱلْأَلْبَٰبِ$$

'He it is who has sent down upon you (s.) this Book. There are revelations within it which are quite categorical and explicit. These are the Book in its essential meaning and nature. Other verses employ metaphor and analogy. Those who in heart incline to deviant ideas have a habit of following these metaphorical parts with a will for discord and tendentious exegesis. God alone it is who knows the interpretation of it. Those who are well grounded in the knowledge of it say: "We have put our whole faith in it: it is all from our Lord." It is only those endowed with real perception who take it to heart.'[7]

Surah 3 is Medinan so that the passage, with its remarkable frankness, belongs many years into the mission of Muhammad. Should we understand from its handling of those *mutashabihat* that mischief-

---

[7] *Muhkamat* almost has the sense of 'decreed', an 'authoritative' thing not subject to any receiving 'surmise'—hence the use of two English adjectives. 'Essential meaning' renders the much debated clause: 'these are the mother of the Book.' The *Mutashabihat* are what tell by 'similitude' or 'likeness'. These are 'other' than the 'decisive' and allow the unwary or the malign, occasion for 'hearts prone to *zaigh*' an ugly term, presuming to discern what is known truly only to Allah. Such are quite far from the 'steadfast' who bring an entire 'taking to heart'. The 'heart' factor belongs here to Chapter 7. The translator needs to be alert to all aspects of a basic ruling.

makers had already exploited them to create controversy? It is clear that, by making the distinction so squarely, the Qur'an was alert to what might well be 'awkward' in the very nature of language and that, therefore, even its assurance about 'a clear and luminous Arabic' might not ensure it safe carriage into a maliciously human world. Thus, pointedly, it has a cautious caveat about words that are 'metaphorical'—despite these being often the most evocative of impact on the heart—as liable to give rein to perverse minds, reading *of* being always prey to reading *in*.

It seems clear that the Qur'an's essential assurance about a sure inherence in its words of meaning and language has to be tempered by the menace of metaphor. This was to lead the theologians, as we must see, into crippling reservations about the very 'Names' of Allah. Was it wise or prudent thus to prejudice the very employment of analogy as prone, unlike 'things categorical', to unhappy treatment on the part of readers? For on 'readings' its whole intention turns. Must it be frustrated in its ends by the risk implicit in its means? For being less than 'categorical' by the tactic of necessary imagery and verbal symbol is inseparable from the language of a faith seeking theology—Allah being in no way abstract in mere cerebral telling.

Surah 3.7 offers no clue how the distinction it makes is to be identified. In every living language what may seem quite 'categorical' hides the metaphorical, something pictorial in its sense-structure, the first imagery in which is no longer evident, having passed into a kind of factuality.[8] Even where this has not happened, something quite 'categorical' lives only by analogy. Thus, example, the change of the *Qiblah* in Surah 2 round from Jerusalem to the Mecca the 'exiles' had lately left, is a command outright. Yet, like *Zakat* also, it has to do with 'seeking the face of God', which—as the verses note—is 'everywhere.'[9] The divine 'countenance' was Semitic imagery going back to Aaron (Numbers 6.25-

---

[8]   Examples are endless. Asking a lawyer: 'What is your fee?' seems innocent of all imagery, utterly factual. The answer will be 'categorical'. Yet the source word *feo* (cattle) goes back to when these were the form of payment. Imagery has a way of solidifying into the factual. What inter-relation belongs between *rahm* ('womb') and *rahmah* ('mercy')? Or how the sense of 'test' in *fitnah* can widen into 'trial', 'persecution' and 'sedition' by means of what its 'siftings' assume? Language-users need to be alive to long hidden metaphor surviving into quite factual usage. They could never be poets otherwise.

[9]   The change of *Qiblah* from the original Jerusalem to Mecca after the Hijrah is decreed in 2.143-144. Prayer-direction to that location did not imply that 'the face of Allah' was not everywhere (2.115). 'Everything is perishing save the face of God' (28.88).

26) and highly 'metaphorical'. However, the truth it has in view is never less than categorical.

Concepts concerning God can never be otherwise. Precisely because God is their theme they must resort to simile and have the conceptual perceptible, with whatever caution may be necessary. The very need for caution indicates how even reservations cannot dispense with the risk of them.

If metaphor is inseparable from the very genius of human language and crucial to its expressiveness, is there something puzzling in the warnings of 3.7 around it? Ought the Qur'an's own frequent allusions to 'lessons in stones', to forsaken camps and shifting sands, to be discounted? Can the natural order be indeed a realm of 'signs' and the instinct that invokes them be excluded from the language of the theologian? Those numerous invocations, mostly in the Meccan period, of day and night, of sun and stars, of wind and wave are surely no spur to 'unstable' distortion but only to kindling imagination and the quickened will to wonder and to worship. These of Surah 77 *(Al-Mursalat)*, almost defying a translator, plead amid winds, tempests and rain-clouds, for 'all that deciphers and discerns' *(al-fariqat farqan)*.[10] That ever disputable English rendering has ground in what follows about 'the Reminder' that pleads and warns, and thus gives the clauses so eloquent with natural phenomena their moral force.

Thus the very rhetoric of the Qur'an would be sadly crippled if the stricture in 3.7 about *tashbih*, the 'similitude' that calls for nature's wildest powers, was taken too harshly. The clue surely lies in the attitude of mind, the good-will that seeks only to understand and scorns the ill-will bent only to disrupt the sense of things. Such good faith with the text on the part of exegesis is not served by clipping the wings of imagination, spread so eloquently as they are in its own pages.

Perhaps there is a strange quandary in the other direction when we are perplexed by the intensity of the pictorial in the Qur'an's depiction of Paradise and the Fire, in its measure of 'the Last Things'. How should the reader take the flowing streams and verdant meadows of the former, the grim conflagration and bitter waters of the latter? What *mutashabihah* is

---

[10] How can any version claim to be definitive, the words being so charged with power? Alternates are: 'those who winnow with a winnowing,' 'the severally severing', 'the separate one from another,' 'those that divide asunder.' The use of two verbs 'decipher and discern' is meant to capture the vehemence of the Arabic. The poetry defies the rubric of Surah 3.7 by the thrust of its passion to underline 'the Reminder'.

here? *Al-Yaqin*, 'the Certain', is categorical but what should we understand by the features we are summoned to imagine?[11]

It is in this context of relating the ethical to the eschatological, of moral conduct with final reckoning, that the burden of religious language becomes most heavy. There the question: 'What can we really mean?' is most acute. But it belongs with all religious discourse. Since meaning has to take to language if it is to be possessed and—being possessed—be also told, how the language is read will decide how the meaning is known. The one must be a worthy servant, if the other is not to be a disserved victim. That nexus with its risk is always present in reading, conversing, trading terms and nouns, analogies and metaphors.

If we try to relate this meaning/language situation in the Qur'an and meaning/language in the Western mind, wide strains and sharp tensions are obvious and forbidding in their range. There are, however, two aspects of the 'burdensome' in these which the present context can take up. One has to do with having a rightly certain mind, the other with giving it a language of inter-human care that makes no aliens. The first concerns the language of theology, the second the rhetoric of religious mission and of *Da'wah* as its 'call'. Perhaps we might link them by puzzling what Franz Kafka meant when he wrote in *The Great Wall of China*: 'The positive is already given: our task is to overcome the negative.'[12]

We resume again the 'point of words' already there in the concern of 3.7. That point recurs in the 'word question' Islam has about *Al-Asma' al-husna*, the 'most excellent Names of Allah'. They were crucial part of their 'certain mind'. Allah 'had' them and the faithful were enjoined to 'call upon Him by them' (Surah 7.180).[13] There is no doubt that Allah

---

[11] Nowhere do the two qualities more pointedly pass into each other than in this field of the Qur'an. For how we are to take the imagery will be crucial to how definitive we take the final verdict to be. Can one say: 'There are thus literal *psycho-physical effects* of the Fire, without there being a literal fire'? as, for example Fazlur Rahman does (his italics), while adding: 'Hence one can speak only of eternal success or failure, of everlasting Fire or Garden.' *Major Themes of the Qur'an*, Minneapolis, 1980, pp. 112–13 and 120.

[12] Franz Kafka, *The Great Wall of China*, New York, 1946, p. 284.

[13] That 'the Names' may be wilfully flouted by false use is implicit in the further warning: 'Keep well away from those who blaspheme with them.' Surah 17.110 notes the 'beauty' of the Names with the same phrase and has *Al-Rahman* as almost synonymous with 'Allah' when used in prayer. That 'Name'—passing into the *Bismillah* (with its partner *Al-Rahim*)—seems to have been puzzling to the Quraish as to how it related to 'Allah' already part of their pagan currency. Muhammad's 'mission with monotheism' was at pains

'possesses' these 'Names'. Islam is not a theism without a theology. How could it be? For without a faith using divine 'adjectives' there is no worship, except to a cipher. Devotion subsists only in doctrine. Crying only 'Thou' is in some measure conceptual. Without this 'nameability' of God religion languishes, its meaning forsaking it.

In its first Arabian world of the *Sirah* no problem arose but with the expansion of Islam a deep paradox became present to the thoughtful. Allah was 'incomparable': 'none is like unto Him.' Those 'Names' that were enjoined upon the believers were drawn from the human scene. How was using them concerning the 'ever Other' compatible with those descriptives having currency and content from their human sense? Must using them in worship not be a form of *shirk* in taking what was not divine as any clue to what was? Could the incomparable share those humanly referent words and be *karim* or *latif* or *wudud* in any comparable sense? Yet to halt and forego their use would mean both disobedience and silence. If, thanks to them, 'the positive was already given,' how were the faithful to overcome the negative, the sense in which they could *not* be true or usable?

By the third Muslim century the theologians had their resolution of the paradox. It stood in the formulae *bila kaif* and *bila tashbih*. The divine 'Names' should be used 'without asking how' they were to be taken, and without 'similitude' intended. They would both mean and not mean and if that situation were thought to be 'unsatisfactory' or somehow less than 'categorical' it was the duty of faith and the task of devotion to take that undeterred in their stride. Language was being used in the sense in which it could be true, and not otherwise. Theology that needed to be certain could only be so this accommodating way.

Many outside Islam have seen this positive/negative stance of faith as a sort of equivocation, even potentially some sleight of hand, a 'confidence trick', in that by taking away it only seemed to give. In point of fact, the subtle distinction has not affected the quality, for behaviour and credence, of a very authoritarian religion. Its assurance is more in *that* Allah is than *who*, except that the 'who' dimension requires our

---

to disabuse all minds of any notion of plurality, such as the pagan mind might draw from multiple 'Names'. 'Cry to Allah … or to *Al-Rahman*' in 17.110 might well be aligned with 'prayer to God and to Christ' in the Christian tradition, as being devotion's 'duality within unity'. *Al-Asma' al-husna* are the clue to the use of the *Sibhah* on which they are enumerated by the fingers of faith.

submission. *This* form of 'knowledge for obedience' is the Muslim's prescript. The 'knowledge and the love of God' is the pairing made feasible in the New Testament.[14]

We need to keep in mind the phrase earlier about being rightly certain, as perhaps of the Islamic order just summarised. First here, concerning 'the Qur'an and the West', we note a strange and unsuspected kinship between these Islamic reservations about language concerning Allah, and insistent motifs in 20th-century theories about language as 'equivocal' and never otherwise—theories nourished in France and proving popular in the USA. The kinship is remarkable, though the Islamic has not enervated faith-assurance in the way the Western has fathered 'disbelief in belief'.

The point here is not about political 'double-speak' or the 'between the lines' onus on readers in learning where the truth lies, nor with the slantedness of 'spin', nor the guile of verbal subterfuge. These served notice of themselves on those they would beguile and adjustment could be made. What is at stake has to do with the very capacity of language, not only for faith and theology and religion, but in each and every writ of words, to deliver meaning not contaminated by how language handles it. 'Equivocity is always irreducible' wrote Jacques Derrida in 1962, of whom an expositor writes on how an author will be:

> ... the victim of linguistic signs richly capable in their combinations of containing meanings he would have taken steps to exclude had he been aware of them.[15]

The affinity with the *bila kaif* formula in Islam is distant yet unmistakable, only that 'steps to exclude' are already taken in the formula itself. The Derrida-style language of 'signifier' and 'signified' is not unknown to the Qur'an's world of *ayat*. Those *Asma' al-husna* inform and yet do not inform. They require reservation concerning what they cannot mean in the very acceptance of what they can mean. The caveat of faith is different from that of recent philosophy but they each chafe

---

[14] The second has the warrant—via Jesus as God's Christ—to proceed from 'submission' to 'love' as the consequent of the 'knowledge' being about 'grace in redemption' rather than about the divine will in law.

[15] Quoted in John Sturrock, *The Word from Paris, Essays on Modern French Thinkers and Writers*, London, 1998, p. 77.

at 'the burdensome necessity of words'. Saying (or writing) what is meant, meaning what is said (or written), is a kindred issue in either realm. What makes the Islamic *bila kaif* different is that it is a reservation about 'the transcendent', whereas for the Derrida mind—as he himself notes—'the absence of a transcendental signified extends the field and play of signification into infinity.'[16]

Aligning these so far alien realms of thought about what is textual in human using via words was not a self-indulgent exercise, only loosely bringing something Muslim and something Western into either's ken. It can suggest a latent sympathy in mental duty and, on either count, it has to do with our concern—via such discourse about language—for 'a rightly certain mind'. The linguistic emphasis in modern Western philosophy, despite turgid and often circuitous exposition, bears no less than the old Kantian attitude on the credibility of theological language. What words can veritably 'carry,' whether we only 'falsify' when we intend to 'verify'—these questions belong with any theological integrity. Islam, as so heavily verbal, so slightly symbolic, a religion, has to take note of them.[17]

Might the *bila kaif* formula about divine 'Names' help it do so, as bringing into faith-assurance a room for reservation inside itself about itself? And, only so, be on the way to 'rightful certainty'?

It is noteworthy that, by and large, those convoluted reservations of the language doubters do not prevent their ready engagement with language and society, just as the *bila kaif*—not 'asking how' divine 'Names' mean—has never deterred the supreme self-assurance of historic Islam.

But is that 'positive/negative' faith-formula, that 'acceding without asking how' satisfactory? Can it be consistent with the human 'caliphate' we have been studying, one that includes the mental trust in 'charge of our own souls' the Qur'an says is ours? Does it imply that the central transcendent reality might still be enigmatic, and as such incapable of love given or received? To be consonant with our full sense of ourselves, that 'not asking how' concerning the 'who' of our worship means a worship

---

[16] *Ibid.*, pp. 79–80.

[17] 'Symbol', of course, is deeply present, being inseparable from liturgy and life. Yet its presence in caring calligraphy and equally caring recital are alike serving the verbal, while the symbols of prostration and pilgrim fulfilment and the fast observed tell the obedience of faith more than the content. The absence, otherwise, of representation or of a Muslim 'bread and wine' are significant.

less than fully expressive of our own identity as worshippers. A right theism has to be fully reciprocal to a right humanism. If the 'who' in the goal of worship is elusive, the 'whether' about worship stays perfunctory, a thing of duty without joy.

The clue to the burdensome business of language telling faith and meaning worship would seem to lie in a confidence that leaves *bila kaif* behind, *not* because God ceases to transcend but transcends consistently with the evident will to create and dignify the creaturely with an under-sovereignty. Could those credentials, present in our being the humans we are, relieve us of an onus about not asking how? For, otherwise, we assume that there is something about human language from which the divine must be immune—and by our having it so, whereas a non-immunity is in the very meaning of creation. Given the right humility about the wonder of ourselves, this will never mean that our faith or our theology become less awed and 'fearing', only mysteriously more so in love for the God who wills to love.

It is notable that the *bila kaif* reserve about words relates to those adjectival terms that concern 'being' rather than 'doing'. As for those of the *Asma' al-husna* that have to do with action, *Al-Wahhab*, 'the Bestower', *Al-Razzaq*, 'the provider', *Al-Musawwir*, 'the Fashioner', the *kaif*, the 'how' about these is manifest on every hand in the 'signs' in nature to which the Qur'an exultingly appeals. Thanks to these, and the perceived meaning of ourselves, we might think the descriptive attributes of God no less evidentially ours to use, alike in thought and praise and prayer.

Perhaps again the clue is caught in the ancient words of the Hebrew prophet to a novice king: 'If you will not trust, you will not be entrusted' (Isaiah 7.9).[18] The language faith uses has its final proving in what happens in the heart.

What, then, we asked earlier, of words in the rhetoric of its mission in the world? Rhetoric is meant here, not in the terms by which

---

[18] Playing on the Hebrew word *aman* the point of which has been ventured in English by, e.g. 'unless you confide, you will not abide,' or 'if your faith does not hold you will never hold out.' Syria and the Northern Kingdom tried to force Judah into a coalition against Assyria but Ahaz made himself a vassal to Tiglath-Peleser III. Did Isaiah advise him during potential or actual besiegement, which would explain Ahaz' inspection of Gihon and the water supply? Taking the paradox in our context we have to hold our 'trust' firm if firmly to discharge it.

it has become suspect in society as only a guileful form of persuasion, but in its original sense of being charged with the worth of that which, therefore, must be published and taught. With that charge it surrenders mind and will to the theme it loves only because it is a theme of love to all. The witness, via its own words, has to be at once the 'signifier' and the 'signified', seeing that the only rightly certain faith is one that is taking its own risk in the way that love does. It witnesses to the Lord of its theism only as knowing Him the shaper and originator of the inclusive humanity from whence, as what it fully shares, its language derives. It speaks peace because it learns patience. Its witness is given as being about this 'givingness' of God to us.

It was in this way that New Testament Christian faith was first present in the world, both in word and life, in terms of what it held to be God's presence in Christ in that same world—a presence which had broken down the 'negative' of 'Gentile' exclusion from divine/human peoplehood by the 'positive' in its language of 'the Word made flesh'. Such was the ultimate reach of the original meaning of creation's mandate to all humankind. Its faith was like a vessel out of harbour and at sea which only then answers its rudder by being thus afloat. Its certainty was only right because it was launched on a corresponding venture risking all that it knew and only consistent in doing so.

The logic now would be that what a faith believes it has to 'say' concerning God must keep patiently within what it ought to feel and hold about man, lest its witness to the sovereignty of the One is resolved into an enmity-making factor in the other. There is in many Western quarters a reluctance about 'witness' altogether, an unease in the presence of 'preachiness' as invasive of mental privacy and in unduly aggressive forms quite repugnant. 'Poetry', it is said, 'never takes sides.'

By contrast, too often the impulses of religion seem, or more than seem, systems of divisiveness by the subtle vested interest in their propagation. What happens—and has long happened—is that the centre of gravity passes from a reverent theme-in-trust to the identity-in-prestige of a structure and an institution. Such is the constant temptation of 'fundamental' things. The wise *islam* becomes the formidable Islam. The Gospel is resolved into Christianity or was known as Christendom. What a study there is in the etymology of the words 'Church' and 'ecclesiastical'. The only rightly spontaneous *Allahu Akbar* is liable to become the would-be coercive *Islamu akbar*.

Thus what the Greeks called *rhetorika* and Paul 'commendation',[19] becomes often a strident or stentorian voice and religious word-usage magisterial with an absolutist referent that will be disowning the 'caliphate' *Ilah al-nas*, 'the Lord of humankind' once for all granted to the people of His creaturely world.

Would it not be fair to think that—thanks to salutary influences in which it has only partially shared with others not of it—Christianity has been enabled to relate its witness more suitably to that human autonomy of mind?

Being vocal under the constraints of a strong and suspicious empire, original Christianity had no occasion to be combative, except in strenuous pastoral discipline of its own moral life. Original Islam certainly began as *balagh* with a purely verbal mission to dispel what it significantly read as 'ignorance'. But its audience, with vested interest in its paganism, had an empowered obstinacy which at length drew a still formative Islam into the combative shape its Hijrah fashioned for it. It is a shape it has not normally relinquished and has found repeated occasion to resume. The will to political power, and the language form to serve and suit it, have characterised its history. These have an instinctive appeal to its genius, one evidently at work still both in private hearts and designer societies.[20]

Its imprint is present in defining areas of the Qur'an's vocabulary.. They bring us round to those laden terms of 'the Last Things' earlier pondered. Throughout, after the Hijrah, the Qur'an's verbal world is sharply discriminatory between 'believers' and 'unbelievers' as a realm of *muhkamat* or decisive categories that leave nothing 'allegorical' about 'gainers' and 'losers', moral 'right-handers' and 'left handers' in terms of how they receive their post-mortem 'books'. These human 'antitheses' make for a very divisive perception of the role of faith in the world, despite the Qur'an's own conviction concerning the Oneness of Allah and His gift of *khilafah* equally to all and sundry.

This bent of language leads to measures of ready congratulation on the one part and hapless reprobation on the other. It inhibits the vital religious virtue of self-distrust and entire humility. It has Allah Himself in

---

[19] The verb Paul uses *sunistesin* means to 'establish together', as of a party seeking to persuade by enlisting an assumed capacity in the other party to respond. This which is his own practice, he perceives also to be God's way 'in Christ' (cf. Romans 5.8).

[20] 'Designer societies' with such intention are e.g. *Al-Ikhwan al-Muslimun* and *Jama'at-i-Islami* and many others invoking terms like *Takbir, Tawhid* and *Takfir*.

an inconsistent image as no longer, somehow 'a discerner of the thoughts and intents of the heart', in so dire a classifying of the burdened human populace.

Thus, sadly, what began as a mission with words set to persuade and convince became also a regime with power minded to rule and preside. A teacher sent to the Yathribites at their request paved the way to Islam's establishment in their midst as the base of a structured *Ummah* coalescing old tribal bonds into a new religious collective ready to do battle. When this moved into regional and then far-ranging expansion it was not notably by the like of the teacher to Yathrib.

It is difficult to tell how much preaching for persuading accompanied that Islamic expansion. The old indictment that 'Islam was spread by the sword' was wilful calumny. It took no account of the option for *dhimmi* status on the part of the conquered. What is true is that folk had little occasion to know what had overtaken them, except the reach of power by which it had arrived. It was a regime to which they had submitted, not a faith-system they had begun to understand and, understanding, freely embrace. Islam, for its part, was massively confirmed in the pragmatic validity of its Medinan ethos. It was historically realised in terms congenial to the most vigorously discriminatory language of its post-Hijrah Qur'an, while it still retained the guiding rubric (2.256) concerning 'no compulsion—no making aversion for itself, in religion.'[21]

What chance in the current century of an Islam renewing its original theme of would-be persuasive words, burdensome as the task will always be, thanks to the capacities of an unheeding world? The fact of an appreciable Muslim diaspora in the West and in India (perhaps no less than a quarter of all Muslims) may help towards the positive, and deter the negative answer. Except in the dream of the fanatical, there is a permanent occasion to participate, a continuing disallowing of unilateral dominance in the politics of statehood. There are significant examples of thoroughly Islamic ventures of compatibility, as on the part of Abu-l-Kalam Azad in post-partition India and of Fazlur Rahman in the USA and Dr Zaki Badawi in Britain.[22] Notable studies emerge of how an 'exilic' Islam can define and

---

[21] The prime root *kariha* means 'to detest' or 'loathe', so that *akraha* means 'to arouse that reaction'. Thus *ikraha* is more than mere 'compelling', unless we conjoin it with aversion. What merits disdain could never win assent. Religions beware.

[22] Data and bibliography on the first two can be consulted in my *The Pen and the Faith*, London, 1985, pp. 14-32 and 91-108. Dr Zaki Badawi, of Egypt, is the esteemed Head of the Muslim College, London.

fulfil itself as a no less valid vision than the contrasted answer of Pakistan. 'Exilic' thinking in this way can influence Muslim minds responding, from within empowered nationhoods, to a sense that even their autonomy is required to co-exist. None can be 'exiles' when the globe is one.

Unhappily there is much in 'the Western connection' that deters deeply committed Muslims from heeding its relevance, still more from adopting its values.

> 'Fie on't. 'Tis an unweeded garden
> That grows to seed: things rank and gross in nature
> Possess it merely.'[23]

Arrogance, consumerism, sexual-exhibitionism, vulgarity and a sheer indulgence of its own esteem dismay the gravitas of traditional Islam. It is important for the West to recognise its capacity to engender anger and to query the assumptions out of which it interrogates the dislike it registers. The career of the late Sayyid Qutb perhaps best illustrates the situation. Reportedly, on ship in mid-Atlantic, on the very Western errand of a study-course in literary criticism, he felt the undertow of an Islam that drew him back into his proper allegiance and away from the *fitnah*—as it must be—of a 'secular' pursuit.[24]

The experience may be somewhat romanticised in the telling but there is no doubt of its lesson. He emerged to be a kind of role-model for a most radical Islam with his many volumed *Tafsir* of the Qur'an, his leadership of the Islamic Brotherhood and his suffering and death as an activist during the regime of 'Abd al-Nasir in Cairo. He gave a drastic personal symbolism to the familiar thesis of 'un-Islamic' Muslim states and politics that is a primary feature of contemporary 'extremism'.

Statecraft in the West has to reckon with this mind and mood in some current Islam and with the extent to which aspects of its own mind and mood play darkly into its hands. 'Islam in danger' is a cry whose fervour loses nothing from the sense of the material—and other—superiority confronting it. Given those brand-marks of legitimated counter power we have explored and the word-readiness of the Qur'an

---

[23] William Shakespeare, *Hamlet*, Act 1, sc. 2, lines 136-37.
[24] *Op. cit.*, note 22, pp. 53-71.

for anathemas on perceived resistance, it is not a thing of riddles that Islam should now be at odds with non-Islam. 'Our task is to overcome the negative.'

What, then, for the present 'burdensome necessity of words'? It is not as though 'the positive is not already given.' It is 'there' in all we have argued in foregoing chapters. It is about recognising God in the human 'caliphate' and the human 'caliphate' duly under God and, by the same token, seeing and serving that human vocation as squarely in the purpose of that 'God and His messenger' at the heart of its *Shahadah*. Such prophethood was always perceived as mediating into that vocation and, by its 'sealing' all its predecessors, doing so to the end of time.

It, therefore, means today a will to speak the language, not of anathema on all 'non-Islam', as if this could be rightly identified, but of persuasion as to what is only rightly certain in itself by being peaceably 'involved with mankind'.[25]

[25] John Donne's 17th-century dictum on human solidarity had to do with 'sending to know for whom the bell tolls' noting some local funeral. 'Involvement with ... mankind' is of a different order now when there is 'a bell tolling' at global incidence of crisis and new dimensions of mortality.

## Chapter 7
## WHERE THE HEART
## HAS ITS REASONINGS

إِنَّ فِى ذَٰلِكَ لَذِكْرَىٰ لِمَن كَانَ لَهُۥ قَلْبٌ أَوْ أَلْقَى ٱلسَّمْعَ وَهُوَ شَهِيدٌ

Surah 50.37 brings together three terms—*dhikra, qalb* and *shahid*. They are lively clues to aspects of the Qur'ans that bear closely also on the impulses of the Western mind.

> 'Surely there is point to ponder here for whoever has a heart
> or who heeds with alert perception.'

The immediate context has to do with the grim lessons of bye-gone history as the Qur'an was many times minded to rehearse them.

> 'How many a generation of stronger mettle than they have
> We brought to ruin before them! They went over the land in
> frantic search for possible refuge.' (v. 36)

The allusion to what past we need not stay to identify. It suffices to learn its present import. For this the text uses a beloved term *dhikra* which, with the kindred and still more frequent usage, *dhikr* is a synonym for the Qur'an itself, as when Surah 7.2 refers to 'the Scripture revealed' to Muhammad as *dhikra li-mu'minin*, 'a reminder to believers.'[1] The English 'remind', however, can be a much diminished word, like some nudge on the elbow. *Dhikra* deserves better than such a casual sense. We need some

---

[1] Surah 7 begins with examples of the mysterious single Arabic letters that preface many other Surahs and intends them as warranting what follows as 'divine Scripture' and adding, significantly: 'Let there be no anxiety in your heart because of it.' *Dhikra* is, therefore, clearly a term by which the Qur'an refers to itself and hardly distinguishable from the more frequent *dhikr*.

neologism, like 'enminding' (on the pattern of 'enhearten' or 'ennoble') to do it Quranic justice. For the meaning is not simply to bring something back into ken, but to have it there perpetually, not merely as a notion in the head but as an affection in the heart.[2]

Hence, in the same context, 'the point to ponder for him who has a heart'—*qalb*, another term precious to the Islamic Scripture. For the heart, with its warm emotions, its kindling impulses of affection, is more likely to be keenly attentive to the world than the abstracting intellect. Mind may only be *shahid*, 'a take-in of things', in academic remove from their true pathos. Surah 50.37 has an evident intensity about its awareness of 'many generations'.

The present hope is to keep these three terms in steady emphasis in an intelligent appreciation of the Qur'an as a text calculated to relate us in lively nexus to the present of our global history, no less than to some hallowed—or unhallowed—past. The previous chapter dwelt with aspects of language usage and the range of metaphor and imagery: this concerns the motives in the society that language was meant to summon and direct. There was never any doubt about the Qur'an's literary eloquence. For what was its excellence intended, if not for an 'enminding by the heeding heart'?

That sense of purpose in 50.37 about the *dhikra* in history—taken as the term must also be into the entire point of the Qur'an—is confirmed by how the text elsewhere appeals for readiness of heart towards it. Earlier chapters have noted its praise of *tadabbur* on the part of hearts 'unlocked' from prejudice and negligence (as in 4.82 and 47.24). The guilt and folly of their *ghaflah* ('negligence') are the frequent lament of the doomed in the Book's portrayal of 'the Last Things'. It could almost be that it is aware of a very modern habit of living where lethargy or boredom or a crippling sense of *déjà vu*, in the otherwise ever avid appetite of society, generate an indifference to worship and a sorry agnosticism disinclined to take better stock of day to day experience. Too many among us have thus attained—on our own alleging—to 'come-of-age-ness' feebly indifferent to 'the mystery of things'.

---

[2] It seems clear that the age-long practice of learning the Qur'an 'by heart' and reciting it—in celebration as well as for education—comes from this sense of things. Perhaps the odd English phrase 'knowing by heart' has a hint we did not suspect. A text to 'cherish' lies, similarly, behind the practice of calligraphy. In both ways the Qur'an is 'beautified' in its own beauty.

By contrast, after assuring hearers that 'the apostle of God is in the midst of you,' Surah 49.7 continues:

> 'God had made faith precious to you and given your hearts an appreciation of its beauty, rendering unbelief, wickedness and rebellion hateful to you.'[3]

This feature of faith as 'endeared' to the heart and 'beautified there' is linked, post-Hijrah, to the claims it made on the cost of allegiance in terms that had their well-spring in the Meccan sphere of initial conviction. It was there that the attraction of Islam, in such heart terms, was first kindled to be, later, the impulse to the emigration. It made the first *muhajirun* far other than those of whom the word is now mostly current.[4]

We might truly say that nothing is more crucial in the current encounter of religions in the tide of international affairs than 'having a heart' about them. For the heart feels more, learns more, yearns more, than the finesse of diplomacy or the case-making of religious philosophies. *Qalb*—'heart'—has in Arabic a high significance. *Sadr*, or 'bosom', which we had 'with its 'whisperings' in Chapter 4, is the core of selfhood, but *qalb*—we might say—is what is within the within, like the kindred word *fu'ad*, the very wellspring of personal being. *Aina dhahaba qalbak?*—'where has your heart gone?' an Arab will ask, meaning: 'What you am I knowing?' 'The deeds of the heart' are the very pith of existence. The verb behind the noun means to 'revolve' or 'turn over and over' inwardly, brooding on a decision. The ancient cry: 'Son, give me thine heart' (Proverbs 23.25) is the plea of all Semitic religion.

That 'heart' belongs centrally to the Qur'an should give pause to the frequent suspicion—or practice—of a 'heartlessness' about it on either side of the present inter-religious scene. It will be well to explore the Qur'an's sense of the 'heart' word not only in 50.37.

---

[3] There are numerous tributes to this in Muslim autobiography. For a very recent example see Muhammad Abdel Haleem in *Scriptures in Dialogue*, London, 2003, p. 2: 'I play tapes of good recitations and intone the Qur'an to myself, letting the words, style and music of the Arabic text lift my mood.'

[4] Meaning at first 'emigrants' or 'willing exiles' leaving Mecca for Yathrib (in distinction from the *ansar* who would receive them there). It has been of late adapted to denote a belligerent participant in an aggressive Islam, of which the first exemplars were in no way minded. Hostilities had not then been joined. A later phrase: *hajaru jahadu*, 'they went out and they strove,' explains the current usage.

But there is a prior duty relating to the entire traditional view which classic Islam has of its Scripture and of the place of Muhammad in its incidence, or *tanzil*. For a deeply religious reason precious to their mind, Muslims have insisted on a literal 'dictation' of this *Kitab* to a wholly passive Muhammad as its recipient. It has seemed part of its 'endearment' to them that this must be so. The celestial *Umm*, 'Mother' (of the Book), was mediated from heaven so that it might be an 'immaculate' text, unaffected by the potential 'corruption' of an active human reception of it, via 'thoughts and intents of the heart', never participatory in its contents. For, it was passionately believed that any such co-activity would forthwith disqualify it as ever being a 'Book from heaven', in which God spoke. That Muslim insistence was based on the prescript: 'the more it is divine requires that it be ever the less human.' For God to speak, there must be no human voice. The source of this conviction may be admired—but not approved—as valid desire to be holding what is 'of God' as exclusively 'by God', or to have confidence in 'God's Word' having no human agency, no human 'mix'. With any such 'admixture' it would cease to be divine and its divine Giver would be frustrated in His giving. To think Muhammad participatory in the incidence would cancel all 'Quranicity'. Faith would be left with the likeness of a cracked bell or a forged cheque.

It has been necessary to state this situation sharply with a will to comprehend its rationale. For it is one that has long attracted either the scorn or the incomprehension of Western minds. It has also been the heavy burden of Muslim minds of the Surah 57.37 order.[5] What all parties need to realise is that human agency *is* there, whether passive or active, and that there could be no Qur'an, from eternity into time, without such human dimension. Indeed, any and every concept of 'revelation' means that, if there is initiative from the one there must be reception by the other. Apostolate in it, Arabicity for it, audience to it—all are human and

---

[5] Many of whom have sensed the need to understand *tanzil* and the *wahy* within it as necessarily engaging Muhammad and no way an abeyance of his set of mind or soul. Fazlur Rahman, of Pakistan and later of Chicago, was 'exiled' in the West over his view of Muhammad's active role in the receiving of the Qur'an. He tells something of his story in H P Little, ed., *Essays on Islamic Civilisation*, (presented to Niyazi Berkes), Leiden, 1976, pp. 284-302, 'Some Issues in the Ayyub Khan Era', He in no way calls in question the 'verbal inspiration' of the Qur'an but seeks a right understanding of its incidence with its *Rasul*.

in time, as the 'wherebys' of the eternal. To exclude such receptive agency would be to deny the *Umm al-Kitab* any entry into its earthly realm of relevance, however passive entry might be.

Not only so, for every evidence of the Qur'an itself tells with emphasis how the reception and the relevance were, indeed, active and in no way passive. Such 'witness of the Qur'an to its own stature and character' is everywhere apparent. To concede the significance of its evidence is not, however, to forego the vital conviction of its being 'from God'. Rather, having it more wisely and more seemly, can establish it more firmly. No one 'who heeds with alert perception' can think otherwise or else he wills to do so, only by ignoring the very 'signs' of the Book itself.[6]

Muslim re-assurance might begin with the plain statement of Surah 2.97: 'By leave of God, he (Gabriel) sent it down upon your heart,' and only so into your ears and on to your lips. For it is Muhammad here being vindicated against calumny and disbelief. Surah 26.194 uses the same words, attributed to the action of 'the faithful Spirit', where Muhammad is to be one of the 'warners', and one using a 'clear Arabic diction'. The single phrase here *'ala qalbak* can only mean that there was 'heartfeltness' in his experience of *tanzil*, a personal factor of feeling and ardour in the onset of *wahy*.

That Muhammad was far from being a de-personalised 'auditor' of words, but instead a conscious perceiver of meaning—and its substance—is manifest on almost every page of the Qur'an. The situation is full of those *asbab*, 'occasions', which *tafsir* would later insist were the key to exegesis. On each of those occasions, be they meditative, circumstantial or activist, Muhammad was their centre and nerve. It is hard to think they could have been the biographical 'text' of the deliverances and he himself a mind-absent cipher in their incidence, their happening and the emotions they aroused. Those emotions, too, are often legible in the context of many a *sabab* ( sing.) or revelatory event.

---

6   Those *ayat* which we studied earlier in the context of the human 'caliphate' which alert and inform our perception en route to our sciences. Significantly, the term applies also to verses of the Qur'an with the clear hint that its contents are to be 'explored' in the same investigative way before they yield to us the 'findings' they present—but present only truly to the questing heart. This equation between Scripture and readership, if thus analogous to the natural sciences, is mystically invoked by Sufism in the distinctive terms of 'inreading' as one might the 'underside' of a Damascene brocade.

What sustains us further in believing so is the fact that so often the Qur'an almost converses with Muhammad, as if noting and answering misgivings, perplexities, anxieties which arose for him as a person in the total context. There are references to past experience as to 'burdens relieved', 'reputation established' or 'decisions vindicated'. The living situation, as only personally transactable, appears alike in commendation, direction, re-assurance and even congratulation.[7] Then—and elsewhere—he is personally addressed in his 'messenger' capacity in ways which it is odd to pronounce as somehow not in his ken, or foreign to his heart's affections.

The constant refrain of *yaquluna faqul*—'They are saying, so you say…' is evidence of a concrete encounter where the very text of the Qur'an comes as a theme between the parties. We need not think that Muhammad is contriving his own answers, as if no *wahy* belongs. We need to see that the abiding *wahy* is engaging with a *Sirah*, a career of conscious spokesmanship under God. What, for example, of 2.186: 'when My servants question thee concerning Me …'? and the text directs him to reply that 'God is near when they call.'[8] There are some fifteen other occasions where 'they ask concerning,' whether it be about 'the Hour', or 'the Spirit', or details in ritual and conduct, and he is given the reply. It seems clear that what is being 'worded for him' (as the classic view has it) is, at least on these occasions, coinciding with a mental pre-occupation present to him by virtue of a world of hearers. Or there is the necessity to comment on the vagaries of that audience-world, as in the crucial verdict about *mushrikun*, namely that 'they did not measure Allah by the truth of His measure' (6.91, 22.74, 39.67). The heart of *tanzil* surely belongs with an inner passion about the grim aberration in idolatry. Is there not a certain anguish in that re-iterated 'perhaps' *(la'alla)* awaiting the response of attention, gratitude or reflection for which it pleaded? The content of the Qur'an is all the time proceeding

---

[7] 'Congratulation' might seem an inapt word were it not for the *Tasliyah* (Surah 33.56), the 'calling down of blessing' upon Muhammad by Allah and the faithful also. See my *Muhammad in the Qur'an*, London, 2001, pp. 114–136., It would seem to signify how Allah's 'pleasure' is realised in and by His *Rasul*, as effectively enlisted to it—the sense of 'pleasure' being that 'will' with which Muhammad's 'will' is aligned.

[8] It is noteworthy that 'I am near' does not directly answer the question put. Things asked 'concerning God' are met by the pledge of 'nearness'—not for questioners but for those who pray. Instincts deep in Islam are here.

in terms of a sustained engagement with its mental world and as a burden on the heart.

Another indelible aspect of this situation is the strange interplay between a first-person and a third party sequence in the pronouns. Muhammad is both a referent 'he', and the speaker 'I'. As the second, he is often heard alluding to himself as the 'other'. This became more marked in the post-Hijrah scene with injunctions like 'Obey Allah and obey the *Rasul*,' and directions about access to his own person and family quarters. It was, however, latent everywhere and came to a mysterious focus in the directive about *Tasliyah*, the divine—and human—'salutation' of the Prophet.[9] As explicit commands in the text itself, and relating to his own person and role, their very nature would have made him implicitly self-aware in the very act of giving them voice. For they had to do with things about himself that were central to the very substance of the Book and to the progress of its theme—of *islam* in the way of Islam.

The duty here for Muslim orthodoxy is not to surrender the precious conviction concerning a Qur'an from God but to amend its classic view of what its 'from-God' auspice and status could have humanly meant inside its incidence 'upon Muhammad's heart'.

To recognise and fulfil that duty, being no treachery to faith concerning it, would have salutary consequences for the whole pattern and temper of exegesis. It would require possession of the text to be more existential than has been traditionally assumed in *tajwid*, calligraphy and *tafsir*. These have possessed words and language, in some measure, for their own intrinsic sake, rather than as by one *wa huwa shahid* ('alert and observant'). Those 'ruins,' for example, in 50.36—though written off as deserving retribution—might be retrieved for more perceptive reflection on their story, more in line with the realities of Muhammad's own struggle over a wayward society.

So much Qur'an interpretation has been devotedly textual, occupied with grammar and with the immediate 'occasions' of its local incidence. Would it not more duly fulfil itself, and better commend itself to the wider world of its (e.g. Western) relevance, if it read its *Rasul* and its *Risalah* as belonging—by Muslim discharge of that duty—in the breadth of human history seeing that Muhammad is understood as 'a mercy to

---

[9]  See note 7. The point here is how that command could be told from the lips of one who was its very party. It is not occurring in a narrative where he is the absent party.

the worlds'? All Scriptures—given the 'time and place' factor in which all are involved—have to pre-suppose this liability to a faithful custody that seeks the art of an inclusive import, one ready to possess them with 'the reasonings of a present heart' and a contemporary will.[10]

A Qur'an readership, thus keenly appreciating the persona of Muhammad through all its surahs, is the purpose of our focus on their 'descent upon his heart'. It will be a readership that reckons with the terms in which the text refers, and frequently, to *al-qulub* (pl.)—those 'hearts' at its first hearing. For there are more than a hundred allusions, with or without the pronouns *kum* and *hum*. Readers can be in no doubt about the role of the private heart in the sundry participants in the years of the *Sirah*, whether as audience, heeding or reviling, volunteers or deriders. There are numerous references to 'hearts' being 'sealed', or 'hardened' or made to 'panic'.[11] Such are 'veiled' from perception (6.25).

By divine contrast, it is 'upon the heart' that faith is 'written' (58.22), one in awe at 'the mention of God' (57.16) among 'hearts' Allah has 'examined' for their *taqwa* (49.3). Such hearts have the faith 'beautified' to them (49.7). To such the Prophet has a closer relationship than they have to their own selves (33.5). While there are those on whose hearts 'faith has been written' by God, there is throughout a firm emphasis on this situation deriving also from the will to hold it dear within—and that in full sincerity. Thus the halting in 49.14 of over hasty recruits into whose hearts 'faith had not entered.' Witness also the role of dilettante folk in false play with 'things allegorical' in the Qur'an as noted in 3.7 and studied in the previous chapter.

The question: 'where has their heart gone?'—though not explicit in the Qur'an—is everywhere implicit in its reproach for the deviousness of 'unbelievers' and their perversity over the appeal of faith. In 2.118 they cavil over why no words came directly to them, in umbrage about being asked to believe in those of one they despised. The auspices of *tanzil* always displease the recalcitrant heart. Naaman the Syrian may have had reason to prefer the 'rivers of Damascus' to Elisha's Jordan, but the Qur'an's 'pure

---

[10] 'With full intelligence'—as one translation goes *(wa huwa shahid …)*—is a rider tested by close attention to the fifteenth Hijri century, no less than to the first in its opening decade up to the close of the Qur'an.

[11] This is surely in line with a Biblical, Semitic instinct to read the end as explaining the process, a divine *telos* in what was also the entail of human action. Cf.2.10: 'in their hearts there is disease and God their disease increases.' See below.

Arabic' did not suffice these heirs to the same language, while also accusing
him of alien sources. The 'locks' they had upon their hearts according to
47.29 were of their own consent.

The appeal against this obduracy of 50.37 is renewed in 22.46:

> 'Have they not travelled in the earth to take to heart such
> things? Have they no ears to give heed? It is not their sighted
> eyes that are blind but their hearts within them.'

It is manifest history this wilfulness is ignoring—'many a city
given to evil ... made to perish, ... fallen on its own towers ... many an
abandoned well ... many a fine palace!' It would seem that the *balagh*
is summoning a lively conscience of what history writes to sustain the
scripted Book. While not itself *tanzil*, it calls no less for a *tafsir* to discern
its commentary on humankind.

The benediction on perceptive hearts is told in the Qur'an's
painful contrast between two heart conditions. The one is *itmi'nan*, the
other *marad*. What sunders them completely raises a deep issue for a
theological readership. 'The heart at rest' or 'in blissful tranquillity' occurs
in 3.126, 8.10 and 13.28 as well as in the famous passage (89.27) which
uses the adjectival *mutma'innah* of the soul called into paradise. On the
first two occasions it refers only to a sense of re-assurance during or after
crisis in the story. The third 'finds hearts at rest' in 'believing remembrance
of God'. The truth of its being so is marked by repetition of the phrase.
The full weight of *dhikr*, discussed earlier as 'enminding', must be kept in
view. The conscious awareness of the divine presence means inward calm
and peace. A New Testament reader might recall the words: '... and assure
our hearts before Him.' (1 John 3.19).[12] By the noun *al-nafs*, 'the calm of
the soul' in 13.28 has to be understood in contrast to 'the soul prone to
evil' of 12.53 and 'the soul as self-reproachful' in 75.2.

This boon or benediction of the God-aware has to explore the
mystery of those who are 'sick in heart'. The phrase *fi qulubihim marad*
occurs some dozen times from Surah 2.10 to 74.31. The setting is almost
always in comment on 'unbelievers' and their 'hypocrisy'. The context, as in
5.52, has often to do with the exigencies of conflict, battle and thus danger

---

[12] The writer John's reference is to the assurance of forgiveness when the heart can feel a
genuine integrity. The *itmi'nan* theme of 'the soul in rest' has been much loved in Sufism as
the 'satisfying' of 'the unitive state'.

where—as in 22.56—Satan set a *fitnah* in such hearts, a snare in which they might be trapped into defaulting in courage and bravery. Or, as in 24.50, the 'sickness' may relate to dissatisfaction with a verdict Muhammad had passed in a dispute between parties, one of whom was disgruntled with it. Again, as in 33.60, there is a crisis of confidence about the way things are going with 'the cause'. A sense of disquiet about dubious or treacherous parties in a conflict situation is inevitable and appropriate, but is it well to see it as 'disease' as in any sense, a physical malady?[13]

Other occasions of the 'disease' imagery raise more subtly the issue from 3.7 about the 'categorical' in language and the 'allegorical'. These have to do with attitudes to Muhammad's verbal mission. Thus 2.10 refers to feigned assenters, while 74.31 has the 'diseased hearts' asking about the *mathal*, or 'similitude' relating to 'wardens of the Fire'. It would seem to follow, from 3.7 applied to the frequent 'sickness' imagery about the humanly perverse, namely that, if there is danger in reading the allegorical—so that the 'unstable' read wrongly—there must have been risk in employing it. So much the distinction in 3.7 implies.

In that light, this *marad fi qulubihim* could have two inferences, the one sound to take, the other not. Its aptness lies in that evil meant breeds evil more. That is the way of disease. It has a pattern of becoming chronic. Maladies worsen. At several points these *marad* passages refer to 'hardening', and 'sealing'. Seen in Semitic terms as Allah's doing, do these not point to the cumulative nature of wrong-doing? As noted in the concerns of Chapter 4, one sin engenders another. The heart grows accustomed to its deceits. The will to innocence fails. The once fine portrait moulders in the attic.[14] The character of besetting evil is to atrophy the will to repent. Conscience becomes the victim of its own compromise. Wrongs gather their own momentum. The gravity of evil has this downward gravitation. The disease analogy has proper force. Law and legislation know well how to detect and deplore it.

There, surely, wise discernment of the *marad* theme has to forebear going further into the other inference. Things ethical, using

---

[13] The translators of Jeremiah 17.9 rang the changes between 'desperately wicked' and 'desperately sick' about the heart of man. The second is preferable. 'Devious' and 'perverse' are apposite too. Thus the *marad* analogy is not unique to the Qur'an. But where-ever used, the analogy between the ethical and the clinical will always be dubious.

[14] In Oscar Wilde's story *The Picture of Dorian Gray*. Cf. Surah 2.9: 'they deceive none but themselves,' the degeneracy is their own story.

this metaphor, do not stay ethical if they adopt it as a charge about enmity to themselves, or suggest a vested interest in the *marad* being incurable. It is not a ripe descriptive for a deliberate adversary unless it has a matching therapy in view. 'Sickness' is no situation in which to invoke triumphalism or to forego a ministering compassion. For lack of one, no disease is rightly seen to be such. By any Hippocratic oath, the capacity to diagnose must evoke a will to serve. The precept of Surah 3.7 allows us to interpret the *marad* verses in no other way. Such is the very logic of their use of allegory.[15]

The sound mind in such situations of confrontation has to resist the will to calumny no less than disowning it when it is incurred. The 'who has a heart and is observant' of 50.37 will know it must be so for honest faith. Can we return to the formula of 'where the heart has its reasonings' in any linking of 'the Qur'an and the West'? The plea to either is for a converse in patience of the loyal mind out of the one into the characteristic mind-set of the other. The first task is for the West to see beyond the dissuasives it registers in its superficial attitudes towards the Qur'an, to perceive the basic 'enminding' in the Book's drama and the core theme of Muhammad's *Sirah*. Despite its severity, its theism has to do with a genuine humanism, with our 'caliphate' of privilege, as being trustee-tenants in a sacramental order. We are neither remorselessly 'on our own' as if 'gods to ourselves'. Nor are we the playthings or the puppets of a malign omnipotence. Rather we are 'associates' of the God who willed to create and then entrust, who cared to invite and inform how such we might be.[16] The severity of the theism in which the Qur'an affirms this humanism may be explained—if not easily allowed—by reference to the immediate locale of culture, economy, climate and tradition in which its definitive human theme was told. That context does not betray and need not now cause the human meaning to be disparaged, being one too precious to be lost to our 'enminding', and too urgent for our present sanity in West and East alike.

That the Allah of the Qur'an dignifies our humankind with the trust of a created cosmos delivered into our reverent custody—whence

---

[15] By a strange irony, do we arrive at a conclusion where the 'allegorical' becomes 'categorical'. As noted earlier, the distinction can break down.

[16] See fuller discussion in my *A Certain Sympathy of Scriptures: Biblical & Quranic*, Brighton & Portland, 2004.

all our cultures and our civilisation—is not in doubt. Our pursuit of the 'expertise' it underwrites proves it with increasing emphasis and liability. The fact of *rusul*, of 'messengers', for its education, is the surest evidence of its meaning as from God. Prophethoods, so central to Islam and the Qur'an, are the divine imprimatur on the human privilege. Thus the truth about us is bound up with Muhammad's having been—and been in the vital role for which Islam prizes him.[17] It follows that a theism told into a humanism is the very heart of the Qur'an. It is one for which, in the sense of 50.37 and 22.46, all of us might 'have a heart.' We perceive the transcendent reference of our existence in the very mandate by which our human-ness is fulfilled. That our sense of its being so is reciprocated from beyond finds its assurance in the fact of confirming Scriptures given for our guidance. By dint of these, to return to Surah 114.3, Allah is *Ilah al-nas*, 'the God of humankind', participating this verbal way with the creaturely vocation He bestows on us. To 'have a heart' this way, as the Qur'an asks, is to acknowledge what—in Christian language—is the sacrament of being who we are.[18]

The quest for such a heart in present time means the surmounting of much prejudice and a foregoing—it must be—of legitimate anger or latent ill-will. Problematics between 'the West and the Qur'an' were noted in the Introduction. But a 'heart' not to be deterred by these might kindle to the sense of history, both natural and political, to which the cited verses appeal. The written and recited Scripture has its implicit otherness for minds that feel themselves alien to its universe. Yet its own frequent reliance is on the 'signs' that abound everywhere in the good earth and meet us in present history. Muhammad was a wayfaring merchant, a cameleer in 'the caravans of the Quraish summer and winter' (106.2), so that the scenes through which he passed and the script of the history they told came into the incidence of the things he preached. Readership can do no less in the setting of its present situation. For that situation is, by virtue—or vice—of its technology, more loaded

---

[17] It is not only in Sufism that there is this ardent quality of devotion to the person of Muhammad. Though it may have mystical form there, it belongs generally in the most zealously 'unitarian' expressions of Islam, aside from the emotions of 'folk Islam'. It is in line with how Surah, 49.7 tells of 'faith made precious and beautified' in heart.

[18] To find, as the Qur'an does, even in 'ruins' something to arrest attention and prompt thoughts of anxiety and scrutiny is to sense a kinship that has us discover in ourselves what is beyond ourselves. We begin to be 'religious', as 'tied' into who and where we are.

than any other age with threatening, or fulfilling, potential for us all. There is no sane meaning for that ambiguous 'and' in the 'Islam and the West' formula but one of mutual openness of heart and a human peace of the divine bond.

## Chapter 8
# THE ONUS OF NECESSARY SHAPE, ART AND RITUAL

Of the two sisters in the Gospel story, it was the practical Martha who was said to be 'cumbered by much serving,' whereas of the devotee, Mary, it might be said that she was 'busied with much ceremony.' The religious mind has ever been pre-occupied with due forms for worship and right shapes for the structures of belief.

The directives in Surah 22.29-30 make the general point and exemplify the principle in the vital context of Islamic Hajj, or mandatory Pilgrimage. They do so the more usefully because translation itself is debatable, just as rituals also are productive of controversy—thanks to the import they carry in a world so liable to deviance. The verses run:

ثُمَّ لْيَقْضُوا تَفَثَهُمْ وَلْيُوفُوا نُذُورَهُمْ وَلْيَطَّوَّفُوا بِالْبَيْتِ الْعَتِيقِ ذَٰلِكَ وَمَن يُعَظِّمْ حُرُمَٰتِ

اللَّهِ فَهُوَ خَيْرٌ لَّهُ عِندَ رَبِّهِ وَأُحِلَّتْ لَكُمُ الْأَنْعَٰمُ إِلَّا مَا يُتْلَىٰ عَلَيْكُمْ فَاجْتَنِبُوا الرِّجْسَ

مِنَ الْأَوْثَٰنِ وَاجْتَنِبُوا قَوْلَ الزُّورِ

How ought the English to read? Much turns on the very obscure word *tafathahum*. Is it their 'lewdness', 'their unkemptness',[1] or that about them which requires the urging to 'spruce themselves'?[2] Such the niceties of ritual often demand. Or is the sense more technical referring to the start—or the ending—of the ritual state of *Ihram* during the Meccan Pilgrimage, the time, with its due garb when pilgrims abstained from sexual activity for its duration.[3] We would then having the following sense:

---

[1] M Pickthall's rendering in *The Meaning of the Glorious Qur'an*, London, 1930, p. 342.

[2] N Dawood in his *The Koran*, London, 1956, p. 390. Arberry's version reads: 'Let them finish with their self-neglect.' *The Koran Interpreted*, London, 1955. Vol. 2, p. 30.

[3] If the ending is understood, as seems to be required by the verb *yaqdu*, the 'circuit' mentioned must be one of 'farewell', since 'vows' and 'circuits' have been statutory parts of the Hajj itself.

'Subsequently, let them terminate their ritual state, fulfil the vows they have undertaken and make the circuit of the ancient House. Such is their duty. Who-ever holds sacred the solemn directives God has laid down, will find good to his soul therein from his Lord.'

The context is certainly about the Hajj for which Surah 22 is named and there are clear instructions about the animal sacrifice. An entire ritual perspective is present—due order, binding vows and soul-profit—all entailing holy place and an obeyed tradition, with an age-long form and formula. Certain things are done that kindred things might be meant and both would be 'religious'.

Readers of John Steinbeck's novel *The Grapes of Wrath* may recall how old grandfather Joad dies during the family's grim trek towards California in search of livelihood after the cruel dispossession of their farm-land by unscrupulous financiers whose identities are inscribed on far-off brass plates on New York banking houses, beyond all reach of justice. Having no money for funerals, they bury the corpse on the wayside with their own hands. Then, alarmed about official suspicion aroused by a newly dug grave as some 'foul play', they resolve to write the story down and lay it on the loose soil to come clean about their integrity, a scrap of paper in a bottle.

It occurs to them, that its bald story needs some 'religious' words to hallow its tale. They turn to a decrepit preacher who has tagged on to their waggon. What would he suggest? Maybe: 'Safe in the arms of Jesus.' That plea of theirs—'So that it will be religious' can add nothing to what is deeply 'holy' already—their grief, their good faith, their simplicity, their sense of seemliness and honour, not to say the sheer pathos of the old man's end. Steinbeck seems to be asking: 'What can any words do, whatever they might be, that could speak better than their actions speak?' The signature of truth is there already.[4]

Yet the question presses: Would they have been people of that quality of heart in the presence of deep crisis, if they had not also been people who wanted the 'religious' text? What they had within them of

---

[4] John Steinbeck, *The Grapes of Wrath*, was first published in 1939. The (Penguin) London ed. of 1992 has the original text. The passage is in Chapter 13, pp. 149-150. The 'preacher' demurring (by secreting himself), they write of themselves Psalm 32.1. 'Safe in the arms ...' it might have been. Each one of the household helps dig, and then fill, the wayside grave.

reverence in the face of mystery and of courage in despair was not a witless novelty. It belonged squarely with a nurture which alone enabled it to be spontaneous when its test came. It had been formed within them before it could inform their conduct.

John Steinbeck's meaning in the novel may seem far from Surah 22, indeed almost a reversal of it. There was pattern in the Hajj, hardly to be called spontaneous nor, there and then, devised. All was a ritual meticulously followed. Nothing came by after-thought as with the Joads. Yet any Hajji would say there had been long forethought and there would be long afterthought because the Hajj was set to happen as a life-time's fruition.

Either way, there is the single fact that religious forms, rites, ceremonies, times, customs, festivals, even buildings contrive to shape what might be described as a 'second nature', a quality of 'taking' life and its crises that arrives to be instinctive and then un-self-critical. Where this obtains, its practitioners (if we may so describe them) are the more puzzled and dis-oriented—though not disenchanted—in the context of a radical secularism by which their 'second nature' is quite discounted as superstitious or malign.[5] It follows that the situation needs to be carefully addressed by both parties, each of them little qualified to do so patiently.

There is perhaps no area more liable to mutual impatience than the strong traditionalism of many in Islam. As with all religion, there is a strange paradox about its features, even contradiction. As we have seen earlier, there may be the menace of self-esteem in the self-assurance, or of unworthy merit in the pride of discipline, with censure of those outside the charmed circle from those within. How should we take the ambivalence in Surah 22.30's pledge of 'good to the soul from its Lord' in 'holding sacred' His directives? This *khair*, this 'well-being', may indeed be authentic in honesty of character or it may be deeply compromised as bland prosperity and vain congratulation. The religious form itself will be caught in the alternative and be unable, of itself, to obviate it. All will turn on the will to integrity with which 'we mind the meaning.' Nor will those 'secularists' who so promptly identify the issue be themselves exempt.

---

5   It is important, for any hopeful relations, that the parties should realise how far 'the other' may be pre-possessed by assumptions and attitudes they have never really thought themselves outside of and so to measure where discourse needs to be. This is equally true of the secularist as of the devotee.. The point here was anticipated in Chapter 5.

What is most urgent for the West is to recognise the distinctive Islamic contours of this situation in all religion and relate to them perceptively and, as far as possible, from Quranic precepts. For their own Scripture, as we are seeing, is apt for their own critique and perhaps—with due caution—the outsider may help to further it. What is then more deferential in relationship will prove more radical in the end.

The element of paradox is so acutely present in the classic Pilgrimage where Surah 22 belongs. It is supremely Islam in ritual self-expression. No other faith has anything comparable. It is annual, in its proper month, with its familiar ritual, its art of focus (geographical, personal, corporate, even dress-wise) and its asset of prospect and retrospect as a 'life-expectancy'. Along with the Fast of Ramadan, it is where Islam is most intensely self-aware.

Yet where it congregates it most surely segregates. Its inclusiveness is a most tellingly exclusifying thing. Any non-Muslim will be present there at risk of instant death. The rest of humankind are excluded even as potential learners of its meaning. The soil of Mecca—and for long of 'the island of the Arabs' altogether—was to be spared the tread of non-Muslim feet.[6] It must remain a hard question whether Islam will ever open up its Pilgrimage or its natal territory to the reverent tuition of a wider world. This would be in line with its Muhammad being 'a mercy to the worlds' and Allah as *Rabb al-nas* and *Rabb al-'Alamin*, 'Lord of humanity' and 'Lord of the worlds'.

It may be said that faiths cannot have the intensity their patterns afford without the separatism they require and that the phenomenon occurs in all traditions, if nowhere with quite the same emphasis as in Islam's Hajj. Certainly the price is well paid. For the universality—as an Islamic one—is effectively achieved. There are many tributes to the egalitarian, emotionally incorporating experience of the Pilgrimage. Islamic inclusion is a supra-racial thing. There is a oneness that ignores rank, tribe, speech, nationality and origin.[7] Even Muslim schisms are in part overcome in the single embrace of Mecca, the more so as all is known

---

6  Does this doctrine about Arabia as 'belonging to Arabs' go back to Surah 90.2:'You (Muhammad) have the liberty of this land,' though exegesis varies and maybe only Mecca is meant?

7  There is notable proof of the efficacy of this aspect in the autobiography of Malcolm X, who undertook the pilgrimage as a 'Black Muslim' from the USA to realise how inconsistent with Islam that movement's version was.

in deeply personal terms—thanks to the *Iltizam* at the Ka'bah.[8] The physical experience of massing humanity transacts profound participation. Emphatically, the ritual works.

The immunity of the land and of the liturgy makes for a sharp self-sufficiency in the soul of the faith, an assurance which does not stay to ask: 'What lack I yet?' But does it need to? Yet, if it does not, has the victory over ethnic separatism been attained only at the price of a more subtle one? Has the crowning asset become the heavy liability?

To bring John Steinbeck's 'so-that-it-will-be-religious' into relation with Islamic Hajj is only to indicate how close, in all religions, is the association of form with spirit, and of shape with intent. In every case patterns become channels. Structures enshrine[9] familiars and familiars transact feelings. Faiths take to themselves their institutions of place and time and image that they may 'be' themselves the more consciously by giving their private inwardness a public narration which recruits the arts and invades the senses, eye, ear and motion. This way they know themselves in telling themselves, believing that their being is to be received. Long before the secular world made it so banal, they knew that 'advertisement' was instinctive to their soul, for that soul's own profit, for which purpose language and culture lay readily to hand.

Their liturgies and ritual acts, and all that waits on these, serve to intensify inner meaning, transacting it so that it may be extensified by dint of where it has been focused. The mosque can be described as 'a gatherer' or *jami'ah*, where people assemble and whence they disperse. The erect form becomes the prostrate form in the act of *Salat*, to affirm the meaning of *homo erectus* as, in that very capacity, a worshipper.[10] The limbs of the body, from head to foot, in performing this liturgy can be understood as a *masjid*, a mosque in itself. Faith proceeds in both intensive and extensive life, being right with itself in the rites of its expression, both fulfilling its ends.

---

[8] The 'pressing of the chest' on the 'Black Stone' in a corner of the Ka'bah during the circumambulation rite.

[9] 'Enshrine' has an interesting, perhaps ominous, etymology. The *scrinium* was a chest or casket in which papers might be stored, or even human relics. Those of a saint would supply the 'holy' aura to dignify the mere 'containing' 'enshrine' would first denote.

[10] The human in supremely power-wielding posture, well-sighted, readily mobile and mentally superior is brought down to the earth in a self-controlled prostration—brow on the ground.

Like all religion, but perhaps with a unique savour, Islam harnesses the twin human assets of solidarity and habituation. These are evident enough in all its 'Pillars', as in Pilgrimage, so also in Ramadan. Calendar and recurrence co-operate. There is an enabling rhythm between duty and meaning.

There is, however, a price to pay, in that the more effective the inner sanctioning of identity via form and rite, the more potentially alienating from humankind at large. What engages and pre-occupies the habituation and the solidarity also sharpens or hardens the postures of otherness. To belong thus is not to belong where 'thus' will not hold.[11] Islam and its Qur'an have this alienating potential in distinctively insistent form. The reasons have been apparent in all the foregoing—hence the urgency of trying to see how its effect might be mitigated from within its own text. The boon of finality—'religion as Allah would have it is Islam'—can be the bane of 'religion as humankind needs it to be.'[12]

We might derive an analogy here to illuminate this paradox from 'ships and harbours'. Philosophers have noted how there is something integral between them, in that ships must always seek, utilise and suit harbours. This law, however, though integral to all shipping, applies only at the mercy of what cargoes are being carried. They will decide which ships and which harbours will actually coincide, albeit all lying open to all.

The voyages of shipping are world-wide. So are the ends and means of religion. The cargoes of faiths will have only fitting ports in their itinerary. The task of faith, by this analogy, must be how to have their forms convey their contents, their liturgies carry their meanings, beyond where the idiom they have for them, in shape of ritual and norm, can travel and arrive as in a global traffic.

---

[11] Here is the old problem crudely now labelled 'acculturation'. Can the African drum be sufficiently detached from some summons to war to become instead a duly local call to worship? Will Christians, if invited to attend mosque prayers, pray by prostration? No Muslims would ever make the sign of the Cross but need that usage elsewhere always offend? The puzzles are endless. What matters is the heart.

[12] Surah 3.19 (cf. 3.85) one of the six occasions in the Qur'an where the noun *Al-Islam* occurs. It is usually thought to mean the whole 'established' creed and regime that is 'Islam'. However, it may be rendered as *al-islam* (small 'i') meaning the 'submission' Abraham brought God as a 'muslim', long before the final shape of Muhammad's *Sirah*. In that simple distinction between capital 'I' and small 'i'—which Arabic cannot make—lies our whole problem.

Some would say that the onus here is one they can never rise to, being so far existing in their own idiom. They would draw another analogy from language and argue that, while language is common to humans, its sundry grammars have no reason to coincide. They remain masters of their own order and sovereign to themselves. Faiths, likewise, can only opt to co-exist in their assertive self-sufficiency, under no necessity to relate. Hindus might contrive a philosophy to have it otherwise, Islam never,

What, then, from a faith that believes itself divinely 'self-sufficient' in duly non-relating terms, a faith which has thereby a mandate to bring all humankind under the sway of its single truth and—in that truth's name—its one political rule? Plainly, it will need disabusing of that sense of itself on two grounds. The first must be on any responsible realism about the human globe in contemporary history. The other will be the relevance of its own sources to its own surer, saner, larger mind. Some of these we nave reviewed. Flanking both tasks will be the potential ministry to them of neighbour faiths—insofar as neighbourhood is accepted—and the stimulus of the secular as explored in Chapter 5.

Whether we drew metaphor from cargoes or from grammars, we must be asking what the cargoes or the rules we find in forms and liturgies intend to 'mean', as mean they must if they are to register for their intensive role. This, we must believe, is a role they cannot play (their custodians being fellow humans) unless it is also extensively accessible outside its own community. How duly can all that is intensely domestic as fully copyrighted faith, legitimate in its own norms, signify beyond itself? Can the content be identified without the shape, the point within the rite where the rite will always be strange? Can such strangeness cease to be perplexing, disquieting, even repulsive, as prejudice is liable to find it?

With minds—as the Qur'an would say—not having 'locks on them'[13] we can consider the questions, as goodwill might, around the familiars of Islam in the art of its theology and the acts of its devotion. In so ample a field the venture can only be selective.

On several counts, it is well to begin with the mosque as the primary physical, architectural and emotive expression of Islam. Every local mosque (*masjid*, lit. 'place of prostration') corroborates the habituation and solidarity achieved in Fast and Pilgrimage. Its niche or

---

[13] Surah 47.24 and the whole plea of Chapter 7 about a 'readership with a heart'.

*mihrab* points geographically to Mecca and thus has all present facing where, soul-wise, they belong. Surah 7.29-31 gives to every mosque a sobering presence that reminds of the brevity of life and bids in all a sense of frugality.[14]

A mosque, named for such *taqwa* (9.108) was built promptly on Muhammad's arrival in Medina, to be quickly followed by the erection of the Great Mosque, with his household quarters on its north side. By its sheer presence, the mosque tells a discrimination against unbelief. For 'polytheists have no right to enter or administer the mosques of God while they bear witness against themselves of their denial of faith' (9.28). The frequenting, the very constructing or furnishing of mosques are the sole privilege of true believers (9.18). Thus, on all counts, the mosque mediates Muslim identity as being possessed in its possession. Visibly and emotionally it transacts community.[15]

Its interior makes for a consecration of space, whether in a colonnade of pillars or beneath some majestic dome. As Surah 72.18 explains 'the mosques are God's, (so) do not make invocation to any but God.' The utter absence of statuary and visual representation or iconography vindicates the solitariness for which worship reaches. Calligraphy (with geometrical or floral design) suffices, with its intimation of how that divine Oneness is prescriptively concerned with us humans.

The *minbar*, or 'pulpit', aside the *mihrab* interprets what the writing tells. In Muhammad's *Sirah*-time, it became a focus of deep veneration. Around and overhead there is what some have thought a *horror vacui*. Let tiles and surfaces carry the text lest their emptiness suggest distraction or contrive a wrong imagination. When fully congregational the edifice gathers its serried ranks into a unison of singular direction quite contrasted with the sacramental focus of a Eucharist. When peopled by a scattered few it ministers deeply to that

---

[14] One verse calls for sincerity in facing any and every mosque, while v. 31 commends due 'decorum' around mosque attendance in respect of fine apparel and good food and drink but warns against excess that is 'prodigal'. Some take the command to be: 'Beautify yourselves.'

[15] This means that, somehow, the edifices and houses of other faiths are inauthentic, Even so Surah 22.40 is happy to list—in its vindication of the use of armed defence—'Monasteries, churches, synagogues and mosques where God's Name is oft remembered.' It is also noteworthy that when in Surah 17.1, Muhammad was transported to *al-masjid al-aqsa* in Jerusalem it was not then a 'mosque' in the sense Islam came to know the term. It had meaning thanks to Abraham and 'Isa.

sense of the personal equation on which its every discipline turns. Its carpetry will often be designed to offer private rectangles to fit—and invite—the physical measure of prostration. On these many counts, the mosque communicates Islam to the Muslim, by the mosque the Muslim understands Islam. The West needs a patience to take in the distinctive terms in which it intends to have the earth also duly and scrupulously our place of worship.

Thanks to the strictly educative purpose of its Scripture, the mosque in Islam has not traditionally known the pastoral aura of the Christian parish church. For the latter derived from the 'shepherd' language of its psalmody and, more tellingly still, of its Gospel concerning God Himself in Jesus assuming the 'shepherd' role of which David only sang. The very features which the mosque, in line with its Qur'an, abjures, i.e. of art and imagery, table and 'the fruit of the vine', come only from their cradling matrix in 'the Word made flesh'. Whence, in turn, that rich pastoral tradition, ministering holy things.

More recently, however, the mosque has become a deeply social agency in caring terms, beyond those of its traditional teaching function and its role as a source of *fatwas* and Shari'ah declamation. The Muslim Brotherhood, for example, notably in Egypt, has made the mosque a strong factor in social concern. It has done so out of a will to demonstrate to a sceptically oppressive regime its 'good faith' as law-abiding. Indeed, where relief of poverty and illiteracy has been less than adequate in governmental form, Brotherhood mosques have been notably active in assuming the urgent task. They have seen their social concern as galvanising their youth in a more deliberate practice of faith as also ethic, to the quickening of its own discipline. Fanaticisms can somehow be usefully tamed by being more socially directed.

If the mosque is the West's prime index to Islam, calligraphy is the other. Arabic, as a flow of linking letters, lends itself to the art of the scribe, as does its rhythm to the skill of the reciter. A text to inscribe, words to 'read' and 'read aloud'[16] were from the outset the prime credential of Muhammad. 'Written-ness' is the single 'sacrament' of the divine will. The text is the token of divine intent as of human duty. Its possession is at once our guiding but also—we may say—our 'savouring'. For the

---

[16] This supreme 'asset' of the Qur'an is often overlooked in the West as being 'music' as well as 'meaning'. But see, for example, *Approaching the Qur'an: The Early Revelations*, trans. M Sells, Oregon, 1999, with recording attached.

devout reciter that which is the divine language is breathed on private lips. There is a conscious participation by the personal in the eternal.[17] That which is of God comes to be that which is in us. God's 'speech' is ours to rehearse anew. The Qur'an is for the voice of man and woman. It will carry exclusively the sound of worship. The Oneness of Allah translates into the singularity of His 'strategy' in Scriptures[18] and both are underwritten in the finality of Muhammad uttering—and so conveying into a scripted thing—the final 'seal of prophethood'.

With calligraphy paramount in art and recitation in liturgy, it follows that where revelation is 'scripted' this way, it needs and breeds a mind-set that reciprocates. The believer is schooled to rely on quotation. Citation becomes the first plea of the lawyer, despite the urgent theme covered in the previous chapter about 'having a heart'. In the way Quranic *tajwid*, or recital, is traditionally divided into *ahzab*, or 'portions in sequence', the reader is more likely to be occupied with which follows which textually than with what logic is in view coherently. A text-keeping faith answers to a text-affording God. Both ways we are given a Shari'ah, apt for conformity.

Of course, the particularity has long required an enlarging emendation, hopefully consistent with it yet additionally to it. It was quickly obvious as Islam spread and persisted in time, that the *Sitz-im-Leben* of the *Sirah* and the Qur'an had not sufficed to cover all emerging issues. Hence the need to gather and to invoke the precedents of Muhammad as a further source. These in turn needed to be amplified by arguable analogy with them and by communal consensus as warranted by expert initiative.[19] These sources had to be 'non-repugnant' to the Qur'an itself but they could speak for its 'silences' and implement its diminishing adequacy to its ongoing years.[20] Yet it would never cease to dominate and control what Islam would be because of it.

---

[17] Some have suggested—but dubiously—that there may be analogy here in Christian participation in 'the bread and wine' of Holy Communion.

[18] 'Strategy' may seem a harsh term here. But clearly if revelation is exclusively 'verbal' and 'textual' and not 'incarnational', it is the plan by which God chooses to proceed..

[19] I.e. what is known as *qiyas* and *Ijma'* via *Ijtihad*, in respect of Sunni Islam and its famous Four Schools.

[20] Only so in that time left behind the context and culture by which the Quranic text had place and date. A continuing 'adequacy', i.e. 'abreastness' of calendar would be had only by responsible interpretation—'holy writ in writ of readers'.

The alert observer, not least if from the West, needs to realise how this faith, thus equipped with mosque and calligraphy and sanctioned by the solidarity/habituation attained by its ordinances, constitutes a deeply self-authenticating whole that has its participants feeling entirely self-sufficient. They are the less susceptible of self-doubt or even of self-interrogation in being on every count the more self-assured. This situation needs a perceptive relation on the part of Western thinking, whether academic or spiritual. The West and its traumas of anxiety or delusion need patient interpretation to minds that have little or no reason to appreciate them inwardly.

This situation may well be relieved by the fact of sizeable Muslim presence inside the Western scene, though its kindred responses may not readily commend themselves to the non-exilic mind-set elsewhere, permeated as that 'elsewhere' is by the superficial influences of the West and its gadgetries.

Either way, these two bastions of the mosque and of calligraphy take us to the authority of the *'ulama'* and the mosque personnel, the contrivers also of *fatwas* and rulings, the custodians of the faith and due 'readers' of the text. The Shi'ah pulpit has long been a potent factor in the kindling of emotion,[21] as well as of enmity towards the reciprocating Sunnis.[22] Both pulpits have contrived to be involved in the political realm—of old with the caliph seated near-by—as collaborating with the regime in place, or inciting to rebellion. Hence the concern of ruling authority to recruit or muzzle preachers and, in many cases, to decide the content of sermons. The points belong here with Chapter 11.

Of present relevance is the vexed question of 'clerical' and 'lay'. Does the mosque pulpit have right to the very definition of Islam or does the vital personal 'caliphate' we have been studying throughout mean a genuine individual liability for the scrutiny of faith and law? If it does not, how is it really entrusted? That it should not has long been the vested interest of the *'ulama'* claiming to be the only valid interpreters. The matter is the more important in that the 20th century brought a widespread

---

[21] See, for example, the recent study from Hyderabad. India, Toby Howarth, *The Pulpit of Tears, Shi'i Muslim Preaching in India*, Vrije, 2001.

[22] As in the mandatory 'cursings' of 'Ali, Hasan and Husain in Umayyad pulpits before and after Karbala' and the answering imprecation against the 'enemy' in Damascus as the Shi'ah knew it. The *minbar*, either way, could not escape the political theme it lived with and had to enforce.

'laicisation' into Islam, when many formative roles in society passed over from the wearers of turbans cloistered in mosques into the preserve of technicians working in laboratories and there engendering new problems societal, of which the former were likely to be ignorant.

Given that the latter are duly 'Muslim', as were their many forebears in the middle centuries of their sciences, have they no say in the shaping of current decisions in Islam? Yet the turbaned cloisters tend to cling to their prerogatives, claiming that only they command the necessary resources of training and expertise in *tafsir*, Tradition and jurisprudence. They have the *Ijtihad*, as the term goes, the right of 'initiative' which can duly serve to promote some new *ijma'*, or 'consensus', by which Muslims could now be guided. Or, even more binding, the 'door' to such *Ijtihad* is now closed, all necessary decisions having been already reached.

It follows that one of the most pressing needs of today's Islam is a more resilient, a less raucous, religious leadership. Must it not then also follow that a gentle nurturing of this quality is the duty of Western intellectual relationship, insofar as outsiders can exercise an influence?[23] Muslim religious studies have, for too long, been in a separate segment from studies in general and from the terms of reference any theology must now give itself. Disciplines, like sociology and international law, have required religion to face new liabilities, but there has been a tendency in some quarters in Islam to strive to subdue their challenge by somehow enclosing them in an 'Islamicization of knowledge' where their 'secular tendency' would be disallowed. Then there is no 'lending our minds out' which Robert Browning felt to be the genius of art and artistry.[24]

The spirit that holds the sacred Shari'ah inviolate is not true to the history of its own formation, enclosing as it did in the early centuries much customary law, as well as those other constituents needed to implement the Qur'an. The contemporary mind of Islam needs to exercise a comparable role in the Shari'ah's rubric and thus disown its imposition in terms of implacable necessity.

In this context, it becomes the more clear how capable of flexibility the Qur'an itself attains to be—not by wishful usage or sleight of hand, but by the ambivalence of meanings questioningly present, in

---

[23] Richard W Bulliet, for example, in his recent *The Case for Islamo-Christian Civilization*, New York, 2004, leaves this issue out of reckoning.

[24] Robert Browning, *Poetical Works*, Oxford, 1941, 'Fra Lippo Lippi', p. 431.

the sense reviewed in Chapter 6. Is not so much implied in the very term 'non-repugnancy' as a negative criterion? It may be too magisterial to say: 'The Qur'an means what Muslims find it to mean.' That will always mean estimating as such the Muslims in the 'finding'. Yet the *magisterium* which demands to be the only one is no less problematic—and for the same reasons. All faiths and all Scriptures incur the same problem, perhaps currently Islam has the most exacting shape of it.

The poet Browning's word about what 'art was given for', as 'telling truth obliquely, do the thing shall breed the thought,' applies vividly to the long pre-occupation of Islamic art with angles, lines and shapes, its fascination with geometrical design. Assessors have detected here a clue to the procedures of its theology. The hexagons or octagons, the self-repeating flow of tracery on the walls of pulpits, the cover of books, or the metal of lamps, speak of conformity and order, a re-assuring continuity forever defined by its own consistency. There will be subtlety, but none that is guessing about whence and whither. All is patterned in a patterned-ness, if we employ that word. Muslim thinking has often abjured all plea of paradox. Truth does not consort with contradiction. Geometry is an art proper to religion. It recommends *Tawhid* in being its own order and unity is self-affirmed.[25]

There is a deep irony in the ambition of Islamic art to represent in the sure symmetry of its geometric design the given order of its Shari'ah, or in the conforming sequences of its artistry the proper claim of its learned hierarchy. That by which life in its living wills to be identified 'so that it will be religious' needs to have place for brokenness and tragedy. The exquisite beauty of the Taj Mahal owes something to the curved shadows in the iwans, or cavern-like recesses, in its walls.[26] Authority is perfectly blended with submission in the precision of the geometrical and the splendour of the architectural, but the religion so affirmed belongs also with the human perversity that nevertheless has proved incorrigible, however blessedly its artists dream it could be.[27]

---

[25] See Issam El-Said and Ayse Parman, *Geometric Concepts in Islamic Art*, London, 1976.

[26] As noted by Titus Burckhardt, *Art of Islam, Language and Meaning*, London, 1976, p. 179. 'These recesses are like vast caves of deep and heavy shadow while the dome draws down upon itself the full light of day.'

[27] Might it be right to reflect in this context on the symmetry of aircraft, the line of fuselage and the spread of wing as an exercise of art as well as efficiency, on the beauty of design and integrity in the jet-engine, on the pure cloudless blue of a New England morning—and all this crashed into The World Trade Centre to advertise so vividly the crime of a religion?

Art and architecture have always proved susceptible to inter-borrowing. Islamic builders in India registered the influences of Hinduism, those in the West often recruited Christian skills and patterns. The material realm in which they excelled took to its neighbourhoods more readily than the theologians or pundits. Yet such borrowings always kept the hallmark that was their own, as its witness to the common human-ness it could never evade.

By its use of the verb *zayyana* and its noun *zain*, the Qur'an suggests an intriguing inter-relation between faith and beauty. Surah 7.31 was noted earlier, enjoining a care for personal seemliness in mosque attendance. Surah 49.7 goes much further in saying how the 'heart', that capacity for love we found central in the previous chapter, holds faith itself as 'beautified.'

> 'God has made faith precious to you and given your hearts an appreciation of its beauty, rendering unbelief, wickedness and rebellion hateful to you.'

The verb might be taken in the sense of to 'endear', as when frequently used in an unhappy sense about Satan beguiling folk into a false and deluding fascination. Even Allah may have the erring 'see their doings fair' (27.4). Art has a capacity to lull as well as arrest, to deceive as well as to disclose. About the artistry of the heavens, the stars as lamps in mansions of the sky, the Qur'an is in no doubt (15.15, 37.6, 41.12, 50.6 and 67.5). These will ever keep their purity even though certain 'beauties' below may prove seductive for the unwary (3.14).

Thus the 'onus' for discernment will always be present in the prizing of the asset. 'So that it will be religious' will always be the vital criterion as well as the possible pitfall in the 'associate' things we devise for the expression of faith, whether the environs where we will to gather, the rituals we enact, the artistry we enlist or the structures we erect. All these will be the more at issue when, in fact, it is not 'we' who will them but 'the faith' itself as only ours as subjects in a heritage. This, however, which we hold to be 'the faith' is always ambivalently ours as the associate of 'faith' itself, of that which wants these 'somethings' to tell what it is.

Since that equation is always precarious the more rigorous it wills or fails to be, it may be fair to conclude that the Qur'an deserves a generous patience from the West. Can its own readers heed where the exchange must go?

However critical the secular aspects of such converse, there can be no evading the things critical for the Christian incidence of that 'the faith/faith' equation. It is right we turn there—though selectively, in the shape of the Christian 'table' to which obliquely the Qur'an itself notably refers.

## Chapter 9
# THE TABLE AND THE MEMORY

According to Surah 5 of the Qur'an there was a request to Jesus from his disciples. It ran: 'O Jesus, son of Mary, can your Lord send down to us a table from heaven?'

إِذْ قَالَ ٱلْحَوَارِيُّونَ يَـٰعِيسَى ٱبْنَ مَرْيَمَ هَلْ يَسْتَطِيعُ رَبُّكَ أَن يُنَزِّلَ عَلَيْنَا مَآئِدَةً مِّنَ ٱلسَّمَآءِ

There is a prior point before seeing what followed their request.

No invitation to the West to reckon intelligently with the Qur'an for its own sake and for the world's can neglect—as thus far by deliberate design in the foregoing chapters—the long Western tradition of Christianity. There are central items of that faith for which the Qur'an has its sharp anathema. It firmly disallows the whole incarnational theology of any 'Word made flesh'. It finds the Passion of Jesus neither truly historical, nor morally sustainable, nor redemptively necessary. With these inclusive vetoes it radically revises Christian perceptions of transcendent Lordship, realised and known in 'Father, Son and Holy Spirit'. It, therefore, also lays its ban on the structures of Christian pastoral ministry[1] and the vital dimensions of Christian worship in 'bread and wine' as where Christians 'offer and present themselves' in the perpetuation, personally and socially, of the living principles to which these summon them.

So radical is this massive Quranic disallowance of things that are ever distinctive of Christianity across all its centuries, that many would

---

[1] It originates with the imagery of a nomadic and flock-tending people about their Yahweh as 'the shepherd of Israel'(Psalm 80.1) and extends into an analogy for their prophets, whether as true, or false, shepherds and has its surest climax in the 23rd Psalm. Whence it continued in shepherd-'hood' as the right index for Christian ministry in its New Testament shape, 'Feed my sheep,' (John 21.16–17) and Paul's charge to 'Ephesian elders,' 'Feed the flock of God' (Acts 20.28) and numerous other passages. The metaphor of 'sheep' may be archaic now for an intelligent laity, but this 'care of all the churches' has always been more than 'teach' and 'exhort'. It has been 'love and belong.' There is no more utterly committed role than that of 'shepherd'—which is why they can muse and sing as well.

122

dismiss out of hand any effort like the present one to plead and present any Quranic relevance to the Western world. We have argued reason in the preceding chapters to resist that counter anathema, by seeking a positive relation with the Muslim Scripture. Unconvinced, and perhaps unpersuadable, as many hard of heart (in the sense of Chapter 7) remain, the uniting territory we have explored will not be gainsaid. Nor can it be denied its bearings on the Western scene without our also disavowing wide reaches of our own Biblical vision of the one human world.

Yet, in a will to keep faith with those who still demur, there is no escape, nor any will to shrink, from a clear reckoning with the deep inter-issues that must pre-occupy the sincerity of any current Muslim/ Christian relationships. Too often these have suffered from a minimal attention, succeeding what was too long a bitter and often obtuse polemic. Having both these failing postures in mind, it is the more heartening to turn to this Quranic text—for all its enigmatic quality—which associates Qur'an-readers with the Jesus of the Gospels in the very context which became the celebratory liturgy of Christianity. It comes in the Surah on which it bestows its title: *Al-Ma'idah*, concerning a 'table from heaven' as 'a memorial' among Jesus' disciples.

قَالَ ٱتَّقُوا۟ ٱللَّهَ إِن كُنتُم مُّؤْمِنِينَ قَالُوا۟ نُرِيدُ أَن نَّأْكُلَ مِنْهَا وَتَطْمَئِنَّ قُلُوبُنَا وَنَعْلَمَ أَن قَدْ صَدَقْتَنَا وَنَكُونَ عَلَيْهَا مِنَ ٱلشَّٰهِدِينَ قَالَ عِيسَى ٱبْنُ مَرْيَمَ ٱللَّهُمَّ رَبَّنَآ أَنزِلْ عَلَيْنَا مَآئِدَةً مِّنَ ٱلسَّمَآءِ تَكُونُ لَنَا عِيدًا لِّأَوَّلِنَا وَءَاخِرِنَا وَءَايَةً مِّنكَ وَٱرْزُقْنَا وَأَنتَ خَيْرُ ٱلرَّٰزِقِينَ قَالَ ٱللَّهُ إِنِّى مُنَزِّلُهَا عَلَيْكُمْ

Before coming to the detail of this *Ma'idah* and its Quranic background, it is well to realise how it links poetically into the whole foregoing saga of a significant creation with its 'serious' human intention. For does not 'a table for heaven' capture the whole scenario of the open face of a planet expectant beneath its sky? Even astronomers must mount their dishes to read those heavens. The landscape in its life-bearing, fruit-yielding capacity is where we are present, with the earth our 'table' and we its invitees,[2] in a sort of terrestrial/celestial exchange.

---

[2] 'Table', as at the Cape of South Africa, and elsewhere has been borrowed as fit to describe territory and the domestic 'plate' akin to 'plateau', while in many cultures seated on the ground is how we eat. There is the usage about those who 'keep a good table,' referring to the fare they provide.

Thus there is deep in the Biblical concept of creation the sacramental principle that is at the heart of Christianity. There are intimations of what is ever spiritual conveyed in what is arrestingly physical, in how this earth presents a bosom of land and sea in naked frontage to the heavens, Seascape and landscape have their dawns respond to the waking sun, their nights saluted by the rising moon. By nature, earth has its being in this canopy-rapport, cherished by reviving rains or buffeted by chastening storms. Thence it has its fertilising rivers from above and offers the face of its seas for the clouds that will replenish them, but only in concert with its own mountainous terrain. Such is the theme of all the moods of heaven.

'Wherein', as the Qur'an would say, 'are signs for intelligent folk.' Perplexities and enigmas abound. We have to live with King Lear on a 'blasted heath', yet only by the kinship of what the Qur'an so often calls, as twain: 'the heavens and the earth'. The instinct of all theisms is to peruse and salute this duality, as though a manifest 'hospitality', in the grateful acknowledgement of a 'homestead'. Be it sullenly or vividly, we know the earth as a habitat and, as the preacher quaintly said: 'if the inn was full, you may be sure the stable was not empty.'[3]

How welcome then, to Christians in the West, ought this *Ma'idah* in the Qur'an to be. With the other passage due to be studied in Chapter 10, it gives occasion to obviate, or better focus, the controversies that have persisted so long and which, on the Muslim side, play their sorry part in the enmities that currently loom politically so large. While it would be irresponsible to relate 'the Qur'an and the West' in neglect of all that is adversarial in doctrine, there is better hope in what is potentially conciliatory. For what Christian theists call the sacramental principle—as the vital clue whether for theology or humanism—can be recognised in this Quranic *Ma'idah* being sought and loved by Jesus' disciples as a 'celebratory festival'. Though excluding the Christian Eucharist (ever to be re-affirmed by Christians) Islam throughout its Qur'an has the shared concept of a 'eucharist' with nature and the earth. Despite a sundering between creation and redemption, which Christianity could never concede, a sacramental sense of the created is the more to be cherished. Why, for the Church, they always belong together was well told in the poem of the early 20th century writer, Alice Meynell.

---

[3] In line with Lancelot Andrewes homely wit in preaching, as his practice was in Whitehall on Christmas Day. *Seventeen Sermons on the Nativity*, London, n.d., p. 201, Sermon of 1618.

'And will they cast the altars down,
Scatter the chalice, crush the bread?
In field, in village and in town,
He hides an unregarded head,
Waits in the cornlands far and near,
Bright in his sun, dark in his frost.
The mill conceals the harvest's Lord,
The wine-press holds the unbidden Christ.'[4]

If the physical order ever became, in history, the place of divine meaning in action, then it was always capable in itself, of bearing the divine image through the working of the divine purpose. It is, therefore, possible to see in creation also the artistry of a will that has undertaken to be 'materialised', just as the musician embarks on the resources of sound and the artist on the yielding in the brush to paint and canvas conditioning the art in the mind. The poet, Robert Frost reportedly called it: 'risking spirit in substantiation'.[5]

From such long thoughts about this *Ma'idah* of the Qur'an, bearing as they do on the heart of theology. we pass to the fact that this Biblical/Quranic 'table' was needed in a 'wilderness'. It is nowhere to be associated with some Grasmere-like terrain as if we were all only thinking the thoughts of a Wordsworth. Even so, if we think sacramentally, on the grounds of our humanity as reviewed in Chapters 2 and 3, we realise how naive and vacuous the sentiments of John Lennon's much admired song:

'Imagine there's no heaven—above us only sky,
Imagine all the people, living for today.'

He goes on:'No countries ... and no religion too ... No need for greed or hunger ...'That 'no need' would have to sing further:

'Imagine there's no dawn, nor sunset,
No need for plough or farm ...'

---

[4]   Alice G Meynell (1847-1922), *The Poems ... 1847-1923*, London, 1940, p. 52, 'In Portugal'.
[5]   T S Eliot, in *Selected Essays*, London, 1965, p. 495, saw 'poetry as a humble analogy of the Incarnation'.

seeing that only as earth-dwellers do we have a sky at all. We see ourselves canopied above because we find a task below. Thus it is only in being responsibly secular that we can be responsively spiritual. Only in 'having countries' are we 'sharing all the world.'[6] This earth with us humans is already 'a table from heaven' by all the sanctions of agronomy. That recurrent phrase, *wa ma bainahuma* 'and what is between them' (i.e. about 'the 'heavens and the earth') could incorporate what the Bible would understand as 'the sacrament of geography' in the capacity of the natural, earthly scene, perceived and received as the realm of human achieving, to be read as 'the minding of a meaning' set 'between the two'.

That being so—and given the fusion of place and time—there could also be 'a sacrament of history' as well as of biography, with event no less than area telling the same exchange of things at once divine and human. The Bible makes this 'history' theme more central to its world, thanks to its reading of tribal migration, an exodus, an exile, a return, a Messiah and thus an 'incarnation'. Islam, however, in the different idiom of its Meccan and Medinan spheres, draws significance alike from time and place.[7]

It is as this double 'sacrament' that we need to read the meaning of the *Ma'idah* and the occasions it brings together. Its point about 'a festival' confirms it. For 'recollection' is always about returning to place and retreating to past time. For just as 'table-celebration' in the art of hospitality, a guesthood offered and accepted, commemorates in food as eaten, so it may also re-enact event and spell participation in its relevance.

What are the Biblical associations that come together in the Qur'an's *Ma'idah*? It reads as reminiscent of the manna in the wilderness through which the covenant-people were travelling and in which they were in jeopardy from hunger. In Surah 5, however, the 'table' is requested by Jesus' disciples, whereas in the Gospels, it is he who plans it for them, directs them to go and prepare the antecedent Passover (recalling Exodus) and bids them renew the rite perpetually in his name.

---

6   The song, July 1971, belongs to the Plastic Ono Band, with the Flux Fiddlers (Apple PAG 10004)

7   Thus the Qur'an's concern to identify the city locale of its 114 Surahs, with no. 9 the only exception. Though incidents inside may be pre- or post-*Hijrah* where surahs are composite, that 'watershed' is crucial and all exegesis must negotiate with narrative.

That would tally with the Qur'an's sense of a 'memorial' for all their 'generations'. There is evidence elsewhere of the Qur'an's awareness of Christian Eucharist.[8]

But, despite that central note of perpetuity, does *Ma'idah* stem from the occasion of 'audience-feeding' narrated in the four Gospels and developed in the Fourth into a deep eucharistic theology?[9] Then those who ate and drank were not a people of divine destiny in historic transit. They were a mixed Galilean ('Galilee of the nations') throng which, by listening too long and without provisions, were in jeopardy had they been summarily dismissed to travel far while homeward bound. The terrain being 'a desert place' is noted—though it is also noted that 'there was much grass in the place' on which the crowd could squat or lie. That precaution: 'Make them sit down' was eminently wise, given how a standing crowd would soon bring likely chaos to a distribution process.

That 'grassy desert' scene was a far cry from 'the upper room' and a small band of disciples' but did it intend to be a commentary on that other desert-place en route to 'promised land'? For now 'They did all eat'—this polyglot assembly going nowhere special except home to sleep, united only in their long and fascinated audition round a preacher. 'The broken baskets' of the over-plus numbered as many as the sacred 'tribes of Israel'. What did the Gospels mean to say by these meticulous details, as in the hinterland of the ancient story, unless an implied contrast between 'two covenants' each differently transacted in the mystery of food?

We can only thus guess in a proximate way at how the *Ma'idah* of Surah 5 means us to understand from what it makes of these strands in the provenance it has. Scholars have long debated the 'what' and 'why' of its presence in the text by speculation on Muhammad's contacts with Biblical traditions or his acquaintance with their Arabian incidence during his travels. For orthodox Muslims the text is simply

---

[8]  Notably the altar lamp in the Surah of Light (24), the favoured notice of 'churches' where 'prayer is made' and its qualified awareness of Christian priests and their potential 'closeness' to Islam.

[9]  John 6, where—as often in this Gospel—an incident in the ministry of Jesus is made the introit into deeply theological discourse. Words like 'eating my flesh ...' or 'the bread of God come down into the world ...' would have had no meaning to 'carry' in the immediate audience on the hillside. They 'meant' profoundly for the early Church in its apostolic shape. Similarly, the encounter with Nicodemus in Chapter 3 prefaces a discourse about 'new birth' that moves beyond his question about 'the rabbi's' teaching, though starting from it.

there, given in the incidence of divine *wahy* and, as such, not apt for academic probing into 'how'.

Whether respect for that posture or a sense of near futility about enquiry[10] the right religious attitude is surely a concern with its theology and with the task of reverent and mutual awareness of the sacramental meaning of place and time, as both are made explicit in what we must call 'the located incidence of history'.

The 'location', both time-wise and place-wise, for the Biblical, Mosaic order of the day, was the Exodus which set in train the journey that needed the table of manna in its wilderness passage. It came to be understood, whether by King Solomon praying at the inauguration of the Temple, or of psalmist and prophet, as 'the place of the Name'.[11] Jerusalem thus came to be a sort of divine/Judaic rendezvous, a city where He chose to 'dwell' and, therefore, where they could 'dwell with Him' by symbol, by pilgrimage and by retrospect. The third allowed the others as being their retrospect on the Exodus where, out of bondage, if not out of Abraham, Jacob and Joseph, all began.[12] That Exodus became in truth 'the place of Yahweh's Name', the assurance of His character. When Moses in his 'burning bush' arrest into the liberator's destiny had interrogated 'the voice out of the bush' about 'credentials', he knew that the folk to be liberated were cowed and listless—if not broken—by years of 'cruel bondage'. Knowing that they too, on being summoned to venture, would also seek 'credentials', he had asked what he should answer.

According to Exodus 3.10f. the answer came only in the form of a seeming riddle—and seeming riddles do not energise the despairing. But the 'riddle' was a pledge: 'I will be there as the "who" I there will

---

[10] This is not to discount the academic enterprise *per se*, though perhaps the main thrust of it should—in the present climate—be left to Muslims, since a Western indulgence may only seem a venture in wilful denigration. The issue of Muhammad's 'sources' and their conjectural bearing on the contents and date of the final Qur'an is too 'loaded' to insert into any serious concern with theology in the contemporary situation.

[11] See 1 Kings 8 and Solomon's repeated words 'this place of which Thou hast said: "My Name shall be there."' Cf. also Isaiah 18.7 and 60.13. (Contrast Malachi 1.11.)

[12] The centrality of the Exodus as where historic Jewry is 'defined' co-exists with the idea that all begins with the 'call' of Abraham. Conjecture persists about how—historically—all should be traced as between mythology and history. Certainly, apart from Joseph—and Jacob's part in 'the going down to Egypt'—there could have been no Exodus. All antecedents should be taken as embraced in the great finale, which was in turn the 'enlanded' beginning, all Abrahamic things apart.

be.'[13] Only Exodus could 'tell' the God of Exodus. The knowing would only be in the going. Meanwhile, all they had was trust. In the very nature of their story there could be no prior guarantee. But, given the trust that ventured, there would follow the exit that vindicated its divine auspices. Ever after, they would learn to say: 'He was there, the He who there was.' The time of Exodus had defined Him: the place of Exodus had located Him. History and geography had been the sacrament of His presence and so of His identity. For ever too, the liturgy of the Passover would celebrate the meaning and, doing, so, would hold it evermore in their corporate ken.[14]

It was pointedly in the setting of the Passover that Jesus inaugurated 'the table from heaven' that would memorialise for his disciples the meaning they should read in the drama that would ensue and so read his suffering and death against the clue in the ancient story. He had himself (according to Luke 9.31—'the exodus he should accomplish ...') taken up this analogy, whence the New Testament faith and Church came to its founding from 'our Lord Jesus Christ' as being, thus in himself, 'the place of the Name'. Realising this way his significance, they read his life and ministry, his nativity and death, his resurrection, by the kindred formula: 'God had been there as who there He had been.' Paul spoke of this realisation as 'God in Christ', the 'in' being in Greek grammar a 'locative', denoting where and when.

This 'where and when' drew their theology—and their liturgy—into the understanding of 'why', for which they reached into the whole inherited Messianic principle of a suffering prophethood, by which the fidelity of maligned 'messengers' upheld the truth and compassion of God, holding out against the wrongdoing of the world that had defied them. By their suffering they vindicated the will of their Lord, ensured that the evil did not overcome the good but, instead, that the good opened out its pardon and peace to penitent miscreants themselves, thanks to its redeeming power. Thus—as they believed—God was vindicated in a historic expression of

---

[13] Such, rather than a philosophic 'I am that I am' is surely the meaning of the Hebrew. See, with profit, Martin Buber, *Mamre: Essays in Religion*, trans. Greta Hort, London, 1946, p. 12. He adds of Yahweh: 'You do not need to cast a spell over Me (by naming My Name) for I am with you by My own choice.' 'You meet Me when you meet Me.'

[14] If we were to borrow a Quranic image, we could say the event was the people's *qiblah*—that which they always 'fronted' and 'faced' in their private and public mind, the memory which gave 'direction ' out of that past into their abiding future. The ritual enacted this significance.

Himself, legible in these eventful terms as the terms of His own disclosing, a disclosing of which this story had been the crux.

Though reversing Jesus' own institution of 'memorial' into being their own request, the disciples of 'Isa in *Surat al-Ma'idah* pleaded that personal pronoun rightly. They said:

> 'It is our desire to partake of that table, that our hearts may be at rest in the knowledge that you have indeed spoken truth to us and that we too may be witnesses to it.'

> 'So Jesus, son of Mary, prayed, saying: "O God, our Lord, send down for us a table from heaven that it may be a festival for us through all our generations and a sign from you."' (v. 112-114)

All the elements of the ultimate Christian sacrament are here—its 'all generations' perpetuation, its incorporation of Jesus with his disciples and they with him ('be to us ...'), its need for the pronoun plural as 'desire', and its adoption of the age-long habit of 'table-ising' fellowship in sharing hospitality. It could be as if the Quranic text is echoing Luke (22.15) reporting Jesus saying: 'With desire have I desired to eat this Passover with you before I suffer.' If the 'table' was in fact spread on the ground for elbow-reclining guests the link we earlier studied of an agricultural import would be complete.

Yet, clearly, it is the redemptive one that must control. Even so, if the 'who' God was, was to be read in 'where' and in 'when' He was allegedly disclosed, why should any event deserve to be so identified? Why, above all, should *this* event be the all-conclusive one—this life-story that culminated so grimly in death on a cross? How could the Almighty be 'there as who there he was'? Did Matthew's narrative unknowingly point up the question by recording of the centurion's men on watch: 'Sitting down they watched him there'? (27.36). 'Him ... there'—this man of those Beatitudes, this preacher common folk 'heard gladly.' Is not the reading, at best 'over-loaded', at worst 'appalling'? Either verdict has been frequent ever since.

Though rooted in a history, the answer has to turn on a theology, a theology that is asking about what it takes for God to be God in our sort of world. The question is the more 'right' because it signals the utter incongruity we feel. Transcendence must repudiate all such ignominy.

Part of the answer would derive from that 'expectancy' noted in Chapter 4 as arising from realist measures of human wrong. Another part must be that, nevertheless, in fact a historic faith did emerge, to be itself another fact in history—a faith ready to have itself accused as a 'scandal' and a 'folly', as affirming 'God in Christ' only because it sensed there must also be 'the Christ in God', a theism needing those dimensions to be—as the later Creed would have it—'very God of very God'.

Yet another part of the answer must take us, via these, into why the Creed needed those words to account for its own assurance.[15] This is an area of Christian theology we await in Chapter 10 to follow. If the Messianic hope—in the human story—hinges on the God whose integrity gave it birth in the human soul, as Jewry knew it, then only the responsive adequacy of God to its measure can undertake its fulfilment. Some aspects here, from the side of the Qur'an must come in Chapter 12.

Meanwhile, we have the fact of emergent faith under-writing the fact of a perceived act of history. That they should inter-depend is part of the nature of things, as of all history.[16] And we have their fusing in continuing liturgy, the 'festival that remembers.' Here it is vital to understand 'how' it does so. In the case of the Exodus, there was generated a sense that it held something meant for perpetuity because it could only be defined as defining them, its people-community, only told in—and as—their telling. They—and they as ongoing—would be its corroboration, just as it was theirs.[17]

It was a comparable quality of 'this and us', the Passion of Jesus and the folk of the Christ event had shown him to be, which gave necessary rise to the Liturgy he had himself 'desired.' There was a strange foresight in his ordaining concerning their need. They had readily acceded to his

---

[15] Precisely because of this persisting sense of incredulity, as when Isaiah (53.1) asks: 'Who believes our report, i.e. our verdict as truth-telling?' 'Very' as an adjective with a noun means to re-assure against doubt it can be so.( e.g. 'I saw with my very eyes' or 'those were his very words.') This—what you are telling—cannot be God. Yet, in truth, it is: it shows God veritably, however 'impossible' it seems! 'Truly God as God in truth'—'very' twice for better re-assuring.

[16] 'History'—in its double meaning of 'what happened, and 'what what happened meant as and when told'—are always in some degree of mutuality. The second amounts to a new 'fact', if not of 'verity' certainly of 'record'. Memory may distort but is never non-existent as a consequent 'event'.

[17] Hence such as Paul reflecting: 'All our fathers ... passed through the sea' (1 Corinthians 10.1), echoing the steady refrain of his Hebrew identity. As in all biography, event is the signature of character. We could almost borrow the form of Exodus 3.14 and say: 'They had been there as who there they became.'

request to them to 'go and make ready.' Their every instinct sought its continuity. They would only be themselves as they 'remembered.' So self-evidently right is this 'Lord's Supper', that we often fail to register why there was never a surmise about some other pattern. There could have been several—a formal rehearsal of his Beatitudes, an oral celebration of his parables, a solemn re-enactment of the opening Sermon in that synagogue in Nazareth, or a folk pilgrimage to Mount Tabor.

None of these ensued. There was no thought of them, only of: 'Do this with bread and wine in remembrance of me.' That directive became their instinct for two evident reasons. It required memory to cluster round his suffering, not to the exclusion of his words (for these could be held in memories to turn at length into Gospels), but as their very climax and the active sign and seal of them. And they required discipleship to make his Cross their theme of living. Those other conjectural ideas about 'readings' could have engendered a sort of patronising pride as 'feasts of admiration', possessively indulged. The Liturgy would have to be 'Communion'— 'Make this your own,' as a summons that was not merely to assent but to discipleship in its terms.

This reading of 'the table' as 'the Qiblah' of soul and society alike seems confirmed by the Easter story Luke has of two disciples en route to their village—Emmaus by name—in the late afternoon. It seems right to think of its import as coming from a more prolonged retrospect than of a single day.[18] For it presents the two dimensions of the Church coming, as it were, to 'be itself' in sequence to all that Jesus and his Passion had inaugurated. These were the precedent of Messiahship in Hebrew Scripture and the 'table shared'. Each was the bequest of the risen Christ but availing for them by his living presence journeying with them—the companionship that was the very heart of Resurrection faith. It was not, however, the exegesis of 'things concerning him' as they walked that made them know. He had taken on where their own deep perplexity had been tossing itself back and forth between them,[19] but in discursive terms he

---

[18] That 'day' in Luke 24 extends into the Ascension, without noting any 'end', while having carefully located 'early morning' and 'that same day at evening' and again after evening return to Jerusalem. Is this a token that, if 'minding the meaning' was thus 'compressed', it would be intelligent to know it as 'extended' over a much longer cognisance in months and years, wherein to give matrix for the writings that would enshrine it?

[19] This seems to be the force of that *antiballete*, soberly given in English as 'having communications', when it suggests an animated 'trading' of conjectures and guesses and anxieties in an unrelieved emotion.

did not resolve it. Only as they sat at table and he 'broke the bread' did they have the finally identifying clue, which point the narrative confirms in telling words: 'He was known of them in the breaking of the bread,' as if to underline how words alone had failed. Yet, in the glow of that 'table-meaning', they realised how all by the wayside had set a fervour in their hearts. It was not that exegesis was inferior but that it would always need the sacramental alliance with 'bread and wine'. Was it not out of the experience of converse as they walked that they had prevailed upon him to be their guest?

Their immersion in the intellectual theme of 'all the Scriptures ... and things concerning him' had its satisfaction when he became again, and would forever be, as he had been on 'the night in which he was betrayed.'[20]

But we need to comprehend this fusion of text into sacrament, of mind-learning and soul-loving as the prolonged experience of the growing and extending Church. Whatever may have been the occasions of a founding day, this was their discovery for all their generations. It was also the logic in the dual growth of ministry as being one of 'word and sacrament' in mutual nurture of 'the body of Christ', where they would know themselves as heirs of a tradition from Jewry and debtors to a future of Jew/Gentile inclusion.

The double role of things written for 'learning', and things done for 'reminding', so well captured in that Emmaus narrative, is central to religious faith. Their dual place in the Quranic scheme belongs with Chapter 7 and a study of *dhikr* and *dhikra* as titles of the Scripture itself and of 'forgetfulness', with 'negligence' as conspicuous notes in its warnings. 'Word' and 'sign', *kalimah* and *ayat*, are one witness there and one summons.

There remains one final point about memory in the New Testament order. Is memory essentially defensive against oblivion, or positive about possession? The distinction is real enough. Recollection is in part a deliberate effort, expressing a sense of responsibility to retain in mind and heart. 'Lest we forget' is then its slogan because it is its fear and

---

[20] The Messianic prospect would have its seal in the Christian retrospect. In Luke 24 the gesture that identified was the one that they remembered. The meal which began with Jesus as the guest continued in his being their host. (Cf. Revelation 3. 20: 'I will sup with him and he with me.')

would be its reproach. Oblivion, into which the past would otherwise be lost, must be kept at bay.

The New Testament faith does not see its Eucharist in these terms, its Jesus being unforgettable. That 'Last Supper', was not because the Beatitudes would cease to be cherished or recalled. By oral cherishing, the emergence of the Gospels proved the contrary. It was in order that the 'remembering'—as we have seen—would be in a certain way and with a right emphasis. Recollection would cease to be an adequate word, suggesting what might be casual or haphazard, dutiful but not passionate. Hence the Greek term *anamnesis*, which meant, not a mere 'recalling' but a 'living again' in the event as 're-enacted' for the heart.

Had the sacrament of 'bread and wine' been only in the sense of defence against oblivion, it would have been unnecessary at least for the founding generation of the Church. Rather, it would be in the ever possessive sense that made it the shape of 'the presence again' of that historic night, that drama of redemption. Thus there was a re-possession of the disciple on the part of Christ, and of Christ on the part of the disciple, because 'bread and wine' were again exchanged between them. It was not that he suffered again or that there was some ceremonial repetition of the once for all history. It was that its 'once-for-all-ness' became 'a here-and-now-ness' in the reality of a personal—and corporate—'communion' in its meaning.

Only in such sacramental terms does memory escape the irony that belongs with purely negative devices. For do not these become themselves the means to forgetfulness, precisely because we have passed our keeping on to a monument, like the note in the diary that finds us forgetting what we meant by it? 'Lest we forget' is then precisely what we are doing. This is the pathos of our mortality when, as the generations pass, there are none remaining who remember directly and poets write about some 'second death' or a novelist thinks for a last time (?) of those 'who lived faithfully a hidden life and rest in unvisited tombs.'[21]

If human memory itself is thus the victim of mortality how right that plea in Surah 5.114 concerning a 'festival' through all their generations. The Muslims of all their centuries have found such in their one *Qiblah* on to Mecca and the long renewed rituals of the Pilgrimage and the age-long syllables of their *Shahadah*. If, then, in whatever ways 'the Qur'an and

---

[21]  Well known as the concluding sentence of George Eliot's novel, *Middlemarch*, 1872.

the West' relate, ought not the shared pathos of our common mortality to mitigate all will to enmity and stimulate an effort after understanding the ordinances by which faith has entertained that pathos? There is no single area of Christianity—unless it be the Holy Trinity—more in need of commendation to Islam, than that table spread alike in the landscape and the sanctuary.

Controversialists in the medieval and early modern tradition of unitarian/trinitarian discourse may well be still unwilling to forego its lure or query its usefulness or allow the appeal here for a priority of worshipful means to meeting of soul. It will seem to them always central that the theme of 'Father, Son and Holy Spirit' should be argued as if number were involved, whereas in fact number is irrelevant. They will say that 'Holy Trinity' is prior to all else in a Christian *confessio* and that Islam must be made to heed it in the absolute terms it demands—this despite the fact that the formula appears in the New Testament as a baptismal form or usage, and otherwise is only implicitly present.[22]

They will urge also that Islam's strict emphasis on 'Unity', on *Tawhid*, sets up an explicit antagonism to Christian theology which must be rebutted. There is then a likelihood that the genuine 'Unity' in the Christian doctrine of God will be made to seem crudely vulnerable to some 'three are never one' attitude, so that witness to the Holy Trinity is made to resolve into a defence of 'three-ness' as if that hypothesis could ever be true and sound. Thus there is need to break away from the numbers question altogether, if 'One' and 'Three' alike are ever to be understood as *both* theological.

But, the controversialist diehards continue, Muslims have such an animus against the Christian case that it must not be left to go by default. It should, therefore, pre-occupy all discourse. The idea of letting a Christian sacrament be crucial, as here in this chapter, is negligent of prior duty. We must relate on the ground where Islam would have us be, even if we come there, in purely discursive terms, without reference to the New Testament experience of Jesus being the Christ out of which the classic formula of 'Father, Son and Holy Spirit', came experientially into

---

[22] The commission to 'go into all the world' (Matthew 28.21) and 'teach all nations' was certainly being obeyed well before its terms about baptism, seeing that these only found formulation in the 'going', to be in being well before the time when Matthew's Gospel set them down. The trinitarian formula was the product of the mission, as it learned fully its own meaning.

faith currency and confessional language. For, as those three terms show, the doctrine was never the sequel to Socratic debate, venturing ideas to arrive at a formulaic truth. It came only from the soul of experience and a mind for history.

There are many areas of mundane living and learning where 'one is ever three,' where 'three may well be one.' Muslims deal in domes which, being circles are each diameter, circumference and area. They had their Al-Biruni (973-1048) who was in his one persona geographer, mathematician and scholar, even as Winston Churchill was equally and consensually statesman, historian and painter and the better in each for being all three. Poems have rime, rhythm and metre, just as music has tone, pace and notation. Oceans have breadth and depth and flux. Examples are legion and exist on every hand, with theatres presenting action, plot and theme, to audiences that relish the mind of a dramatist, the portrayal of that mind's theme in action and, therefrom, the experience of a verdict they must render.

In all these cases, there is a necessary inter-relation, even an inter-definition, between the elements. One might almost say with the poet, 'number there was slain,' were it not, rather, true that number there was mutuality. The Muslim 'unitarian' might want to say that all these examples are unworthy of Allah—and, to a point, he would be right. But in invoking 'oneness' about Allah he comes on numbers-ground and must concede the number-liability of doing so.[23] He, with the Qur'an, has to mean that 'one' *qua* number with intent for the 'One' *qua* Allah—a necessity for him out of mere 'unit' discourse (where so much of his concern may merely be)—and into a 'Unity' where the sheer numerical is ousted by truly theological criteria of sovereignty, compassion, mercy, majesty and grace. With these mere number has no converse in mathematical terms.

It is very arid for us all to bring 'wonder, love and praise' into these ruts of discourse, however congenial to habitués in fee to them. It were better if all of us, East and West, Muslim or Christian, let our discourse about God be more worthy of the transcendence that both alike explore as beyond the reach of mere number as number obtains among us. Then there might be occasion for a 'unitarian' comprehension of the

---

[23] That liability is no less present with the first number than the third. In both cases what is meant theologically, either way, is not of numerical order.

significance—for others no less 'unitarian'—of faith in 'Fatherhood' as God's, 'Sonship' to that 'Fatherhood' as realised in Christ and 'the Holy Spirit' 'proceeding' from these as alone the origin, the experience and the reality in their co-inherence.

The Christian trinitarian Unity of God belongs squarely with the Islamic unitarian Unity of Allah in respect of an identical reach of either into the human enterprise of creation, our human creaturehood therein and measures of guidance for it. They differ—without compromise to Unity—in the length of that commissioned history over which Allah presides. If so, the defining 'greatness' these three referents proclaim will argue the even further dimension of an adequacy to the human drama which has ensued from them and has long threatened to advertise their frustration. The West has sundry poets and pundits who read the human scene in pointless terms. Muslim society and Muslim history have no lack of evidences that tend to the same grim conclusion. Some Muslims in their contemporary incidence have been prone to a like disquiet.[24] Plainly the 'greatness' of God remains a dire open question if we cannot relate it with reverent realism to where we humans find ourselves in the sorrow of our casualties and the reach of our perversity.

Perhaps, in the relation of the Qur'an with this uneasy realism in the Western mind about our global selves, we have to let the issue rest and stay. That to suffer redemptively will be a dimension of any 'greatness' in divinity will always be the conviction and the witness of the Christian society. For, without this measure, divine 'greatness' would be wanting in the realm that most pleads for it. It may be that the mind of Islam will always require itself to hold to supreme divine immunity from human hurt. The issue, though never one from which witness is discharged, may well remain at stake between two faiths, sponsoring and professing what must part them from each other.

But, if so, there are themes in the contemporary scene, stresses between what—too eagerly—some have willed to call 'clashing civilisations', which will inexorably bring us back to theology, the doctrinal reading of divine intention in our story and whether or not its meaning points to the necessity of love, God's and ours, either as the costly measure

---

[24] A salient example would be the Egyptian and Nobel Prize-winner, Najib Mahfuz (b. 1912); see a study of him, with Bibliography in Rasheed el Enany, *Naguib Mahfouz: The Pursuit of Meaning*, London, 1993, and my *The Pen and the Faith*, London, 1985, pp. 145-64.

of the other. A final Chapter 12 has the further onus of reading from the Qur'an's own perception of a divine 'liability'. Meanwhile, there is another Quranic/Christian area of common reference in the mysterious journey of Muhammad to the Jerusalem of Jesus.

But, spelling as it must a 'holy communion', what of its rebuke to a blatant consumerism, an arrogant industry, a planetary exploitation and a management attitude to the world? How are global politics to be made 'divinely liable' in the sense that they are pursued by those who know themselves 'under God' with a power that is only in trust? How, in that awesome 'caliphate', do we comprehend 'the humanly liable lord' who gave us the sub-sovereignty? Those are the themes of the two final chapters. Meanwhile the Christian mind 'has other duties that arise from all the foregoing in the deep hinterland and the near foreground of this 'table from heaven'.

# Chapter 10
# JOURNEYING THE DISTANCE

The task now is to delve further into the Christian factors in any study of a 'Qur'an in and for the West'.

The preceding chapter began by justifying and relinquishing the focus earlier on themes over which the two faiths were not seriously at odds but in truth firmly at one. The passage where it did so was bound to lead to further questions. 'The Table and the Memory' perpetuated in the Christian Eucharist as the Church believed, gave to memory the content and dynamic only ensuing from its 'Upper Room' location in the New Testament narrative. It became an *anamnesis*, more than mere 'recollection' (as of what might otherwise be readily forgotten). It meant a present re-enactment of its once-for-all meaning in the heart and in the community.

Thus at the heart of Christian Liturgy stood 'a table', visually affirming the hospitality of God to humankind in the sustaining yield of the created order, had by dint of the due exercise of their colonising, fructifying privilege. It was a hospitality thus fashioning community in the age-long togetherness of food and drink.

These societal meanings had been deepened for the Christian 'table-people' into a history of redemption. They culminated in the Passion of Jesus, told and made their own in 'bread and wine'. If there was to be honesty with 'The Qur'an in the West', its Christian mentors must go beyond 'the table' of Surah 5 into that 'memorial festival' of which the disciples told. This would be a far larger, harder task by reason of those harsh anathemas earlier noted in the Qur'an's version about Jesus post-Gethsemane. For, as the Qur'an sees it, it certainly brought him there as the very prelude to his allegedly having no Calvary.

The idea is to broach this task in an imaginative way by engaging with an equally pivotal Quranic event in the *Sirah*, or 'word-career' of

Muhammad. It concerns what we may figuratively measure in 'The Night Journey' of which Surah 17 writes—the symbolic access by which he was brought to *al-masjid al-aqsa*, 'the more distant sanctuary', namely Jerusalem. There now stands at the southern end of the sacred mount the edifice that bears, from this passage, the name Masjid al-Aqsa. Lying deep in the meaning of the Journey was the place Jerusalem had from the outset in Muhammad's sense of vocation to be, in potential likeness to the Hebrew prophets, a bearer of divine words.

Since, and in a different debt to those prophets, the Jesus of the Christian faith via the New Testament narrative is for ever known in the significance of Jerusalem, is it not a duly Christian instinct to take the 'distance' of this Journey, as a figure of whence and whither the Muslim mind passes into any full appreciation of Jesus and Jerusalem as the Christian narrative possesses them?

Such are the hope and intention here. Or if not the distance to be covered between Mecca and Jerusalem in any Muslim reckoning with Christian faith, then the distance inside concepts of theology and of history which any Christian interpretation needs to undertake, if the exegesis is ever to arrive. No inter-relating of 'the Qur'an and the West' could fail to recognise its explicitly doctrinal tasks, given how far renewed theological conviction is vital for either.

Here, then, is the resounding opening verse of Surah 17.

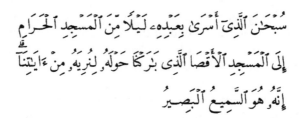

'Glory to Him who betook His servant by night from the Sacred Mosque to the more distant Mosque, the precincts We have blessed, in order to show him Our revelations. He is the one who hears and sees all.[1]

---

[1] 'Betook' may seem an archaic word but it fits the Arabic sense of *asra' bi*. 'Carried' or 'escorted' would be too pedestrian. The verb enshrines the idea of 'by night', though the verse itself wants that phrase too. The significance of this *Isra'* is central both to Qur'an exegetes and to Sufi mysticism.

A physical measure of the remoteness of Al-Aqsa in Jerusalem from the inviolate *Haram* of Mecca would be some eleven hundred miles. One sanctuary is the very shrine and citadel of the faith of Islam—Mecca the *Qiblah* of all prayer-direction, the focal point of Muslims in the West, aligned thereby with all a Muslim East. The other sanctuary belongs intimately with the climax of Jesus' story. Over what mental territory must the heart of the one pass in reaching the heart of the other? What of the obstacles that strew the way there? The route was one Muhammad had likely traversed years before the onset of his vocation, in his ventures as the trusted custodian of Khadijah's commerce. For Mecca traded in those 'summer and winter caravans gathered in convoy' of Surah 106. They plied their goods from the Yemen in the far south to the markets and the shrines of Gaza, Jerusalem and Damascus. The ardours of those journeys and the hazards of that commerce are fair analogy for the transactions of faiths that 'go between' each other. We might even borrow from the old preacher, Bishop Lancelot Andrewes (a treasure of the West), and his sermon on the journey of the Magi:

> '... an uneasy journey for their way lay through Arabia Petrea and the craggy rocks of it ... a dangerous journey through Arabia Deserta too and "the black tents of Kedar" famous for their robberies ...'[2]

The Qur'an knows about desert tribes who might extort a share in the profits of the caravans by exacting otherwise the toll of their raids upon them. There are analogous deviants and dastards in the negotiations of religion.

Those problematics now for meeting minds are symbolised by the issues within the Qur'an around what we may perhaps call a Mecca/Jerusalem axis. Until shortly after the Hijrah, or migration from Mecca to Medina, Jerusalem had been the original prayer-direction of the first Muslims, betokening the place of Hebrew factors in the genesis of Muhammad's preaching career. After the transition into a power-structure and a political expression, it was important, as Surah 2 directed, to turn around to a *Qiblah* in Mecca. 'The face of God was everywhere,' and it was

---

[2] Andrewes, *Sermons on the Nativity*, London, n.d, p. 243, on Christmas Day in Whitehall, James I present, 1620.

vital to demonstrate that Mecca, albeit—for the time being—abandoned, had been in no way forsaken.

From Medina, however, that turn-around meant a facing away from Jerusalem and a more ambivalent relation to its Judaic/Christian meaning. Medinan Islam became a more studiously distinctive faith, alike in its self-understanding and ritual expression. It still held tenaciously to the Abrahamic associations of that Mount Moriah where its Al-Aqsa was,[3] but it became less in kinship with the Judaic 'peoplehood' with God under ethnic covenant.[4]

If the change in the *Qiblah* suggests a loosening of the ties with the Christian bearings of Jerusalem, why then the crucial place of 'the Night Journey' thither in the *Sirah* of Muhammad and the definition of Islam? The answer would seem to be that it signalled both a confirmation of the early association and an independence of it. The paradox is confirmed if the point in time of the Night Journey is placed just before the migration to Medina, so that Muhammad was made mysteriously present in Jerusalem when the *Qiblah* would need to be forsaking it. It would seem he was 'possessing' it—or being attested by it—but in terms that would be Islam's alone.

Muslims in general understand the meaning of Surah 17.1 which they know as the *Isra'* or 'conveying', preluding the *Mi'raj*, or 'Ascension' into heaven, from the rock of Abraham into rendezvous with his many predecessors in the 'messenger' role, and the 'planting' of truth, as it were corporeally, into his heart by that heart's 'opening' to its full reception.[5] Thus his divine—and final—illumination was from a Jerusalem point as event, only to transcend, in a different finality (as Jews and Christians must hold) what that city had meant and been and witnessed, whether of Davidic purpose, Solomonic wisdom or New Testament salvation. The debts, we may say, and the self-sufficiency of Islam stood in the same place,

---

[3] Though the Qur'an understands the Isaac/Ishmael 'offering' to have been located in Mecca, the Abrahamic connection has more to do in the Qur'an with his being a great iconoclast, demolishing the idols of his kindred, than the progenitor of a 'chosen seed'.

[4] The Qur'an's reproach of Jewry became much sharper in the post-Hijrah time as thinking themselves God's 'beloved ones' and narrowing the Noahid 'covenant' of universal 'seedtime and harvest' into the Sinaitic theme of 'land and people' uniquely and mutually 'assigned' together as Yahweh's different ones.

[5] There is a careful discussion of the *Isra'* and *Mi'raj* in Muhammad Asad, *The Message of the Qur'an*, Gibraltar, 1980, Appendix iv: 'The Night Journey', pp. 996-98.

clung around the same city—whence stem many of the burdens of inter-relation now. These the stance and story of the West have done little to lighten and much to reload. The Night Journey came to Jerusalem laden with many meanings. These were overtaken by it in a super-session which became thereby a different and independent theism.

Hence the onerous tasks we now carry in either direction—that of a Christ-exegesis to Muslims and of an Islamic role in the West, travelling as we are between Mecca and Jerusalem. Our best discharge of that duty from the Christian side will be to discard many and long controversies and focus—with help from the Qur'an—on the single theme of Jesus as Messiah. This keeps us centrally to the theme of Christianity as the New Testament found and told it. It is the more apt because the Qur'an so firmly excludes it.

Saying so may seem odd, since well nigh every Quranic allusion to Jesus, always named 'Isa, is followed by the matronymic Ibn Maryam 'son of Mary', and *Al-Masih*. Though occurring nine times, that title never carries the connotation of New Testament faith—that of redemptive action read in that Scripture from the precedent of Isaian and other imagery concerning 'the suffering servant'. It was an imagery gathered by Jesus into his reading of his own ministry, in the light of its travail with hostility, as signalling what he must achieve. It was by those lights he saw and took 'the cup his father gave.' Those dimensions are all occluded in the Qur'an by its negation of the Cross.

In stead, the 'anointing' of 'Isa in the Qur'an's sense is one familiar enough in Semitic tradition from the ceremonies of kingship and, by extension, to the calling of prophets and messengers, marking them as recipients of an 'agency' with words. It was just such *ad hoc* anointing that Hebraic tradition deepened into the more ultimate vocation to a divine 'agency' that was more than education, more than verbal mission, and needing to be vested in personhood and biography itself—hence the final language of 'Sonship' foreshadowing the doctrine of Incarnation, for which the Qur'an has a passionate veto.

All this was explicit in the Jerusalem to which Muhammad came but not in the Meccan aegis of his journey as its antecedents fashioned it. The duty and the theme, in that sober imagination we proposed, must be how to envisage his 'escort' (as the *asra' bi 'abdihi* of 17.1 has it) bringing him—if only in these conjectural terms—into 'the farther sanctuary' where 'Christian Jerusalem' attained to be, with its gardens of Gethsemane and

Resurrection and the Cross between them, the place of realisation of the 'suffering Messiah'.

Such a task of imagination only embraces what Christian/ Muslim dialogue has also to take up, if it is to be true to the potential significance of 'the Night Journey'. It may best be ventured here by way of the clue in a second pivotal text, namely Surah 4.172.

$$\text{لَّن يَسْتَنكِفَ ٱلْمَسِيحُ أَن يَكُونَ عَبْدًا لِلَّهِ}$$

> 'Messiah will never disdain to serve the Messianic role as though it were beneath his dignity as a humiliation he would for ever repudiate.'

In letting all turn on this salient theme, we are deliberately bye-passing or ignoring the vexed formal controversies around 'the Trinity', only to handle them more intelligently.

For the faith in the Oneness of God as a triune Lordship derives from the role of Christology and Christology—as always inside theology—stems from the person and deed of Jesus as the Christ. In the sense we must realise from 4.172, 'Sonship', with or without a capital 's', underwrites them all. Given the predilections of Islam about Allah, which we can also approve on their own ground, we do well to let the thrust of Surah 4.172 take all else that matters into its scope.

For it is one of the rare and precious occasions when a Quranic meaning-in-place dramatically coincides with a counterpart in New Testament vocabulary. There is a veritable meeting of theme and fact. Here for both is the truism that Messiahship involves a daunting costliness it might well count unworthy of its honour, demeaning of its pride and a scandal even to imply as ever fitting to the role or due from it.

Such is the case-making of Paul in writing to his Philippians in Chapter 2.5-8. He sees in his Christ, *not* the pride of a status clutched lest it be forfeited or a disesteem no Christ would ever tolerate, but—on the contrary—an honour he would gladly assume, a task—albeit humiliating by alien reckoning—he would assuredly fulfil and find the fulfilment his true and noble destiny.

The affinity of meaning with Paul's Greek term *kenosis*[6] is clear, coupled with his *harpagmos*, meaning a 'prize', a 'status' one could never

---

[6]   The 'self-emptying' is in no way that of a mere vessel out of which, e.g. liquid contents are

let go. Not counting him superior to, or discountenanced by, the lowly role, Paul sees his Messiah as readily undertaking it as the very fulfilment of his identity, his office and his whole being. It is clear that we are in the same realm of thought as Surah 4.172 concerning a like refusal to 'scorn' or 'disdain' what an office, or calling, requires in the act, or art, of its discharge.

The point of abiding tension between them arises from an ambiguity around the word 'servant' used both in Surah 4.172 and Philippians 2.7 as describing 'Messiah'. In the Surah's case the 'servanthood' is seen as alien to 'sonship', in Paul it is 'sonship' which 'servanthood' constitutes and by which it is fulfilled. In the former the idea in mind is clearly that of a pampered 'son of the house', on whose every whim all servants must wait but who, himself, would never stoop to be himself menial in their role.

There is a kind of conceptual astigmatism between the two passages. What 4.172 envisages about 'servanthood' with 'sonship' as utterly incompatible, Philippians 2.7 sees as totally fulfilling. 'Messiah', for Paul in his Letter is 'the Son' (we now need the initial capital 'S') in the very act and art of being 'the servant' because that 'servanthood' is one only 'a Son' can bring. That it must be so takes us to other New Testament criteria, including the vexed word 'begotten' and the resounding Hebraic theme of 'the pleasure of the Lord prospering in his hand'.

Meanwhile, it is well to note that the ambiguity we have identified between the passages belongs also, and for the same reasons, to the Qur'an's usage of *Al-Masih*. The latter has, for the Qur'an, nothing humiliating to undergo, nothing bitterly costly to himself, no dark travail, no Gethsemane—because all honour abides implicitly in being 'a messenger', a bringer of good words, and never a sufferer to redeem. The Quranic term *Al-Masih*, as we saw, refers to what equips, i.e. appoints to this task. The oil anoints to dignity and stature bearing the beauty and the wealth of words. Despite its provenance, the term in the Qur'an draws very close to that of *rasul*, differentiated by the matronymic (which. never occurs with any other Quranic 'messenger') in token of 'Isa's signal birth, of which the Qur'an has extended narratives in Surahs 3 and 19.

---

poured so that they are no longer there. With personhood what is foregone—for a task's sake—is truly forfeited while the identity that willed its abeyance abides, still—perhaps the more—authentically itself. Such is *kenosis*.

This vital distinction between the two Scriptures in the meaning of 'Messiahship' as applied to Jesus/'Isa makes for what we have called the 'astigmatism' around the 'servant/son' theme. For, in the case of the Qur'an, what the 'office' (if we may so term it) fulfils stays purely verbal—albeit with the consequences words can entail, while in the New Testament it belongs inherently with action, with radical encounter vis-à-vis the wrongness of the world, with the vocation into suffering and death, which these will exact in the full logic of their meaning.

In this Jesus–reading of being 'Messiah' what is 'radical' has to do with two realities which take it beyond a 'servanthood of words' into 'a servant–Sonship' of redeeming grace. These two, in their inter-relation, are a deeper expectation of what is God's and a fuller reckoning with what is ours as humans in the world. It is on account of both that what Christianity holds to be 'Sonship' in Jesus achieves the 'servanthood' the Qur'an accords to him. The one realises the other only in greatly augmenting its range. The 'servant' in 'Isa needs the 'Son' in Jesus as the ultimate measure because of how far in our wrongness we humans are and, therefore, how far reaching into God must be what answers it. Here are aspects of thought and faith which belong further with an ensuing Chapter 12.

In present context, it is well to see how the situation here summarised belongs also with the much distorted meaning of the term 'begotten' concerning this 'Sonship' of Jesus. It has nothing to do with 'begetting' in the physical sense, nor with involving 'God in Christ' in any chain of contingency such as Surah 112 has in mind in disallowing the word.[7] Nor does it signify the *Ittikhadh* or 'adoption' for which Surah 17.111 reprobates the Christians as allegedly holding that 'God takes to Himself a son.'[8]

---

[7] Where the chain of mortal contingency is clearly in mind. The clue is in *huwa Allah al-Samad*, where the *Samad* word, used only here in the whole Qur'an, means One who has all resources in Himself and neither 'derives nor bestows' His being as contingent generations do. *Lam yalid wa lam yulad* can only have this meaning. It is one which clearly neither intends, nor avails to deny, the Christian sense of 'the only begotten Son.' That 'only' also is indeed quite akin to *Al-Samad* in that the divine 'Oneness' is fully, entirely there, unrepeatable and 'Once for all' as—we might say—'one-ly', such being the sense of 'only'.

[8] The charge occurs elsewhere in the Qur'an. Christianity knew it as 'Adoptionism' and rejected it as an improper reading of what 'God in Christ' could only duly mean, namely a divine 'doing' entirely integral to divine 'being'. This purposeful 'human indwelling' of the divine was not a recruiting or adopting of what did not belong to its nature. Hence the formula-caring faith as to 'Incarnation'.

The meaning has a long ancestry which may account for the misconstruings its Christian significance has suffered. When, in Hebraic mind-set, the psalmist in Psalm 2.7 has the Lord saying: 'Thou art my Son, this day have I begotten thee,' the allusion is to an already adult 'agent' of His will, 'a king upon the holy hill of Zion'. God's delight in how—whether in fact or in prospect—that figure will 'perform' the task-in-trust of being the Lord's 'factor' or 'personal instrument' leads to the celebratory greeting: 'Great! It is as if you had here and now become My son.' In the fulfilling of what has been willed, through one sent to effect what that will desired, it is as if the common 'pleasure' in the partnering tells of what is 'heir-making' and thus 'heir-becoming'. The unity of purpose, desired and transacted, means that an 'imperative' has found its 'affirmative'. We are back in the language of how 'the pleasure of the Lord has prospered in his hand,' i.e. His hand in the willing and his hand in the doing, one in the incidence of both.[9]

'Agency' of course, is no less present in the Qur'an's world of 'messengers' and *rusul*. Their verbal task, however, does not engage them with Allah, nor Allah with them, in the kind of 'intimacy' that Christian faith understands in this 'begotten' term. This, emphatically, is how Islam wants it and steadily insists it must be. It is a difference in the very heart of theology, concerning what the human situation divinely calls for and what the 'divine situation' (if we may so speak) holds for answer.

Let it not be thought that this is theological subtlety far removed from 'the Qur'an and the West'. For it reaches deep into the onus of all the things between. It also belongs squarely with that other classic theme between Muslim and Christian concerning the 'properness' to Messiahship of the Cross of Jesus.[10]

For the 'begetting' language simply salutes the 'obedience' that has accomplished what the divine intention had in view. It is as when the

---

[9]   As in Isaiah 53.10—the will that effectuates being one with the will that ordains. There is a proximate idea in the Qur'an's concept of Allah having a 'Benediction of satisfaction' in Muhammad as the accomplishing agent in *Tanzil*. On *Tasliyah* and its enjoining in Surah 33.56, see note 15.

[10]   The coined word seems necessary, since 'propriety' leans towards mere aspects of etiquette. The point is that Islam and Muslims instinctively recoil from the theme of a prophet's humiliation, at least to this utter degree. It implies some divine failure in due rescue, succour and deliverance (which on Christian ground is not to read the divine quality). They are in tune with much modern—and Jewish—disdain for a faith clustering round as dark and grim an image as a cross and thinking it might somehow belong to God. We go far into Christianity in learning to rethink that response, recalling Chapter 4.

musician finally has in place the score for the theme-idea he has 'conceived', providing it for the instrumentation by which—and by which alone—his theme-idea is implemented and avails for the listening world. The music in which the musician is fulfilled is given birth by his very conception of it. The language of Christian faith is very akin when it confesses how 'the Father sent the Son.' That which, in this sense, is 'begotten' is about the twin aspects of a self-expression, which could not be otherwise than a partnership of its two integral dimensions.

It is the more tragic that the 'begotten' language has been so sadly and wilfully misunderstood, as if 'conception' could never be other than physical, least of all in what had to do—via this analogy—with the 'music' of God. The notes are in the instrument because they are in the mind. The mind that wills them is fulfilled in them and, in their hearing, once thus 'begotten', the listener has that mind in knowledge and in love. The sequence from mind to musical notation-rendering is like the sequence from the Eternal where Allah is into the temporal where we humans are.[11]

If, instead of the musical, we think of the dramatic, we find the same 'begetting', by an authorship into writing, whereby in turn an understanding is conveyed, but conveyed only because it took shape (shape inherent to its nature) in expression accessible to readership. This could in part have been the case for readership of the Qur'an, had its entire format and instinct insisted that, although 'the Book of God', and 'His Speech', it did not purport to 'tell' Him but to tell only of His will.

It is in line with its faith in divine 'self-giving' (in the sense just studied) that the New Testament has to be taken in its own terms, as quite contrasted with the Scripture of Islam. Since 'the Word was made flesh' the book-text that presents this 'Word' is itself 'the Word of God' only in a derivative sense, as where the ultimate revelation is had as God's 'truth through personality'—the personhood of Jesus as the Christ of whom it adequately tells, without being 'infallible' of itself.[12] It would, therefore,

---

[11] The Biblical/Quranic language about 'sending' has just this sense of 'rendering' in the idiom that is appropriate to the purpose. We can think of what is 'between the heavens and the earth' (a frequent Quranic phrase) as 'spatial', only as being 'relational'. 'Distance' there is none but there is need of 'reach'.

[12] The distinction is important. If 'faith' is essentially 'trust' and 'reliance' the demand for the 'infallible' has no place. 'Sufficient' is the word many use here, to denote an entirely 'reliance-able' text as sufficient for all that faith should want—faith that finds itself 'secured'. The point is very close to the Qur'an's *hasbuna Allah*—'Allah suffices us.' See Surah 9.129

be sadly awry for Christians to handle their hallowed text in the way that Muslims receive and handle their Qur'an. The terminology of *Tanzil* as 'sending down', or 'sending forth (His Son)' may point to the same sense of a transaction from heaven to earth, from eternity to time, but with this disparity between what either faith understands it has received thereby. The music/drama analogy would hold only for Christian understanding of Allah as being in the 'authorship' of Christ, the 'Father' known in and through the 'Son', even as musician and music co-inhere.[13] How well it would be for 'the Qur'an and the West' if the valid negative: 'Far be it from the Eternal to take to Himself a son,' could give way, once and for all, to the positive salutation: 'How blessed in the Eternal to take Himself to music for His humans.'

Read aright this way, it is easier to understand how the Messianic 'Sonship' of Jesus deserves that phrase which echoes through Hebrew prophethood: 'The pleasure of the Lord prospers in his hand.' Can we imagine Beethoven not rejoicing in his own 9th Symphony? When at crucial points in the Gospel narratives we find the words: 'This is My Son, my beloved, in whom I am well-pleased' what meaning should we understand? It cannot mean some idle 'pleasure', a sort of mild admiration fondly observed on an unrelated object. It has instead to do with a congruence of wills. 'Whose pleasure is my pleasure' is the only apt translation. It tells of a trust realised by means of a trust fulfilled. As with music, what the one party meant lay in what the other party told.

In this field of theology, it would be wrong to suggest a merely mechanical metaphor, where one did not fit well. If we imagine two gear-wheels, perfectly aligned, the one transmitting a motion which the other receives, whereby perhaps a circular motion is turned to a lateral one. This could be a right image of 'In whom is my good pleasure,' a thrust imparted and a thrust accepted. In some such way, what is intended by God is realised in Jesus. 'His good pleasure prospers', in that it makes its way effectively. The Eternal is transacted in the temporal.

---

which has the *la ilaha illa Huwa* of the *Shahadah* (using the pronoun 'He'). There and in 39.38 'In Him have I trusted' as if echoing the Christian *Te Deum laudamus*. Such is the mutual way of 'trust' in the 'trustable'. Cf. also *ni'am al-wakil* in 3.173—'the most positive of trust'. On *hasbuna*, see also below, p. 184f.

[13] It is in there being the 'musician' that there is any having the 'music.' The one is by definition self-fulfilling and self-expressing in the other. This theme of the literary/musical analogy in theology is well expounded in Dorothy L Sayers, *The Mind of the Maker*, London, 1941, often re-issued.

Something of the same meaning belongs with the term 'my beloved', frequently linked with the 'Son' language in the Gospels. If the whole is the original of love it partakes of its origin in its story. 'The Son of His love' comes squarely in the Letters of John as well as in the four Gospels at focal points in the story. The Letter to the Hebrews confirms all the foregoing from Surah 4.172 in its language about 'the Son learning in suffering' and thus, in active terms, 'becoming' the Son he always was.[14]

The theme is not one to be pursued here, but there is something akin in the Qur'an's concept of Allah's *Tasliyah* upon His *Rasul*. The meaning there of how 'God and His angels call down blessing upon him and greet him with peace' has provoked much debate, with the injunction that believers are to do the same. Hence the salutation, in word or print, after every devout mention of his name. This must surely express a 'satisfaction' Allah registers in the faithful discharge of his vocation to preach by Muhammad who, the *Tasliyah* apart, is frequently encouraged and commended on other occasions.[15] The divine 'pleasure' is distinctive in either case, in line with what differs sharply in the tasks fulfilled. We might even say that the 'pleasure' divinely *there* belongs either way with the will divinely meant, even though so disparate as to make any parallel remote, if also none the less illuminating.

Perhaps in tracing the 'distance' from Mecca to Jerusalem, as covered by Muhammad's 'Night Journey' and by any Christian mediation of meaning, we only register how *aqsa*, 'most far', the Masjid remains, despite the fact that its eastern prospect looks over Gethsemane. We have to recognise that the old controversies around 'Father/Son', 'Begotten', 'Beloved', 'the Incarnate Word', have to be taken into the ultimate theology where alone they can be resolved. For they all have to do with what it takes for God to be God, with what we may await from, expect of, or find in, Him as 'Lord and King and God of humankind'. It concerns what 'esteem'—to use the Qur'an's phrase—we hold Allah in, what measures

---

[14] The Letter to the Hebrews, Chapter 5, v. 8, where the writer makes a play on words, with *emathen, epathen*, (in Greek)—'in learning he suffered, suffering he learned.' Here also as well as in Philippians 2, 5-11, the inter-association of 'Sonship', 'suffering' and 'servanthood' is pivotal to the whole argument. Truly 'this Messiah never scorns the servant role' which is his in being the divine Son.

[15] On this invocation of Allah's 'blessing' of Muhammad see Constance Padwick, *Muslim Devotions*, London, 1961, pp. 152-166; also in my *Muhammad in the Qur'an*, London, 2001, pp.114-136. The verse is Surah 33.56.

we take of His omnipotence, what criteria we bring to the reckoning of our theism.[16]

All these, however, have to be reciprocal to the measure we have of the human scene, the human crisis, the human story. A larger sense of these must mean a larger expectation. Is the world sufficiently comprehended as a 'school', or—more—a 'surgery', a haunt of ignorance only or a place of wounds? We must keep in constant view the realism to which we are all summoned by the perspective of our human capacity for wrong and hypocrisy we studied in Chapter 4. That case has to be carried forward into Chapter 12.

Is it seemly, one may ask, that two theisms should be at odds over whether humanity is more in need of a divine intervention that brought redemption and healing, rather than one which brought command, prohibition and inclusive education? Are not either somehow a tribute to the other? Should we not forego the controversy, that must divide them and focus simply on that 'Glory be ...' of Surah 17.1 that praises what, in both, greets a divine initiative taken on behalf of this one world? 'That we might show him our signs' is the Qur'an's perception of Muhammad as the recipient of Allah's 'guidance' and 'exhortation'. 'That he might verily be our sign' was the New Testament's comprehension of Jesus as 'the servant-son'.[17] By the one, humans learn God's will for their concurrence in submission: by the other God's nature for their experience of His society.

Christian faith, from within its own ethical discipline, can readily belong with what counterparts it in Islam as found, for example, in the extensive Quranic 'Decalogue' in Surah 17.22-39, the very Surah of Muhammad's *Isra'*. Islam, for its part, has only an unrelenting ban on the Christian conviction concerning 'the Word made flesh'. This it stubbornly sees as derogatory to the majesty and sovereignty of Allah.[18] Since that

---

[16] The comment on the 'disesteem of Allah' in Quraishi paganism comes in Surahs 6.91, 22.74 and 39.67. *Ma qadaru Allaha haqqa Qadrihi.* The question must always follow: How may we learn whether what we think about God 'thinks' of Him duly, fully, rightly and honestly?

[17] The Qur'an uses the term *ayah* often of 'Isa in this sense of a meaning that is in him and through him, alike in birth and in incidents like the 'table from heaven' in Surah 5. This 'truth-in-the-person' passes into Paul's language when he speaks of 'having the mind of Christ'. 1 Corinthians 2.16, Philippians 2.5.

[18] 'Derogatory' seems exactly the apt word here, from the root 'to ask', something we would be entirely wrong to 'ask' of God Most High, or—as the *OED* explains: 'having the character ... of lowering in honour', 'to be depreciatory of'.

conviction enters so far into Christian reading of what that sovereignty is, it cannot loyally be renounced. All, therefore, has to be left where it belongs, namely in the mystery of the divine reality and of that reality's bond with humankind. For, on either premise of faith, the Islamic or the Christian, bonded it surely is.

All must return us to Allah and His being *Al-Rahman*. It would seem that there was some open-endedness in the *Sirah* itself about reference by name to God. The word 'Allah' was already current as denoting a—or the—'supreme Being', regnant over all. But if and when *Rabb* was used to denote this 'Allah', *Rabb* might readily be pluralised as *arbab*, the many deities of a pagan and plural worship. It was, therefore', urgent to have *Al-Rabb*, 'the Lord', understood as referring to 'Allah' in total singularity. When the terms *Al-Rahman* and *Al-Rahim* came into use—to be at length invoked in the *Bismillah* as *Allah al-Rahman al-Rahim*—the Meccans seem to have been perplexed, asking: 'What is *Al-Rahman*? Are we to worship whatever you bid us? And their aversion grows' (25.60). There are times when *Al-Rahman* becomes a noun and synonym for Allah and can stand alone as the referent. Was the Quraishi 'aversion' the reason why Surahs 20.5 and 25. 59 declare *Al-Rahman* as 'seating Himself on the Throne'?

Study of the incidence and the frequency or rarity of the several words, Allah, *Rabb*, *Rahman* through different periods of the Qur'an's *Tanzil* might yield interesting data, if always speculative, about the vicissitudes of theological language within the *Sirah* and their place in the progress of Muhammad's mission. Certainly, in 'terms of terms', there were hazards about 'how to mean', in the context of a hostile paganism, at odds about concepts and bitter about the preacher.[19] Whatever the tasks here of textual exegesis they wait on scholarship. Our concern is only for their being analogy of the ever underlying question: Of whom is our theology thinking? Whom is our adoration celebrating?

In Surah 2.186 there is a striking shift of the verb about 'asking' from its sense of 'query' to that of 'request'.

---

[19] See an analysis of how sundry terms differ in frequency (or may even be quite absent) at different points in the sequence of Surahs, Meccan and Medinan—assuming their periods can be rightly detected—in J Chelhod, 'Note sur l'Emploi du Mot Rabb dans le Coran', *Arabica*, Vol. V, No. 2, 1958, pp. 150-167.

وَإِذَا سَأَلَكَ عِبَادِى عَنِّى فَإِنِّى قَرِيبٌ أُجِيبُ دَعْوَةَ ٱلدَّاعِ

إِذَا دَعَانِ فَلْيَسْتَجِيبُواْ لِى وَلْيُؤْمِنُواْ بِى لَعَلَّهُمْ يَرْشُدُونَ

'If My servants question you (sing.) concerning Me, in truth
I am near. I answer the call of the suppliant who cries to Me.
So let them hearken to Me: let them believe in Me that they
may be rightly led.'

Those who are insistently querulous will say: 'This is evasive.'
Interrogation is invited to pass forthwith into prayer. But prayer is never
made to a cipher, nor can we ever worship an enigma. Faith cannot
abandon its yearning for an understanding.

Yet there is wisdom in turning all due theological discourse into
an awareness of His 'nearness' of whom we speak. 'So let them hearken.'
We must still pray for comprehension, lest we worship 'a God unknown'.
But there is a comprehension that comes only with the will to love and
serve. If our theology is like that of surmisers on the Areopagus, some
'whom it may concern,' it will bring no authentic worship.[20] It will be
like T S Eliot's watermill 'beating the darkness'.[21] Prayer is truest from 'an
understanding heart', while being ever 'the call of a suppliant', for whom
the God of belief can only well be the God of the soul's homage. This 'I
am near' of 2.186 has to sober all else in that mental distance between
Mecca and Jerusalem, all else between the continents of faith those two
cities symbolise.

When the Qur'an in Surah 17.1 names Jerusalem 'the Farther
Sanctuary', 'the one that lies beyond,' it is fair to assume that Medina was
'the nearer one.' It was bye-passed on 'the Night Journey', so that only
the sacred rock in Jerusalem became the site of the *Mi'raj*, the 'heavenly
ascent'. Even so, whether before or after the *Isra'*, Medina and the Hijrah
which led to it had a vital role in the ethos and destiny of Islam. The
second city stood for the inevitable political dimension in human affairs,
whether or not also in the minding of religion. To that dimension with its

---

[20] Paul's listeners during his 'Lecture' there according to Acts of the Apostles, 17, 16–33.
[21] T S Eliot, 'The Journey of the Magi', line 23.

sharp problems both for weal and woe the chapter following has to come. The divinely liable humanity we have studied throughout, whether East or West, has to learn its divinely liable politics, religion relating rightly with power.

## Chapter 11
## DIVINELY LIABLE POLITICS

It follows from all the foregoing about human *khilafah* and 'dominion', that politics are divinely liable and that all such liability is set to be humanly fulfilled. Our inclusive human investment with the world must pass for corporate exercise into an investment of organs of authority as duly governing. This human/divine situation is tersely told in two Qur'an passages.

$$\text{يَـٰٓأَيُّهَا ٱلَّذِينَ ءَامَنُوٓا۟ أَطِيعُوا۟ ٱللَّهَ وَأَطِيعُوا۟ ٱلرَّسُولَ وَأُو۟لِى ٱلْأَمْرِ مِنكُمْ}$$

$$\text{وَمَن لَّمْ يَحْكُم بِمَآ أَنزَلَ ٱللَّهُ فَأُو۟لَـٰٓئِكَ هُمُ ٱلظَّـٰلِمُونَ}$$

'Believers! Obey God and obey the Apostle and those of your number invested with authority.' (Surah 4.59)

'Those who do not judge by what God has sent down they perpetrate evil.'(Surah 5.45)

But how does 'investing with authority' happen, and what is 'judging' by the dicta of revelation? Centuries of Hebrew religion have been the story of Yahweh and His Torah via His Moses. When Christianity became Christendom its history was 'Church and Empire' and 'the divine right of kings'. Broad, and often painful, developments in the modern West have sought to separate the two realms, foregoing the divine referability while still holding the political tributary to the ethical, since power could never properly be a law unto itself. Whether or not such ideology could be the shape of being 'divinely liable'—an ever open issue—the human liability was only the more insistent in the very fact of being 'secular'.

'Obey God and obey the Apostle' by contrast seems utterly simple. The simplicity is elusive. 'The Apostle' died, to be—as it were—perpetuated in the caliphate, but only then in his governing Medinan role. Abu Bakr's assumption of rule was crucial to the ongoing faith, but the Quranic terms of what 'Allah had sent down' now belonged only in the community. Prophethood had been finally 'sealed'. Muhammad's whole *Sirah* had yielded a religio-political amalgam as the founding theme of Islam. A text that was not yet a 'canon' passed to its faithful in double trust—to all as their 'Scripture' and their 'religion' and, for their politics, to 'those of their number invested with authority'. All for Islam then and since turns on this sense of *Al-Rasul*, that dual role Muhammad in sequence played during the *Tanzil* of the Qur'an, first religious and then political.

In that Scripture there seems to have been no explicit injunction for the Hijrah.[1] Nor does the Book have any alternative word other than 'Apostle' for that martially different office, thereby shaping the whole perennial issue for Muslim things religious and things political. Nor was there any precise injunction in the Qur'an—but only a pragmatic logic—for the political Caliphate. Indeed, as we have seen in Chapter 2, the only 'caliphs' there are are all of us, we mortal humans, 'ruling' by divine behest in our persons and our society and our ecology, in earth-found environmental trust. Only David (38.27) has the 'caliph' word as a 'messenger who rules' and the Qur'an is much interested in his skills as a 'sweet singer' of psalms.

Something of the same issue is latent in the Surah 5.45 passage which has been rigorously applied—with greatly disruptive political effect—as disqualifying all Muslim regimes that do not pass muster in 'true Islamicity' as gauged by the sectarian judgement of such incipient rebels. However, in the verb *yahkumu* there is not only 'judge in rule' but 'judge in wisdom'. The immediate context favours the latter as concerned with moral and social reading of the code of the Decalogue which it cites, about the 'tooth for a tooth' limits of retaliation. Such rulings doubtless become the business of enforcing courts and courts (as the English word

---

[1] The cognate verb in 73.10 refers to breaking off from harsh encounter courteously. Surah 59, entitled 'Exile', refers to another occasion some years after the 'emigration' from Mecca. In general the plural verb *hajaru* is descriptive of those who did so, not imperative about the one event. The one potential allusion would seem to be the note in 9.40-41 about the protecting *Shekinah* over the two departees, the Prophet and Abu Bakr. (Cf. 36.9.) These are not about an actual command.

has it) the tool and province of regimes in power, but they will also be in the purview of scholars and exegetes in their *zawiyas*, the 'courts' that are mosques, busy with pretensions—and vigilance—of their own. Between these sundry courts of claim, appeal and verdict we are returned to the near enigma—as it may contrive to be—of 'those of your number invested with authority'.

Having that dilemma in common, however they resolve it, is at least the shared quandary both of the Qur'an and the West. For the one there is a very explicit religious liability with politics, for the other a steady diminishment of it in long traditional form. Yet in some measure, however attenuated the word 'divinely', they might concur about 'divinely liable politics', as meaning that statehood and power are accountable beyond themselves to criteria of justice, truth and compassion worthy to be sovereign with state sub-sovereignty in a serving role. The burden for Western/Muslim relations now, in political terms, is how well—and on what score—Islam's tradition of the religio-political can appreciate, and reckon perceptively, with the more secular one. Conversely, there is the issue of Western attitudes, in thought and practice, to Muslims in the present crisis as they find it to be. For any reckoning is highly fraught.

That present Western ethos is a far cry from how Islam found and kept itself centuries on from its defining years. 'This nation under God' of Lincoln's Gettysburg Address was differently meant from the Qur'an's *al Mulk li-Lllah*, 'the sovereignty is God's.' When presidents, after their manner, conclude with 'God bless America' they mean other than *Allahu akbar*. The words 'In God we trust' are carried by the ubiquitous US dollar into every corner of the globe, but with a message scarcely akin to Muhammad's '*Alaika tawakkaltu* (42.10) or, indeed, of the *Te Deum laudamus*, concluding long centuries before him with the same words: 'Lord, in Thee have I trusted.'

Europe, too, has its own recession in the sense of God and the practice of worship in perhaps more incisive forms than the 'God-fearing' USA[2] but—to the puzzlement of traditional Muslims—a patient, if challenged Christianity lives critically with this diversified secularity,

---

[2]  Perhaps it would be fair to say that the American commitment to the expression and practice of its (manifold) religions has been less affected than the longer European scene, in exposure to the intellectual factors in the older culture, on which see, usefully: Owen Chadwick, *The Secularization of the European Mind in the 19th Century*, Cambridge, 1976. Was there not, however, a latent 'secularism' among the Founding Fathers of the Republic, notably Thomas Jefferson?

still—however—concerned by its own lights for 'a liable politics', liable for values by which all must be judged. Some of tie intellectual factors in that transition were reviewed in Chapter 7. These, whether sceptical or despairing, have yet to reach Muslims of traditional mind, outside the scope of Western literature or the significance of Muslim diaspora.[3]

Classic Islam, by the long-lasting constraints of its origins, is far removed from these dimensions of religious vulnerability (if we may so describe them) and remains so in its deepest, self-defending instincts. When Muhammad failed to dissuade what was, in the Quraish, a local political hegemony, from its strongly sanctioned idolatrous religion, he attained to dislodge and dispossess it of its pagan religion by dint of its martial/political surrender to his force., That 'manifest victory' emphatically sealed a religio-political pattern as the very theme of Islam. When, by the expanding success of its armies, regimes beyond 'the Isle of the Arabs' capitulated, it was in military guise to a 'stateless' future. What mattered by the Medinan precedent was the changed hegemony. Islam could be contentedly gradual about a changed religion, given that the conquered were not the Quraishi pagans. The *dhimmi* system was contrived whereby 'approved' religions could survive, strictly on the condition of political non-entity. Only Muslims must rule, and only ever under Muslim rule would Muslims be.

It is this founding story that makes the Western formula of being 'just a religion', without the sanction of its own power, so instinctively high a hurdle for Islam to take. *Din al-Islam* (the Qur'an's own formula, 3.19, 5.3) integrates only with *Dar al-Islam*. That 'realm of Islam,' contrasted with *Dar al-Harb*, the realm yet to be power-absorbed into Islam, itself a single *Ummah*, under the due Caliphate of the Prophet's successor in ruling terms. In attenuated form it abides in the form and the ideal of 'the Islamic State', witness the creation of Pakistan.[4] The abolition of

---

[3]  Agnostic, or simply non-committed and critical, attitudes to Islam are evident enough in contemporary writers, doubtless from the 'contagion' of their Western counterparts., Authors like Sartre, Camus, Beckett, Kafka have their Arabic, Urdu, Turkish and other 'echoers', with the extremely influential *The Wasteland* of T S Eliot in their near ancestry.

[4]  The half century of its 'being' has only served to indicate how difficult was the definition of what 'Islamic statehood' meant as a goal, still more the burden of ever reaching it. In the build-up to the grievous partition of the sub-continent it sufficed, for Jinnah's pragmatism, to insist on the objective while tactically deferring its religious rationale (which could only have been divisive). The event and its sequential history are eloquent enough of how 1slam 'needs', instinctively, to be 'political', yet with abiding problems!

the Caliphate in 1924, by a secularising Turkism, and the rapid failure of attempts to renew it, have only partially diminished the passion for political aegis as the indispensable factor in a true Islam. The West has, therefore, to appreciate that—if we may so speak—the global *modus vivendi* it proposes or commends is radically destructive of classic Islam, even given the utmost tolerance for and honour to, its 'religious' Qur'an.

The situation, if we are honest, must also be read as radically subversive of Western political order where-ever, in any diaspora, an Islam of classic mind-set is present.[5] In this lies the ultimate significance of Usama bin Laden and his kind—all other factors apart that stem from culture or global tensions. It makes relatively naive the question: 'Why should they hate us so?' unless we realise 'why they dispute us so,' and the deep patterns of classic Islam which require the dispute.

It is, therefore, idle only to insist that the West has no 'quarrel' with Islam and that, blessedly, there are vast numbers of 'exilic' (from *Dar al-Islam*) Muslims dwelling peacefully and constructively with Western political societies. That is truly emphatic and emphatically true and—as we must trace—these have had to reach, or are reaching, a Muslim ideology of 'minority existence' as sound Muslims. Aiding them without patronage or compromise is a crucial duty on non-Muslims in relation. Yet 'westernism' as a whole still reads as a provocation to surrender in the mind-set of the Islam which clings tenaciously to the old *Din al-Islam/Dar al-Islam* nexus as, world-wide, the one and only authentic Islam, the Islam that first saw the Quraish as duly converted only when they were physically subdued.

We have tried to see in other chapters how the Qur'an itself might—by wise reading—minister to the measure of 'de-politicising' of Islam the situation needs and how, on other Islamic grounds, it might

---

[5] Happily, innumerable diaspora Muslims *de facto* give the lie to this charge that that their presence is subversive. They seek—and deserve—to be trusted. Theory, however, unless it is disowned, has it that *de jure* their duty—if they remain—is to work for the 'making Islamic' of the local regime. Cf. Zakaria Bashier, *Hijrah: Story and Significance*, Leicester, 1983, 'Islam is not like any other religion because it lays clear and unambiguous claims to government. Non-Muslim societies will never accept nor enable a truly conscious Muslim, a Muslim who is fully aware of his identity as Muslim, to realise the ideals of Islam,' pp.103–05. There is need for the notion of *Dar al-Harb* to keep this perception clear and active, as of that which—being inhibiting—requires to be not only disowned but displaced. The irony is that this author is published by an Islamic Foundation eminently realising, in the England of its loyalty, the Islam he deems impossible. 'Sterile communities that refuse to heed the divine call of Islam' can only be 'challenged', in power terms (p.105).

proceed. But that it should happen, and means 'hard going' on all counts, are not in doubt.

Where, in modern nation states (as never now in global *Dar al-Islam* terms)[6] Muslims are in a 'national' form of power control they have a different task. They do not have, as ideally 'exilic' Muslims do, either to return forthwith into the nearest *Dar al-Islam* or work subversively to turn their host-habitat into one, as basic theory holds. They are already in it, but in the ambivalent terms of statehood in tension about what being Islamic means for it.[7] But as 'nations' there is the question of non-Muslims in equal(?) citizenship and, thus, of the range and spirit of Shari'ah, and the forms of an inclusive Islamic democracy. Can the Islam of these states happily and loyally accommodate an inter-faith equality of share and status? By dint of them can *Dar al-Islam* become instead a kind of 'confederation' for mutual counsel, a loose but real 'commonwealth'?[8] If so, what bearing on its working would be apt for Western policy? Is there a partial viable 'de-politicisation' of classic Islam in all these national situations?

For, emphatically, there is a real 'de-politicisation' of 'exilic' Muslims in their now widespread, mainly Western-world diaspora. Indeed, it is estimated that a quarter of the entire Muslim world-population is now in 'exile' from its 'home-ground' of *Din* and *Dar* in any former sense. These Muslims, as it were, are back in the original Mecca, without benefit of power and identified as 'Muslim' by their faith alone. Could that Meccan analogy not now make it utterly congenial, despite everything Medinan in their legend? For there is one sublime difference. Theirs, broadly, is now a 'Mecca', not of obloquy and affliction, but of tolerance and liberty, of potential participation in suffrage and common political order. If their security is seen as precarious, the present factors lie in the suspicions engendered by the 'other' Islam we have reviewed. Western relations—and

---

[6] 'Never' because the fragmentation they assume in the single *Ummah* runs counter to the conceptual and actual 'unity' of Islamic humankind. That very word is ambiguous in the Qur'an but for the 'faithful' (in its proper terms) it flouts the true oneness by appeal to *watan*, or *sha'b* or *qabilah*, the homeland, people, tribe—or other—identities which should all be 'gathered' indiscriminately (as in the Pilgrimage) into Islam.

[7] The tension (here in 6) poses the urgent question re the due integration of their own minorities, or whether a true *dawlah* should 'minoritise' at all.

[8] As is notably happening in the Islamic counterpart to UNESCO and Islamic 'concert' for self-interpretation, protest, protection or 'demonstration' across its several major diasporas.

values—are thus alerted to a discerning—lest it be a panic—attitude to the Islam with which they must co-exist as majority towards minority, with consequences laden for both. For the onus reaches into how well, in Western terms, Muslims everywhere might be 're-politicised' as 'believers' by sharing in a kindred effort, from and beyond Islam, towards 'divinely liable politics' by whatever consensus comprehending it their ideologies might reach. In that engagement with the 'secular', as reviewed in Chapter 5, what wisdom might be drawn from the Qur'an, seeing that to the Qur'an, on Muslim part, it must go?

One prime necessity, in negative terms, is that such willingness be never regarded as some kind of treachery whereby the Shari'ah is forsaken or the essence of Islam betrayed, still less as some concession or capitulation to Western advice or example.[9] It will not be yielding sullenly to some 'clash of cultures' in which it consents to be a failing party. On the contrary, it must and can turn on its own Islamic warrant and worth, founded as these are on the *islam* of a human 'caliphate' summoned to its volitional character, as party in a divine enterprise of inter-association with divine ends by *muslim* means.[10]

That vocation demands that 'judging by what God has sent down,' albeit 'invested with authority' in some of 'their number' must mean that these are responsible to and for the faith community at large. For, otherwise, the personal Muslim forfeits the political measure of an inclusive *khilafah*.[11] There is this built-in principle of an anti-authoritarian quality in the very nature of authority. It has deep relevance for the practitioners of authority whether in mosque or state. Muhammad's dictum was: 'My people will

---

9   The West, in turn, needs to forego its instinct to imply its own exemplariness as a pattern ever worthy to be emulated and favourably contrasted with what it would better 'educate'. For, as seen from outside, there is much that deters or displeases and there is always the factor of envy for its ability to be consumerist and/or of jealousy for the world-role it too blatantly assumes. The human psyche does not take to being 'shamed' in order to be refined. Imperialism can be suspected in more than in its physical forms even when these are honestly absent.

10  Using the italicised significance of the personal terms as the inner, apart from the structured, identity of the 'capital' meaning of 'Islam' and 'Muslim'. The essential point in either term is a genuine act of will as the verb *aslama* has it.

11  For the personhood on which it is bestowed is denied part of its exercise in the absence of political rights. A tyranny, whether of dogma over the mind or of rule over society, usurps something of the sovereignty which belongs to Allah alone and does so by also flouting the due 'surrender' to God of the private soul.

161

never converge (in agreement) on an error.'[12] Muslims have to be the ultimate monitors of their Islam as fulfilling their *islam*.

To know it so does not resolve the crisis within their present history. It does place it where it belongs and where alone it can be faced.[13] Placing it elsewhere will only disserve the task. The West, for its part, needs the wisdom to hearten Islam towards its own Islamic vision of liability to Allah in a *khilafah* that is contemporary. The contemporary awesomeness of that 'dominion' in the current techniques of its global range makes us all contemporaries in terms never hitherto so binding. They are no occasion for studied confrontation. It belongs with our humanity in present history that Allah too is our great Contemporary. As Surah 21.105-06 has it:

> 'Truly have We written in the Book of Psalms in line with the Reminder: "Verily the earth is the heritage of My righteous servants." Such indeed is the message for those who will to worship.'[14]

The 'caliphate' is not withdrawn because it has become so dire in its wayward and malign potential. For this too is evidence of divine fidelity and, thereby, calls us the more urgently to our own. For has not creation made the divine/human scene and story something reciprocal? What was always so is now uniquely claiming the sanity of the faith that knows it, a sanity and a faith that can give no place of a 'clash of cultures'. For 'cultures' have to be themselves as human enterprises with divine creation.

That, by the same token, engages them in politics, to the task of cultures finding in themselves the will, and the logic, to forego the notion that humanity is only right in terms of their supremacy. Ways and means

---

[12] The oft-cited tradition of Muhammad which underwrites the concept of *Ijma'*, or 'consensus', for long a major source of Shari'ah, among the Sunnis— however controversial the *Ijtihad*, or 'initiative', which might pioneer and engender it.

[13] It is evident enough that 'mutual nuclear deterrence' and 'weapons of mass destruction' ('crass' as WCDs) have conveyed us to a time and world for which old categories are obsolete. The more hazardous the world the more urgent its sanity.

[14] The passage is directly quoting Psalm37.29: 'Verily the earth is the heritage of My righteous servants.' Is the psalm echoed in the third Beatitude? It certainly takes up the *khilafah* theme of a 'trust' anticipating a 'right *qua* righteous' tenure. It hallmarks the mortal as being the moral, the world's laboratory as a sanctuary and its economies a sacrament.

have long been military but these are ever more dubious and perilous, given the horrific refining of nuclear weapons and their likely proliferation. The means may also be economic in deliberate or casual manipulation of advantage and disadvantage in the mechanics of trading and resources. Or they may well be cultural via the pervasiveness of an information-world ruthlessly or carelessly pursued.

All these will come also within the writ of the political order, its criteria of civic conscience and its organs of law and society and the exercise of government. How far and how well can all these envisage and ensure a 'peace of cultures', in which religious witness is not muted or forfeited but withholds from all avowed or implied alliance with those other factors in arms, or social strategies or manipulative means? That the West has toils and temptations in such realms is evident enough. That the fabric of the Qur'an[15] makes the tests for its faithful presently more strenuous because they are more directly 'scriptural' is no less clear.[16] Yet, as explicit everywhere in these chapters, the Qur'an also presents an inner case to serve its custodians—God, as just argued, being their 'Contemporary'.

That time factor was always crucial to the Qur'an's meaning. The 'occasions of revelation' were invoked as clues by which to 'read' the passages concerned in them. It was a document gathered into the sequences of a *Sirah* which 'informed' its reading. The division into 'Meccan' and 'Medinan' mattered. The 'point of' had to relate to the 'point at'. Allah was their 'Contemporary' in that 7th century in that Arabia. He remains unchangingly so still in their 21st across a global humanity.[17] Hijrah to

---

[15] In that there is still the instinct not gently to commend but to enjoin a witnessing faith, while there is a Western opportunism in religious propagation that overrides the peace of 'cultures' by exploiting its opportunities too crudely.

[16] In that the martial mood of Islam, its capacity for enmity, e.g. to Jews and Christians, is written into the very text so that it warrants what other aspects of the Qur'an would seem to cancel. The Bible, to be sure, has enmity-inducing strains as in the Books of Joshua and Nehemiah (or the precedent of Samson) but these—for the heirs of the New Testament—are nullified as quite obsolete for any apostolic faith. The fabric of the Qur'an is thus in no way susceptible of Biblical style comprehension concerning its enmities and the writ they run.

[17] The Qur'an's emphasis on the changelessness of Allah surely means the intrinsic constancy of divine purposes. Surahs 8.53 and 13.11 observe that He does not 'change the state of a people unless (or until) they change what they have at heart.' There is that sense in which it waits for (or waits on) the human *islam*. 'Point' here plays on a double meaning around 'when, and 'why'. Calendar-wise the present is the 15th for Islam.

Medina was feasible then: it cannot similarly be now. The *Jihad* from it could achieve mandatory peace then—over against precarious tribal truces by impressing on pagan pluralists the sole sovereignty of God. It will not do so now in those terms.

Their trust of the translation of a 'there-and-then' into a 'here-and-now' is precisely a trust with the unchanging wisdom of God. If some Muslims see this as 'abrogation in reverse' that rubric may well serve in that what the Hijrah did and meant then is seen as invalid now. It is not 'abrogated' in what it believed its trust to be but only in the way by which that trust was then pursued. The founding 'religion' of Mecca has its abiding place as the more eminently suited to a global age.

So to argue tallies with the 'finality' always understood to belong to a Muhammad 'sealing' prophethoods where 'irrepeatability' threw the whole weight on communal self-possession.[18] By these lights of its own, Islam no longer rightly couples militancy with ministry. It can fulfil itself, free from the compromises and wrongs that always accompanied its imperial expression in non-Meccan terms. The making of *dhimmis*, as a sadly ambiguous tolerance of some inter-humanity, did not obtain and was never glimpsed in the Meccan years.[19]

Even when Islam was most assuredly militant there was no doubt on whose 'behalf' it was, namely the message, the *balagh*, of its Meccan origin. That priority was there and the 'arming' was its ally but never its cause.[20] Contemporary Muslims can never be seen disloyal in holding their faith to its Meccan self, and doing so with an inclusive will for the world.

Such loyalty returns us squarely to the political order, no less duly than the original logic of the Hijrah, but differently. For the political order is inseparable from a civil and viable human society as the only form in

---

[18] Divine *wahy*, or 'revelation', was believed to have ended—and so completed—its task (cf. 5.3). While Muhammad could be partially replaced as political leader or ruler (his Medinan role), he could in no way be emulated as the 'messenger'. The faith's significance would evermore be in the trust of its community, both supplementing and interpreting its law, its ethic and its total meaning.

[19] The making of *dhimmis* is 'ambiguous' in that it concedes some rites and rights religious, but withholds all others deemed indispensable to its own Islam. It may have contrived a quasi 'peace of cultures' but not their unbiased human occasion.

[20] Playing on the word 'cause' as, here, serving its success in *not* being of its mind. For the *balagh* had always been forbidden such powered resources. There was to be no place for constraining people to belief by forceful means (cf. the question in 10.99).

which ethics keeps faith with concepts of common good—concepts that are 'performative' in concrete terms, both deploying and disciplining the organs of power. For power that is trustworthy can never be uncritically trusted. Its necessary ministries can never safely be left a law unto themselves or they will cease to be ministries and corrupt into tyrannies. Power is only rightly *over* humans in being duly *under* God, its task being, in the familiar Muslim rubric: 'To enjoin the good and forbid the evil.' It has this ethic to fulfil. Such is 'its divine right', only conferring a rule that itself obeys.

It must follow that the prime claim on religion of political authority is for the nurture and the moral stamina of ordinary folk, seeing that the quality of personal character is the first requisite of a right society. Selfhoods in all their human variety, through youth and age, in their capacity for mutual care, for social compassion, for private integrity, are the crux of 'good feasibly enjoined' or of 'evil soundly prohibited'. Mere injunction, either way, or law by law's own claim, avail little in the absence of the inner will to good, whose evoking and sustaining must be the primary moral and pastoral ministry of religious faith and social caring.

The ground is already there in the privilege and dignity of our *khilafah* as that creaturely 'high calling' into which we must lift our sights and gird our minds. That truth is fundamental but 'rising to it' is so far impeded by sceptical suspicions of absurdity, by lethargy and 'low esteem', by false estimates of God as either tyrant or jester or absentee. The Quranic text has already taken care of these calumnies of human weariness or dismay, in its clarion affirmation of the 'trust of being'. Yet dynamic as that truth is, it readily becomes static in our jadedness and a *jihad* has to be urgent and unresting in renewing its meaning from atrophy and neglect.

'Divinely liable politics' can only well begin and belong in this realm of pastoral religious nurture of the sense of sacredness. It has to remember the Qur'an's own warning of how our selfhoods are beset with the glutting sins of ever attending *shuhh*.[21] We are creatures of envy, avarice, greed and self-will. The best devices of a political order serving an ethic which 'enjoins and forbids' will always fall foul of human perversity, in

---

[21] Surah 4. 128, human 'souls as being ever beset (dogged?) by self-serving passions,' i.e. selfishness in its grossest forms. We should be wary of what, from within, is present round our path.

face of which law can only fulminate and power be in default either by ruthlessness or sloth. The making real and making good of human wills, of ordinary citizenry, of each and all in their sundry offices, must surely be the radical role of religious faith vis-à-vis the political realm, one prior to any discussion about 'democracy', any 'sciences' about the arts and ways of power. For 'the only categorical good is the good will.'[22]

Here, further, must we not locate what we might call 'the reach of dialogue'? The cult of it between religions is in vogue with themes like 'One God for all in many faiths'. There has been Muslim participation but less readily than by others. Ought not such 'dialogue' to be much more sharply focused on the inner judgement of religions and on the temper of their leadership? All too often there seems to be an implicit welcome to, or sanction of, everything that is 'religious', as if all was always well with religious. There needs to be more inward self-criticism, becoming thereby the more ready and honest to be inter-critical, lest we be found bestowing a careless *approbatur* on much that deserves to be deplored. For not everything we label 'religious' is either commendable or desirable. 'Judgement must begin at the house of God.'

Further, are we being too cosily 'religious' in our 'dialogue' with those who 'religiously believe'? What of any concert with those who do not? It is superficial to suppose there is nothing between 'scepticism and Catholicism',[23] or between 'atheism and Judaism or Islam'. Shakespeare's word in another context: 'There is much valour in this Welshman' might be applied to many an agnostic by a Christian discerning of an ally, if also by repute an alien. To talk of 'atheism' wisely is to know what 'God' is being denied and the 'denying' of many so dubbed is urgent. The *Shahadah* itself in Islam needs boldly to begin with 'There is no god ...' before it can add '... except Allah.' The first Christians were accused by Rome of being 'atheists' in withholding worship from the emperors.

Theists need to recognise that they have no unilateral guardianship of the ethical.[24] The fundamentals, therefore, of politics in the ground of

---

22 Echoing the famous dictum of Immanuel Kant in his *Critique of Practical Reason*. Can we be so sure of it in practice as we may think to be in logic?

23 A formula in John Henry Newman's thinking on the verge of his submission to the Church of Rome. Fearing in his questing that he might lapse into scepticism, and viewing 'liberalism' as a deadly menace, he resolved to withdraw into the security of an 'absolute'. See V F Blehl, *Pilgrim Journey, Newman 1801-1845*, London, 2001, pp. 391-92.

24 There were few more ethically anguished and intellectually gifted 20th century 'atheists' than Bertrand Russell (1872-1970) who wrote: 'I have lived for the pursuit of a vision,

ethics call to be shared with 'unfaith people' no less than with people of faiths. Broadly, Christians in the West have been more ready for this than, thus far, the mentors and monitors of Islam. The reasons are evident enough and have concerned us elsewhere. Any readiness to venture will need to re-think the characteristic—and theist—self-sufficiency of Islamic faith and Scripture. These have been categorical in their differential between believers and the unbelieving, as only and always a radical otherness alike of identity and of destiny. The need now is to conserve and interpret what can be valid and what cannot in the sharp divide.

The impulse, or the instinct, are there in the *Fatihah* itself:

'Guide us in the straight path, the path of those whom You have blessed, not of those against whom there is displeasure or of those who go astray ...'

While it is important not to discount the significance of particular revelation, it is well to keep the distinctions it makes firmly inside the common 'caliphate' bestowed by God on each and all. That first creaturely identity needs to condition all subsequent ones turning on unique pedestrians on *Al-Sirat al-mustaqim*. There have been 20th-century thinkers in Islam, like Muhammad Iqbal and 'Ali Shari'ati, who wanted to read Muhamnmad as one who galvanised his people into full engagement with their real world, who sought to be 'renewers' in the immediate incidence of a present time. Their emulation now could mean a more alert engagement with the contemporary intellectual scene as a first requisite of political relevance and the task of government.

Such moral activism inside the political order sets itself two inter-related tasks. The one is the due exercise of divinely right power in the legitimacy of constraining force to serve all 'enjoining and forbidding'. The other is to preserve that power against its own temptations in which it ceases to be divinely right. The negative duty is often the more vexing, while the efficacy of the positive one is always turning on it.

---

both personal and social. Personal in the care for what is noble, for what is. beautiful, what is gentle. Social, to see in imagination the society that is to be created where individuals grow freely and where hate and greed and envy die because there is nothing to nourish them.' *Autobiography*, p. 728. Is there no element of *islam* in that *confessio* or a potential kinship with 'enjoining the good'?

The two together are the whole reason why what a religious faith may do bravely by its moral and spiritual ministry to the positive, and what its zealotry may do darkly in the negative, require that it *not* be unilaterally identified with the body politic. What is often called the 'separation' of Church from State, of religion from politics, is no 'separation' to equal irrelevance. On the contrary, the relevance is the more duly brought when the ethico-religious dimension remains only such, critical not manipulative, the genuine scrutineer not the intriguing practitioner.

This is why the long tradition of Biblical prophethood had its seers addressing kings and powers, never themselves assuming thrones. The very charge of 'treason' they sometimes incurred told how radically their ethicism was apolitical in the very fervour of its political relevance, as a ministry that could only be honest faith-wise by being independent of power's organs. Aside from its fittedness to their religious task *per se*, this 'separation-the-better-to-relate' also admits of the free participation of all faiths, within their will and capacity, in the making and mending of the moral citizenry.

Religions are most truly 'political' in these objective terms, their 'distance' is the surer form of their bearing on statehood. Only so are they best immune from the subtle snares lurking in the direct exercise of rule and power, the urge to bend these to serve their own cause and violate the *khilafah* of all. *Din* and *Dawlah* best serve their abiding mutuality when neither usurps the other. If either becomes the other, neither is truly itself, each, we might say, surrendering to the other their conscience before God.[25]

But what, it will be asked, of that directive to 'judge according to what Allah has sent down'? and what of 'those of your number (i.e. 'believers') set over you'—the texts with which we began? Has not Islam always assumed 'only Muslims ruling Muslims'? Was it not always so *ab initio*? Do we not have the salient example, in Pakistan, of a state explicitly created in 'the Name of Islam', to be unambiguously Islamic? The Qur'an indeed has verses commending human cultural and religious diversity, but can these obtain post-*Tanzil* itself?[26] Has not Islam inseparably wedded, as

---

[25] In that a religious faith immersed in power forfeits its critical judgement of it, and the political compromises its equal justice in discriminating exercise of power.

[26] Verses like 5.48, 11.18, 16.93 and 42.8 say that 'a single, i.e. a non-diversified, human community' was not Allah's purpose. According to 2.148 'every community has a *wijhatun* of its own' and would have it co-exist in mutual well-doing, under His ever availing aegis,

never rightly asunder, what we have here proposed as needing 'a certain separation' the better to be fulfilled?

That is true. It is incontestable that since the recourse to Medina the precept that Muslims alone always rule Muslims has prevailed. There are, however, three facts about that rubric in today's world. One is the hard fact of a segment of 'exilic' Muslim populations outside its feasibility, required in India, the West and elsewhere to live beyond it. Another is the demanding fact of large nations, like Nigeria with mixed religious elements requiring equal citizenship within agreed laws. The third is the daunting fact that the Islamic quality of Muslim rule and rulers has rarely been fully agreed. 'Those of your number invested ...' has long been in equivocal debate, with some disavowing others by different readings of the same Islam. There have been seceders and insurrectionists or quiescent disavowers in every century.[27] The rubric being hard to verify to satisfaction, it must have the sort of pragmatic reckoning, covered by that ready calculus: 'non-repugnant to the Qur'an', appreciating how diversely or congruently it might now be obeyed.

Given the necessary present urgency for an avowed 'inter-humanity,' is it not possible that an *islam*, so liable already to an interior diversity, might move towards what Russians describe as *sobornost*, namely 'the free and integral unity of human beings in the love of God'? It already has the concept of an *Ummah*, a single *(muslim)* humanity that purists see violated in and by separate Muslim states. May it hold a clue to a humanity inclusified as not to be violated by its own separatism? A common denominator that could deplore political separatism, as that *Ummah* does, might conceive the 'human' as common in the same terms and deplore a religious separatism. Divinely liable politics indeed, with the '*muslim*-human' co-liable with all.

That including Muslim *Ummah*, moreover, would still have political statehoods, sobered by it and yet operative within it. A *sobornost*

---

or power. Surah 21.34 sees every community having its own *mansak* (or ritual) for recalling the divine. But do even those 'late' verses abide after what seems the final verdict of 5.3 announcing the finalising of 'your religion'—the divinely 'chosen' Islam? Even if so, we must still be asking whether to read *islam* or Islam? In the former case a non-restrictive meaning becomes possible. See further, Chapter 2, note 4.

[27] Seceders, like the Khawarij at the outset, the Shi'ah throughout developing the art of *Taqiyyah* whereby they conformed under regimes they steadily disowned inwardly. It was a revolt of Muslims (Arabs) against Muslims (Turks) that led to the demise of that most cherished institution, the Caliphate.

of humanity will still have its faiths–with–cultures, its religions with rituals, which returns the argument to their separate existence as willing to co-exist. What of, what from, an Islam then 'judging according to what is sent down'? Who, and how, are 'those of you invested with authority'? We have to conclude with the texts where we began.

Strictly, 'what was sent down' was the Qur'an, yet it had so little to say about the nature of government or its precise ordering beyond its moral task. The classic Shari'ah only arrived by long emendation, addition and customary accretion to what the *wahy*-given Scripture 'brought down.' Has that process been finalised? May the 'sent down' come to incorporate what time will require it to say concerning what lacks all explicit presence in it? 'Ruling by it', therefore, will be more like using a language than consulting a dictionary. In that communal vocation there are two related points. One is that the *Tanzil* term is used in the Qur'an not only of a 'scripture' as guide but of commodities as 'trusts'—'iron', for example in Surah 57, named for it, and so underlining the central truth of our creaturely *khilafah*. How we handle our sciences, our ores and atoms, comes with the text of our *islam*.[28] The other point is that Surah 5.45's 'judge according to what is sent down' uses the verb *yahkum* which has root meanings about 'wisdom' as well as 'rule'. The passage adds that not to do so makes a *zalim*—a 'tyrant', a 'miscreant', 'wrong-doer'.[29] Clearly, the 'governing' it enjoins is no 'rule of thumb' Shari'ah but a discerning task of mind in serving a critical justice.

What then, finally, of 'investing with authority'? Answers are many. Tribal custom, emergent leadership, eminence in religious learning, 'counsels of people' (Surah 42.38), popular suffrage, *coup d'état*, violent seizure, despotism—benevolent or vile. Only some of these could be described as 'invested' *(uwli-l-amr)*, unless we are to translate: 'those who are in authority', in a *de facto* sense with no *de jure* warrant.

There are many counts on which the Qur'an would want the *de jure* version—Muhammad as no 'usurper', the 'hallowed' political Caliphate,

---

[28] Iron—girders for bridges, or barrels for guns, scalpels for surgeons or cases for bombs—that versatile earth-product avails for us by divine 'sending' (57.25: *anzalna al-hadid fihi ba'sun*). It is significant that the same term covers our 'artifice' and our 'guidance'. For without possessions there would be no performing, matter being thus sacramental as all *ayat*.

[29] Politics is 'divinely liable' (i.e. properly under God) because law must needs be ethical. There is no 'ruling' that can be 'right in its own eyes' as if exempt from the judgement of moral wisdom.

the sanction of *shura* (42.38) and, most of all, the privilege of the personal *khilafah*, Allah's dignifying of each and all, and the strong individualism rooted in the *Shahadah*: 'I bear witness.'

Yet 'judging by what God has sent down' must give pause to easy sanguine notions of the West's much vaunted 'democracy', if only because there are no panaceas, no devices safe from human perversity. The private vote, the secret ballot, 'government of the people by the people' may be sound to seek, and apt to recommend. But elections can still be prostituted, presidential campaign budgets sway electorates by massive advertising and heavy donors await their post-election trade-off. There are manipulative devices aplenty and the power of vested interest in lobbies to distort all suffrage. Democracy is not 'the famous stone turning all to gold': gold too often turns it near to dross. The West should be more discerning about what it commends to Islam, unless it can present again a Lincoln.

Moreover, democracy pre-supposes a population literate enough to discern the issues and caring enough to sift the wiles of politicians and, hopefully not so poor that votes are a thing to sell or suffrage a privilege to bribe. Nor are all societies governable without some measure of duress. In that event, *de facto* structures may prove reasonably viable even by lack of *de jure* stature, seeing that—as the cynicism has it—'politics is the art of the possible.' Where the 'possible' is less than satisfactory—and may be meanwhile satisfying—the concern must be strong to 'tolerate' only uneasily and never to forego the sound ideals in present tribulation.[30] That such concern should have international reach when alerted anywhere belongs with the meaning of international community, as also a squarely inter-religious duty.

'Clean hands and a pure heart' was the revered formula of a Biblical world. Politics has always struggled to have the one, while religion could presume to commend the other. Power has somehow always been self-inveterate,[31] drawn into its own excess or at necessary odds with gentleness and grace, thanks to the onus in all wielding of force, the

---

[30] It is not seldom—as Shi'ah Islam so long exemplified—that 'imperfect' situations may stay viable, while—in mind and conscience—their 'imperfection' is never absorbed in complacence. Such is no mere pragmatism but a setting of the will towards a different future. It has the latent answer in waiting.

[31] This seems a right 'word' with 'inveterate' meaning—by progression from 'aged'—'settled in the groove of habit', surely a chronic condition familiar in religion.

harshness that must go with justice against the violent. Thus it pays the price for a feasible society, while religion can charge itself with the prescripts for an ideal one. On either count, they must keep a certain distance from each other lest the duties political stultify the task of religion, or compromises religious fail the divine liability of politics.

That situation is captured in the reading, by many of Shi'ah mind, of the heart and will of Husain in the expedition that had its tragic end in his death at Karbala' and gave to Shi'ah Islam its most telling ritual and the *qutb* of its devotion. There was no doubt of its political origins. Caliph Mu'awiya in Damascus had died. His son Yazid claimed to succeed him, despite assurances, earlier given to Hasan and inherited by Husain, that it would not be so. There was no doubt that political action was needed and that it would have to be military. For whatever reason, Husain had long delayed to assert his right.

Even when he acted, something of that reluctance seems to have continued inwardly, dismaying his most ardent followers. As the narratives have it (and there is point in their being so) Husain wanted the political right he asserted to be somehow, also a moral cause, a spiritual intent not to be thwarted in that by which alone it could be pursued. The issue had to be known and lived in its deeply religious terms, terms that must reserve their character and worth and be preserved from the overtaking requisites of the power they invoked.[32] If, 'in Allah's Name', he came, his coming was to be known in its worth as beyond the martial thing in which it moved. Only as a genuine penitent could he be an authentic claimant. From such a stance, given the final tragedy, only a doctrine of vicarious suffering could ever perpetuate the memory, though historians will never know with surety how far Husain's demeanour contributed to what ensued. He had memorably personified the burden of political religion, the paradox of religious politics.

Divinely liable politics need the theme of 'our humanly liable Lord'.

---

[32] The political action had a theological dimension in the hereditary imamate believed to have the sanction of divine will. The martial Husain was also the spiritual Husain whose calling was to 'unsully' Islam from the violation it had suffered under the Umayyads.

# Chapter 12
## OUR HUMANLY LIABLE LORD

William Caxton, the 15th-century pioneer of the printing press, in describing the feudal system, explains that if it demanded upward allegiance from the peasant and the yeoman, there was also a downward obligation of the lord. Using the language of his day, he notes of the underling: 'the more is the lorde beholden unto him.'[1] Our final task, resuming all the foregoing, is to see rightly this truth of theology concerning 'God beholden to humankind' and to know it also the Qur'an's conviction. For Muslims, no less than Christians, could hardly believe in creation, creaturehood and prophetic 'sentness' to us, without a divine liability to us that counterparts the stature these confer on us.

The inclusive plural 'Our' is vital. For it has been characteristic of Hebrew faith somehow to arrogate this divine solicitude for humanity at large to constitute a 'special relationship' to their kind and kin alone. The instinct to be 'chosen people' has been widespread, whether by dint of race, or history and its interpretation, or of geography and its favours, or of native aptitudes.[2] The concept has been contagious. 'God bless America' spells a fond and frequent invocation on the part of its presidents. 'Blessing'

---

[1] Cited from the Oxford English Dictionary which adds: 'in duty bound to do' as used in 1502. Caxton (1422?-1491), was a notable merchant between England and the Low Countries and a prolific translator who had presses in Bruges and Westminster to disseminate his own numerous works and stimulate the translator's vision in the likes of William Tyndale, born just after Caxton died.

[2] All have been invoked in the Hebrew case, as fitting 'a land of corn and wine and oil' (Hosea), the drama of an Exodus to it out of 'hard bondage' and (often stressed since) the liability to produce genius. 'Chosen-ness' is also a recurrent theme in American literature. It fascinated Abraham Lincoln and the novelist Herman Melville. A sense of 'election' is also deep in the tradition of 'Mother Russia' and Holy Kiev. For an African example one might take Jomo Kenyatta's study, *Facing Mount Kenya*, New York, n.d., relating the tribal life of the Kikuyu people to the mountain they were 'given'.

is understood to be somehow reciprocal to how well 'America blesses God,' as its dollar witnesses with 'In God we trust,' meaning the 'we' that has the currency.[3] The note echoes from the previous chapter.

Earlier and remoter centuries found it natural to 'specialise' their peoples and their climes, being more self-contained and isolated in severe localisms, where frontiers stayed forbidding and languages more cruelly 'frontiered' cultures. It needs, on our part, an effort of imagination to think ourselves back into the Qur'an's world, where—by and large—Europe was unknown and things trans-Atlantic still more out of reckoning. By its presence on the margin, the Bible had more cognisance of a Mediterranean mediating the diversity of many lands. The eloquence of Ezekiel—albeit in his detestation—parading the far-flung commerce of the Tyrian coast is witness enough to the cognisance of more than what lay between Dan and Beersheba. Into that neighbouring Europe, the New Testament betook itself, driven by its will to transcend the ethnic denominator of any 'people of God'.

Neither Bible nor Qur'an comprehend the global scene of our current century, nor the troubled inter-bondedness of our technology, its annihilation of distance and its making for an obsolescence of terrestrial privacies. These have conspired to bring other 'distance' into play, namely the mental measure of how we can no longer inhabit a Biblical/Quranic world in the terms its first peoples knew, from whom we are further than we are from Caxton's feudalism, to which, even so, we can usefully return for the analogy he provides.

There are many who now think that this situation relegates these Scriptures to the archaic and the superseded, so that it is pointless to betake ourselves to them for more than academic or antiquarian fascination. To rebut such complacent negligence has been the aim here throughout. It makes urgent reason for emphasis on the divine/human situation of realities beholden to each other. To study now the 'humanly liable God'—albeit

---

[3] There is clearly a distinction within this word 'to bless,' between divine 'Blessing' and human—in the one case to 'cause to prosper' or 'to bestow the good', in the other 'to give thanks and praise'. Yet the fact that one word, can expressly cover both underlines the very mutuality we are arguing. The ascriptions in the Bible: 'Blessing and honour and power …' are on human part addressed to God as in the psalmist's 'I will bless the Lord at all times.' Yet it is also true that God alone 'blesses,' the sole initiator of all that responds. Perhaps something of this double meaning is present in the 'Name' *Al-Shakur*—'the Cognisant of gratitude'—Islam has for Allah, though it is also, in Surahs 25.62 and 76.9, a descriptive of grateful humans.

differently so in each Scripture—is plainly reciprocal to the 'divinely liable politics' of the previous chapter.

Yet it has long seemed excluded in popular Muslim reckoning—a reckoning which has allowed itself to overlook both the evidence of its own sacred text and the logic of its own theology, as confessing faith in 'the Oneness of Allah and the apostolate of Muhammad'. The reason for its obscuring lay in the weight of the Qur'an's emphasis on divine 'sovereignty' and utter 'omnipotence over all things'. It was a necessary note in the Meccan scene of the 7th century, when, Muhammad's audience were stubbornly wedded to their plural deities in whom their economic interests were also vested. That emphasis can be understood, perhaps validated, in its time and place. Yet the very success of Islam in enthroning Allah as One[4] might be pleaded to argue now a balance of theology more presently alert to its creaturely corollary.

Accordingly, it is to the Qur'an itself that we must go for the explicit case, though we have been extensively making it throughout. It turns textually on the Qur'an's usage of the Arabic particle *'ala* or 'upon', with Allah following. It means what Caxton meant as something 'beholden' by which the party in a relation was 'in duty bound' to certain liability, a liability by which alone relationship existed—something not only congenial but mandatory. It may seem invalid an our part to attribute such necessity to God—and indeed it would be, had not there been warrant given in creation itself to think the contrary, not to say also these sundry occasions of the Qur'an's word. Moreover, God as 'callous', a mere spectator of haphazard will, would be also a total irrelevance. 'Absent minded Deity' is a contradiction in terms. The ancient question: 'Shall not the judge of all the earth do right?' can have only one answer. The Qur'an would have us know that justice and compassion are the divine nature and the nature of the divine.

Thus, for example, we have in Surah 6.5 those who heed Muhammad's message coming to him and saying: 'Peace to you! Your Lord—*kataba 'ala nafsihi al-rahmah*—has written mercy upon Himself,' or 'prescribed mercy on Himself.' There is, then, a 'law of His own nature' by which Allah is guided and by which He is 'decided'. The constraint of 'mercy' is not from beyond, as if to compromise the 'greatness' of God, but from within.

---

[4]  This is to speak historically. Theologically, the sovereignty of God was in no need of 'establishing' by man. It certainly awaits recognition.

The thought, however, that clinches the case is Surah 4.165 about us 'having an argument against Allah'. Few in traditional Islam would think of such an irreverence as a 'case' against God.

Only the Biblical Abraham, the Biblical Job and the Biblical Habakkuk thought that they might do so, while the Biblical Jacob considered he might drive bargains with Him and Hosea and Micah spoke of 'a controversy' Yahweh had with the nation.

Surah 4.165 refers to the sending of 'messengers' (*Rusulan* with no governing verb), tidings-bearers and warners and continues:

'... so that humans would have no case to bring against Allah after the messengers.'

$$\text{رُسُلًا مُّبَشِّرِينَ وَمُنذِرِينَ لِئَلَّا يَكُونَ لِلنَّاسِ عَلَى ٱللَّهِ}$$

$$\text{حُجَّةٌ بَعْدَ ٱلرُّسُلِ ۚ وَكَانَ ٱللَّهُ عَزِيزًا حَكِيمًا}$$

The *Hujjah* word here means 'an argument', 'an arraignment with due cause', a legal quarrel almost.[5] There is no mistaking the *'ala*, meaning 'against' (not *li* meaning 'for'). What 'ought to be done by Allah' had indeed been done—witness the long sequence of prophethoods in His Name from Noah to Muhammad. In their sending God had discharged a duty incumbent on Him. It must then follow that had they *not* been sent, Allah would have been culpably in default of divine obligation and we humans would have had a legitimate case to bring against His failure. The reason is very Islamic. Without the 'guidance', 'warning', 'reminder' and 'ministry' of those vital 'apostles', we would all have been left in *Jahiliyyah*, that state of 'wild ignorance' from which the Qur'an understands them rescuing us all. God clearly had this duty in relation to our waywardness, lest we go on 'thinking ourselves untethered' to our fearful cost (Chapter 5). Our 'caliphate' in creaturehood over the created order would have been in jeopardy for lack of comprehending. In turn, the whole 'Let there be' of history would have faltered in confusion or corruption and Allah would somehow have forfeited his purpose and the meaning of things. Prophethoods were all the time 'minding His meaning' that we in creaturehood might mind it also.

---

5   There is a similar use of 'argument against ...' in Surah 2.150 concerning those who disputed the (new) directive concerning the *Qiblah* toward Mecca. Those who resisted are said to 'have no case against Muhammad'.

This sense of the sending of the messengers having fulfilled what was humanly due from Allah seems confirmed in Surah 42.16.

'Those who want to argue about God after they have pledged their faith in Him will find all they say pointless in the presence of their Lord.'

The completion—and the completeness—of prophethoods has ended all argument. Islam via the Qur'an should rely on its own finality. All 'case-making' against Allah can terminate.

What then of all we tried to study in Chapters 9 and 10 and of the human dilemmas thrown up in Chapter 11? In Surah 4.165 it is not only the particle *'ala* ('against' God) that is important. There is also that *li-nas*, 'to humankind'. The 'case' is not about what argument in theology there might be on the matter of volcanoes or earthquakes, or avalanches or deserts: 'Why have you made us thus?' Such questions do not come *from* them, but only about them from our sentient selves. What makes the mystery of evil is truly in these, but what makes their evil a mystery is in us alone. Would humans then be right—as for Surah 42.16—in settling for a faith that meant ceasing to feel there was a case? Might they then have believed too cheaply, with too ready a will to end all reservations about faith? Might a more 'answerable' God befit a more interrogating faith? Vigilance to keep its perplexities alert would belong with a more reflective theology.

How satisfactory should we require our theology to be and what are the tests it would need to bring, before the case for faith was right, honest and inwardly entire?

Burdening us humans thus the more are the evidences of human wrong which prophethoods themselves have known so well in the deep antipathies that greeted them. It is clear from the Hebrew centuries of Amos to Malachi how obdurate their hearers could be. There had been precedent enough for such wilfulness when Moses came down from the height of Sinai, bearing the tables of the law, to be greeted by the obscenity of 'the golden calf' under the presidency of his own brother, Aaron, to be designated 'High Priest'.[6] There were aspects in the ministry of Jesus of

---

[6] Surely among the most arresting of Biblical episodes. No wonder that the logic of the sight before him impelled him to a shattering of the tablets. No less eloquent was the return back whence he had come, to receive the undeterred law anew. 'Worship' of 'the Golden Calf' was not the destiny for which they were meant.

the human capacity to greet its highest good with its harshest disesteem, prompting—as it would seem—the growing sense that it must be read in Messianic terms.[7] Muhammad, too, during the Meccan years, endured what—as the Qur'an frequently reminded him—the long sequence of messengers had known, so that his experience was no exception and that the realisation might sustain him. 'The whisperer in the human bosom', whom we studied in Chapter 4, had always been busy with innuendoes and deceivings, hard on the heels of divine summons.

Faiths in the heritage of ancient Scriptures are only honest and realist if they attend to the histories with which they have consorted through long centuries and reckon this human capacity for defiance of their witness concerning the Lordship, measured against these human evidences. Otherwise they connive, to their own discredit or undoing, with the obduracies that suggest their irrelevance. How will faiths fare, if the 'argument against God' they have in hand to counter and disprove deepens into a human mood to see it confirmed in their own failure? In that context, only God, more ultimate than 'custodians', could save us from despair. Faith, as argued in Chapter 8, must always transcend 'the things of faith', though it will need to return to them.

Heirs of the Qur'an and the chronicles of the West have their comparable evidences of human perversity. Writers in the 20th century inside Islam have doubted whether the *Jahiliyyah*, the woes of sinful ignorance the new faith was set to abolish, has ever really ended.[8] They see their contemporary society as if Islam had never informed it. Nor was the immediate aftermath of Muhammad's *Sirah* impressive in its spectacle of discord and division, with three of the first four Caliphs assassinated and the emergence of the Shi'ah schism in the context of the Umayyad versions of Islam in its first century, sanctioned by bitter imprecations in the mosques. Its deep internecine strife in this its fifteenth century gives pause to human confidence in its being the radically final and fulfilled liability of Allah to His human world. Our human vagaries have sadly thwarted its promise in the outworking of its story.

---

[7] New Testament studies are not unanimous, but it would seem from citations Jesus made and from the plain logic of events renewing the situations that had generated a 'suffering Messiah' theme, that the reading is sound. For my part, it is argued in *The Education of Christian Faith*, Brighton, 2000, Chap.1, 'Jesus in His Christ Experience', pp. 3-20.

[8] Often such charges came from the pens of the Muslim Brotherhood accusing regimes they saw as treacherous to the true Islam of their perception. Among them was Muhammad al-Ghazali, *Jahiliyyah al-Qarn al-'Ashrin*, 'The Jahiliyyah of the 20th Century'.

If there must be doubt about Islam ever ending the wilfulness of human *Jahiliyyah* some 'spirit of the years'[9] might read a similar miscarriage in the history of the West. Was not its most signal experience the crossing of the Atlantic Ocean and the new dispensation the old Europe was set to find on virgin soil? That old Europe was chronically compromised by wars and wrongs, by oppression and bloodshed, the bitter proofs of its incorrigible *Jahiliyyah* under emperors and popes and divinely righted kings. Renouncing these, a new breed of human liberty under Jeffersonians would retrieve their European story in the open territory of 'a new and vibrant world'. 'All men', they held, 'were created equal' and could realise themselves so, once delivered from their manacles by the spreading invitation of their new abode with its strenuously fulfilling freedoms.[10]

The vision was genuine and wonderful but had the ocean sufficed to ensure its achieving? Was human nature susceptible of migratory correction? Had not the ideal a European provenance despite the old continent's flawed story? Would its new locale keep itself immune from old contagion? Honest history cannot answer with a positive assurance.[11] The eternal enigma abides concerning the liability of God inside the *imperium* of man. The Qur'an's theme about the 'case against' must still remain, insofar as any Christian reading of the answer had been present in the trans-Atlantic saga.[12]

It begins to look as if this 'case against Allah' we are drawing from the Qur'an is in fact a 'case against us' from God's side, seeing we

---

[9]  Echoing Thomas Hardy's phrase in his epic poem, *The Dynasts*, as they comment on the 'vast imbecility' of the Napoleonic Wars as a 'history of human automation', where 'the Weaver' nonchalantly weaves a tapestry He cannot read.

[10]  See the penetrating analysis of their sense of destiny and their high resolve in Daniel J Boorstin, *The Lost World of Thomas Jefferson*, New York, 1964. They wrote in the Preamble: 'created equal ...' because they believed, in their pre-Darwinian time in humans as a single, special creation, in man as a unique species. Yet that doctrine, however set to be disproven, was the sure factor in the abiding truth they used it to undergird and warrant. Thus they exemplified how a faulted doctrine will, nevertheless, uphold a vital truth. Perhaps, therefore, we ought to query Boorstin's title and read simply: 'The World of TJ', for 'lost' it surely is not.

[11]  The logic here takes us back to the point of Chapter 10. See also Reinhold Niebuhr, *The Irony of American History*, New York, 1952.

[12]  The nautical ventures that founded Massachusetts and Virginia were deeply 'Christian' in their driving impulse but never purely so. The argument in this chapter is not that the 'redemptive' in God is more 'successful' than the 'tuitional', but that it is more expressive of His nature and more realist about ourselves.

humans are so far unruly towards His rule and obstreperous against His authority.[13] Could it be that somehow the two 'cases' belong together, so that we only have this theme of God being liable to us because we are liable to Him? In that event, could not an atheism escape the burden by denying both and leave us conveniently 'on our own'? That, however, would be chaos unless some moral law prevailed to which the conscience of society was bound—which would be returning us to the theism we thought we had escaped. Faith, whether Biblical or Quranic, always held that any such human accountability had to be partnered by a divine relationship in which alone it could obtain. The question always was in what reciprocal terms that divinely responding activity might be and to what lengths it might go.

Dag Hammarksjöld finely discerned the point when he wrote of the distinction between being responsible to God and being—if impossibly—responsible *for* God, the first being the ethical, the second the theological.[14] Perhaps the moral law itself, understood as the holy writ of God in Islamic terms, has to involve an intellectual and spiritual decision on our part about the holy nature of God—not that any decision of ours *made* Him so but only found Him needing to be so on His own proper part, as duly related to all that holy writ meant and asked within us by way of obedience and worship.

This inter-liability between God and ourselves, between the submission we brought morally and the worship we rendered essentially, must then be, either way, in the terms most ultimate in our experience, namely terms of love and tenderness, grace and gentleness, if these blessedly belonged with us because these were enthroned in heaven. Divine liability to us could not be less than our human liability to each other, but infinitely more in being other. We would have to conclude that 'God is love' for the same reason by which we said that 'God is great.'[15]

---

[13] The ungainly word seems right, being defined as 'clamorous, noisy, turbulent and unruly'.

[14] Dag Hammarskjöld, *Markings*, trans. Leif Sjoberg & W H Auden, New York, 1964, p. 156.

[15] This was the central point of Browning's Christianity. See *The Poetical Works*, Oxford, 1941.

> 'We had such love already in ourselves. Knew first what else we should not recognise.'

'A Death in the Desert', p. 488.

> 'Do I find love so full in my nature, God's ultimate gift,
> That I doubt His own love can compete with it?
> Here the parts shift?
> the creature surpass the Creator?'

'Saul,' p. 231.

It is just this measure of things divine/human that took the historic Christian faith to its reading of 'God in Christ' as the evidence in time and place of 'the Christ in God'. The antecedent Hebraic tradition spoke of 'the place of the Name', as where it detected, in event and so in accessible locale,[16] the criterion of Yahweh's character. That tradition deepened under the harsh pressures of history into the Messianic hope, the conviction that Yahweh's human liability would be vindicated in a response of deliverance that had the measure of the wrongfulness they knew only too well as the truth of their story.

It was this founding hope that New Testament faith believed realised when it contemplated the ministry of Jesus and how it came into a Gethsemane at the hands of sinful human nature at work in his rejection. That faith was bold enough to recognise a Gethsemane in the heart of God and to read because of it the shape of the ultimate liability He had fulfilled as Creator of the world and master-architect of the human situation. It completed and made good all that the moral theism which Islam would later enshrine, while still thinking of Allah as committed only to prophethoods that taught and preached, as His full liability towards all we humans are and all we need. Allah would be shown 'adequate', as Surah 4.165 said, by our education in the messengers.

If we held, for converse sake, with that schooling role of messenger-borne Scriptures, we could think it one still present in the teaching ministry of suffering also, the ever urgent 'lesson' in 'a man of sorrows'. Yet having 'truth' that way 'through personality' would still leave urgent all that was meant by the Gospel's phrase: 'Yea, I say to you and more than a prophet.'[17] What could this 'more' be if not the travail

---

'So the All-Great were the All-Loving too ...
Love I gave thee with Myself-b love.'
'An Epistle,' p. 426.

[16] The phrase is much loved both in psalm and prophet. (Cf. Psalm 76.1: 'In Jewry is God known; His Name is great in Israel,' and Isaiah 52.6-7.) The Exodus was 'read' as 'where' Yahweh had disclosed Himself by name as the 'liberator', having been there as who there He had been (Exodus 3.14). That history was 'the place of His Name,' i.e. His caring character. After the possessing of the land and the Davidic capture of Jerusalem the building of the Temple 'located' that sponsoring 'presence' after years of a wandering people's 'ark of covenant'.

[17] Matthew 11.9. The 'more' had to do with John's being the 'herald' or 'forerunner' 'preparing the way' for the Messiah. In the Qur'an's understanding of Allah's concern with humans the phrase could have no meaning, 'prophethoods' being all and Messiahship excluded, with the title *Al-Masih* applied to 'Isa only as the 'anointing' of a 'messenger' in the sequence.

of the 'servant', the 'more' that on two counts there had to be. The one count was the reach of human wrong as more than could be met by education. The other was the capacity in God for that costly 'more' and proving it in the reality of a revelation that redeemed. The inter-play of these two would be the whole truth of provenly divine liability.

It has to be said that this faith-decision can be fully trusted and dearly commended, but it cannot be guaranteed. The third must be true of any and every theism. Indeed, there is a strange irony in the fact that negation of God is also an elusive and nebulous idea. Anyone who says: 'I am an atheist' needs to clarify *what* deity is being denied. For the statement might belong with the firmest Christianity, as with an alert Islam. There are 'gods' either faith is at pains to disown. The *Shahadah* had good reason evermore to begin in negation: 'There is no divinity but ...' seeing that the Oneness of God was being affirmed in a setting that wanted Allah disqualified, not as 'existing' but as 'existing as One alone'. He had to be urgently 'dissociated' from 'those that men associated' with Him as peers in His governance or partners in His sovereignty or addressees of His human world. For all these there was a necessary Islamic 'atheism', an urgent 'Let it not be thought so.'

An 'atheism' in Christianity, east and west, when fully discerned because of Jesus in word and deed, denied all gods of negligence and dis-involvement with the world, gods content to be 'gods unknown', remote, indifferent, only supreme in being agnostic, 'not-knowers' of humankind. Islam too repudiated all such. For none such could have willed creation, nor commissioned messengers, nor sent a last Muhammad to seal that sequence. Allah had allowed a 'case against Himself' had it been otherwise. He sought a worship that would correspond with who He was, who He would ever remain. For the world He willed to fashion He had His Qur'an to send. He might be 'rich without them',[18] in showing that He was rich in them.

Such 'wealth' in our 'weal' holds the surest clue to how a Christian 'atheism' of these 'false gods' goes beyond Islam's kindred 'atheism' concerning them. It consists in the New Testament measure of that 'wealth and weal'. First it gratefully outgrew its heritage about a singular

---

[18] God's being 'all-sufficient' without humans is indubitable, yet this 'non-necessity' to God of us might be somehow a contradiction of the meaning of creation and of His many 'sendings' to us. Surah 39.7 balances the point by its stress of 'gratitude' *(shukr)*. Thankfulness on our part seals a relation that would be frustrated both ways by our thanklessness.

'chosen people' in seeing how that destiny could belong with 'all nations, kindreds and tongues'. All might aspire to 'bring their glory and honour into the one Kingdom', and the stigma of being merely 'Gentile' would end. Given endless gratitude to where the tuition had come there was here no 'supersession' but only a wealthier inclusion, under-written by the 'God who was in Christ,' and there 'reconciling the world'.

Such is the final Christian word. But do we need to return to Muslim disquiet about ever reaching there, from Surah 4.165's 'argument against God'? We must seem to any Muslim reader (if patient thus far) to have strayed into Christian territory and impossibly far from his mind-set. Is not Islam incorrigibly set against any notion of divine vulnerability to humankind which seeing Him mirrored in 'a man of sorrows'—and those sorrows at human hands—entails? Is not the whole exercise, then, as futile as it is naive? It can be no sane part of our inter-religious situation to locate it in a place where one party can never come. Yet, if we fail to relate centres of gravity in either case, how are we meeting at all? The whole onus of any dialogue must be where those centres are and how they might ever converse.

Suppose we let such total estrangement meet around a single word-idea, in this context that of 'adequacy'. The Qur'an's word is *Hasbuna Allah* (Surahs 3.173, 5.104, 9.59, 'God our adequacy', with *Hasbuka Allah* directly to the Prophet in 8.62 and 64.[19] Thanks to Allah, the addressees, we may say, were 'made equal' to the situations they faced. To be 'adequate'—from Latin origin—is precisely that, not 'commensurate' but matching what confronts.

It is evident that there is something reciprocal here in two directions, namely between the doer and the duty and, thereby, between God and His humans. Thus, on either part, all is about what either is to the other, so that neither's 'adequacy' can be understood unilaterally but only in their mutuality. In this way, Allah's 'adequacy' is tested by the human situation, and our 'adequacy' by what that situation asks of us. There is this clear measure of inter-definition between the two. *Hasbuna Allah* has its meaning in respect of us and, in context, not otherwise. There is no

---

[19] 'Sufficiency' in the usual translation. The concept is there also in the Christian Greek Testament where *autarcheia* occurs in 2 Corinthians 9.8, and *hikanos* ('sufficient') in the same Letter 2.16 and 3.5. 'Autarchy' seems close to the autonomy, or *khilafah* we have studied throughout but here only in its due exercise under God. Again, as with the Arabic *hasb* there is the same inter-activity divine and human in one.

exempting of divine competence from relation to the human scene and from that scene in its evidently tragic measure.

So much we have already argued in comprehending the central doctrine of creation and of our creaturehood within it. If God is 'never at a loss' about us in our history, how is the adequacy proven in remedying our *jahiliyyah* in its mental sense by law we register about 'the evil' (to shun) and 'the good'(to obey) when our *jahiliyyah* in the moral sense persists so darkly?

That cannot be a right theology that discounts or ignores the reality of the human tragedy which it purports to explain or resolve. Given the whole structure of Islam as 'law', 'guidance' and 'reminder', it cannot be Quranic to deny something inter-defining between Allah and humankind, between eternal sovereignty and temporal creatureliness. Or, in the words of old Francis Quarles: 'There is none that can read God aright unless he first spell Man,' and spell him in the light of all his story.[20]

It is significant that on one of the occasions of *Hasbuna Allah* (3.173) it was Muslims speaking when they were in a tight situation, confronted by a hostile host, whereas in 5.104 the word was on the lips of miscreants invoking their pagan traditions and false worship. Thus there was a direct, explicit challenge to Allah over the 'enoughness' of the same boast—the kind of challenge which the whole meaning of Islam was set to refute. Those contrasted invocations of adequacy could never be reconciled. It follows that the clear vindication of the only valid Lordship of divine 'enoughness' is imperative—as the whole being of Islam requires and intends.

By that same token, then, its vindication must be complete by the measure of that which calls it into question, not by pagan pluralism but by human sinfulness. If the former could be overcome in the physical terms by which Islam had its teaching triumph over a pagan Mecca, these are not available, nor could they avail, for the righting of human wrong. Are we back on Christian ground and that from an Islamic case to come there?

But, if so, the urgent criterion of divine 'greatness' demands to intervene. *Allahu akbar* (the only ground of *Hasbuna Allah*) must for ever forbid this notion of the divinely vulnerable at human hands. 'Exalted be He above all that you associate' and such unthinkable things most of all.

---

[20] Frances Quarles (1592-1644) a contemporary of George Herbert and author of *Emblems*, a moralising poetry but with pointed insight and sagacious commentary on human foibles.

Yet thus to invoke divine 'greatness' is only to ignore the root issue around how that *akbar* is to be construed. Short of some measure, some referent, it cannot be understood. If these are to be 'beyond all that we associate' will they not take us out of this world and so into a vacuous theology? Must we not 'associate' divine 'greatness'—inside this very world—with those things that will most rigorously test and esteem it? Must not these be the things that belong most intimately with the creation Allah has willed, the creaturehood Allah has manifestly placed in our *khilafah* and with how that divine/human enterprise has historically miscarried?

Can the truth of *Ilah al-nas* now avail to promote an over-all human community and do for humanity at large what Islam did for Arabness? That such community is urgent the current global scene with its technology loudly commends to its religions. But these, hitherto, have almost always served to divide and set at enmity global ethnicities and give them asperities and vehemence they might otherwise escape.

But the more impossible the notion of a peace-making, peace-affording Islam appears to be, the more pressing the need it should be. Can it make good its own Qur'an's *Ilah al-nas*—the God in whom it might 'take refuge' from the 'strife of tongues'?

Islam is scarcely a unifying principle even among those who know themselves its adherents, despite the deeply bonding, uniquely Islamic, experience of Pilgrimage to the one Mecca. Those Muslims who hold to a single Muslim *Ummah* worldwide and exclude from it the nation-states they see as its violation, exclusify Islam in very adamant terms. That *Ummah* must needs be at odds with all else human until that all else succumbs to its political control. Hence the responsive 'clash-of-cultures' in Western dismay or apprehension.

Moreover, there is a rejectionist principle in Islam's impulse to categorise all non-Muslims as 'unbelievers'. The contrast, we note, is sharply there in the opening Surah, *Al-Fatihah*, between those seeking to be 'guided on the straight path' and those, being 'deviants from it', are they 'upon whom divine anger rests.' It is an anger which, in terms of enmity, the devout Muslim would have to corroborate.

It is a kind of human apartheid different from that which Judaism applied to all non-Jews by the ethnic and ritual distinctiveness as 'Gentiles'. The Qur'an's apartheid lies in its magisterial proprietorship of final truth. Like Christianity, it is missionary and all too ready for access into its belief-system and structure of worship, but is it so as presenting an ultimatum or offering an invitation? It was broadly the former to which its history points, while persistent unbelief merits a posture of antipathy from an alert custodian of given truth.

But how will that inter-human issue bear on the divine reach, whether within such guidance and law–giving alone, or into redemptive action where law has faced defiance from human perversity in guilty violation? It was a longer reach of the divine into the human predicament which found its expression in the language of a 'Fatherhood' that moved via 'Sonship' into saving action figuratively so described in that intimate language about divine 'Being' in divine 'doing'.

That 'less or more' about such divine doing out of divine Being is the clue to the disparity between two theisms. Perhaps the ethos of Islam will never allow Muslims to consider how it might be welcomed among them. If, on the contrary, it remains always the more excluded from their reckoning, there is all the more reason why what holds it true in conviction and witness should not have its meaning 'perish from the earth,' but ensure its faithful presence. Not then, because controversy is congenial or argument engrossing, but only for love's sake—love for God so understood and love for its truth's sake.[21]

Other aspects of this shorter/or longer divine reach into our humanity emerged in the earlier Chapter 10. Meanwhile, in the sacramental focus of this one does not a wisely gentle 'resting' of the numbers–business, take us to a quite different dimension of faith in the unity of God? We go back to the *Ilah al-nas* theme with which the book began. How might the 'Oneness of the God of humankind' bear upon the contemporary world scene?

It was evident in the Meccan cradle of Islam that the preaching of Muhammad and its Medinan sequel achieved a marked unification into one Arabness, of the sundry tribal loyalties and rivalries of the *Jahiliyyah*. The reasons were not far to seek, inasmuch as tribal identities were fostered and

---

[21] Salman Rushdie's delight in 'hybridisation' of culture is no apposite instance where, with its sardonic cynicism about the human meaning and its reluctance for any constructive evocation of the answers from the resources of the Qur'an. A more articulate and earnest example of disquiet over the human scene is in the numerous—and often translated—novels of Najib Mahfuz (b.1912) the Egyptian Nobel Prize-winner for literature, notable his *Awlad Hawratina* (Beirut, 1967, trans. Philip Stewart London, 1981, Washington DC, 1982, as *Children of Gabalawi*).

sanctioned by tribal deities who patronised their divisive interests. To unify their heaven under one Lordship was to unify society on earth below. It was this which Islam massively achieved, so that Mecca no longer needed precarious 'months of truce' to suspend the operation of *lex talionis* and its feuds, but could look for safe passage for all 'lawful occasions'. Islam itself, to be sure, generated bitter religious sources of strife. What for these now, in the wider issue of global co-existence? They have to live with immense new dimensions of where Allah has conveyed us all, a world's trustees. These surely ask of Islam new assessing of its loyalty.

Thus the contemporary issue is the degree to which the Qur'an can nurture or, at least allow, an inter-human co-existence. The concept of a single *Ummah* incorporating only Muslims will not avail. For it censures Muslims who hold on to nation-loyalty, even though their current frontiers are owed to earlier non-Muslim imperialism. What of an *Ummah* that carried still further into global terms a sort of 'commonweal or wealth' in which Islam thoroughly participated? Then its own inner, bonding exclusiveness could co-exist and co-administer in a single order of inter-cultural community.

It is obvious that something like this is already happening, *de facto* in the wide dynamic diaspora contriving to be an authentic Islam outside any classic *Dar al-Islam* in the original sense and, perhaps better, making a spiritual *Dar al-Islam* where the old, literal one will never be.[22] All turns on how diaspora and non-diaspora Muslims consent now to view the world.

The reader of the Hebrew Bible becomes aware of how Jewry there grew steadily more conscious—if still only distantly—of the wider world of other humans. Initially all had been severely tribal, with 'others' the Canaanites and then the Egyptians and then the great powers of what is now Iraq, with whom Judaic fortunes had to do. By the centuries of the great prophetic tradition and the psalmists of those times, the reader notes an awareness of 'the nations' at large, 'flowing' to Jerusalem to learn from Jewry. Even 'the isles' are waiting for Yahweh's law. There is Micah's great

---

[22] Though there is that 'mind' in some Islam which would have it so. By their lights and the authority of law, as they hold it, the duty of any Muslim who finds himself in *Dar al-Harb* is bound either promptly to move back out of it to the true *Dar* or urgently work to Islamicise the state-power where he is living. He cannot be its guest in any peaceable terms. He must be loyally subversive with Islam the mentor of that paradox.

vision of a war-free humankind, when 'Israel walks with her Lord' and 'all the nations walk in the name of their gods' (Micah 4.1-5). Has Micah somehow interiorised his people's faith-identity? For he concludes: 'We will walk in the Name of the Lord our God for ever and ever.' There is no surrender of particularity or of its validity but there is a new theology of co-existence. The 'Lord of hosts' language which once applied only, either to the starry heaven or Joshua's army, now—it seems—might denote the human multitude in its diversity.

Can something akin now happen in Islam, namely an ongoing interior fidelity that co-exists with an honest recognition of religious diversity, a recognition which no longer has to be suspect as compromise nor vetoed as disloyal? To have it so means a radical revision of every historic instinct of Islam. It will mean a sort of 'abrogation' of what has long of doctrinal necessity obtained.

Appeal, then, will have to be to the 'abrogating' idea which, as *naskh*, already exists in the Qur'an but where it relates—and with much controversy—only to legal and ritual matters. It would be a major enterprise to invoke it on behalf of something so radical as, virtually, a de-politicising of Islam. The matter has been discussed elsewhere in terms of the priority of Mecca over Medina in the assessment of Islam.

The other hope would be a steady accent on those passages in the Qur'an, noted earlier, which enjoin mutual emulation between peoples and races, and which stress that human diversity was divinely meant and willed.[23] This emphasis is important, precisely because the Qur'an neither underwent, nor does it record, the kind of growing awareness of the largeness of the world we noted in Judaic experience. The Qur'an's own *mise-en-scène* was so much more circumscribed in narrow time scale and localised in place. Muhammad was no Ezekiel brooding darkly on the far-flung commerce of a Mediterranean Tyre. The Qur'an's perspective was with ruins and vestiges in its own Hijaz and its Red Sea

---

[23] Allah made communities as plural (5.48 and 11.118; cf. 16.93 and 42.8). 5.48 finds each appointed to a different way (cf. 2.148). Surah. 2.148, with 5.51-52, suggests emulation between each other as the positive point in diversity. There should be a competing in goodness. Even *qiblahs* of ritual devotion may be diverse. The central duty is to establish *al-khairat*, 'good works by co-operation' (2.148. 'be ye forward in good works,' says 5.52). There is urgent need to maximise the potential of these passages to counter the deeply enmity-creating passion evident in other verses. If this implies some measure of explicit abrogation the idea is implicit anyway and the current scene requires it be exercised against all things prejudicial and rejectionist.

as a source of analogies from sailing. It did not converse with the Ethiopia to whom, at one point, Muhammad sent his refugees nor did it note their story there.

Yet surely there is a compulsion in the current world scene to be alert to a whole, globally and privately. The Prophet is understood as 'a mercy to the worlds'. That plural about Allah also as *Rabb al-'alamin* firmly sets Islam in a human ecumene, the 'worlds' of cultures, peoples, traditions, mores, even religions.

Some in the West have tried to commend this co-existence of religions in terms of a subtle distinction between 'faith' and 'belief'.[24] 'Faith', which on this score should never be a word in the plural (there are no 'faiths') means a worldwide sense of a sublime moral order, a transcendence which must be 'had in awe,' or a sense of the 'numinous' which demands to be revered. This is the unitary thing 'faith' denotes. It is, however, by this reckoning, housed, told and transacted in 'belief' and in 'beliefs', legitimately plural, which capture its claim and incidence but do so variously and even contradictorily. It is pointless to try to reconcile these patterns of that single 'faith's' expression. They are unassailably plural by their very matrix in culture, society, and all the other forms of ethnic identity.[25]

It is unlikely, for manifest reasons, that Islam will ever be open to this version of inter-religious mutuality, even though this philosophy concedes, indeed expects, faith to be in propagation. That is part of the thrust of 'faith' itself with which 'belief' is in trust. There is here no formula for silencing witness.

Nevertheless it cannot commend itself to the mind of the Qur'an, since it seems to relativise truth itself and subject truth-belief to something beyond it, so disputing its authority. Islam, in this like Christianity, will always be wanting to have its 'believing' bear on all 'faith' elsewhere. Moreover, the 'faith/belief' distinction itself is dubious on two counts. One

---

[24] Its chief exponent in the West was the eminent Canadian Islamicist, Wilfred Cantwell Smith (1916-2002) in *The Meaning and End of Religion. A New Approach to the Religious Traditions of Mankind*, New York, 1963. Also *The Faith of Other Men*, New York, 1963, and *Belief and History*, Charlottesville, 1977, and *Towards a World Theology*, London, 1981. See also *On Understanding Islam*, his own issue of selected studies, The Hague, 1981.

[25] In this way Smith could argue—and sincerely intend—to legitimate mission and a freedom to propagate. Diversity was itself a warrant for witness, given his co-existence theory which took away the absolute necessity.

is that it ignores the actuality of resolute 'irreligion' not least in the West, and the cancellation of the 'awesome' which insistent unbelief attributes to the wild behaviouring of religions themselves.[26] The tragedy is that 'awe' and 'wonder' and the 'numinous' have died with some 'death of God', to the tragic impoverishment of human society and sanity.

Furthermore, the radical distinction between 'faith' and 'belief' ignores how the former can be articulate or active without some measure of 'belief'. There is no evading the necessity of doctrine if 'faith' is to be transacted in worship and registered in mind. In its way the thesis concedes that by coupling the two. But 'faith' and 'belief' must be more than a loose 'couple' if either is to survive and belong with an exacting world.

Yet, in one particular, the theory can enable co-existence in that it expects witness, holds it legitimate but disowns its ever being compulsive. Since a compulsive witness is a contradiction in terms, it may not be outside the Qur'an's own rubric of 'no compulsion in religion' (Surah 2.256).

At all events, admitted discrepancies in theology need not argue, need not conduce to, enmity-creation, as was so often the case in the strife of the Qur'an with the Quraish and has long been so since in the long centuries of *Da'wah* by Islam. 'Surrender' to God will always be one thing, 'surrender' to Islam another—if surrender be what Islamic witness seeks or wills to have. Can it not, must it not, suffice a contemporary religion to have its meaning expressive and present in the world and let its contents bear compassionately on the making of social norms and manners? It is only in making itself gentle that a faith makes itself great.

Perhaps there is point in this context in noting how there is no laughter *(dahak)* in the Qur'an. There is the precious truth we noted earlier (Surahs 21.16 and 44.38) that there was no frivolity in creation itself, no 'jesting Creator' intending a plaything of the human scene, no divine puppetry of us humans. That purposiveness in our status and dignity is the vital ground of all else. But the possibility, within it, of a human place for humour seems quite absent. Yet, it is said, humour makes us all kin and laughter occurs when we see things incongruous happening (though comedians learn that regions differ in their joke appreciation). Islam has

---

[26] It was one of Smith's hopes and aims to re-authenticate religion and present it as free from the sinister features which so alienated the 'secular' mind. He was firmly a champion of 'faith' via 'believings' to counter the spread of the rank irreligion he so much deplored. He feared for the future of a 'faith-less' society, hence his urgency for the right 'faithing' as he saw it. But did he under-estimate how far 'faithless' Western society had in fact become?

long had what the Latins called a gravitas. But why is it so humourless? Or why are the faces of suiciding self-martyrs and suspects always so unsmiling, so grim, so dour and menace-laden? Perhaps there needs to be a seriousness that can take itself less seriously in order to be its authentic self as forever saying *Hasbuna Allah*.

However that may be, these chapters have focused on the Quranic, Biblical/Christian 'earth tenure', believing that ecological trust and environmental duty are where faiths have their crucial test in today's world. This sacrament of divine hospitality is the clue to all human kinship, the proof-text of our mutuality. To read it also as 'the bread and wine' of divine suffering to redeem is to bring two dimensions into one converse. We learn the divine inclusion of our diversity, all 'liability' fulfilled in undifferentiating grace.

Then they knew how that 'never indifferent' of its Biblical Lord had dimensions of 'engagement' with our human situation thus far unknown, unless they had been hinted in the suffering prophets, with whom Yahweh had suffered too. The Lord who had been known as 'walking in the garden' calling: 'Man, where are you?' was to be recognised in one who knelt in another garden, with words about 'a cup not passing from him'.[27] The logic between the two scenes was one with the nature of God as the New Testament was bold to perceive and tell it. There could only be a final 'theism' this way, the 'God-dimension' that belonged with the creation of the world and human enterprise upon its landscape under heaven.

---

[27] What should we understand by 'the cool of the day' in Genesis 3.8-9, or its relation to 'the dark of night' in Gethsemane?

# AFTERWORD

We have reviewed the intellectual case for the open discourse of 'Islam and the West' as it might more aptly be sought as 'the Qur'an and the West'. But is the venture somehow forlorn, given the politics with its 'negative indicatives'?[1] Is it all an academic project doomed to the margin of a mutual prejudice in powerful fates that have no heed for it? The signs of a will to mental and economic supremacism on the one part and seeming obduracy on the other, do not augur well, or only 'augur' in terms of long and weary cross-purposes. 'Mark twain' we might say, the White House, Washington in current hands and an *Al-Qa'idah* eluding effective counter and presented with occasion in Iraq born of Western blunder. The encounter is no 'Innocents Abroad' though there are present features that—without the innocence—might tally.

When the pseudonymous author, Mark Twain, wrote his whimsy in 1869 he regaled readers in America with ridicule of 'foreign' sites and manners, sharing his native amusement at the follies or foibles of a European and eastern scene, magnified by his own failure to understand. The exercise was a lark in which he could indulge. We are marking twain now in a grimmer disesteem, each more deadly when contemptuous of what it has not understood.

Mark Twain, however, had one salutary use. He exposed the 'innocence' of 'tourists', of visitants who never arrived. He had his readers appreciate the risks of inefficient guides, of customs half misread, and the tribulations in uncongenial hotels. The Western trouble now is that taking 'Innocence abroad' is taking guilt as well. Without the humour, there are custodians of Islam the more deceived by their imagined acquaintance with the West. Prescriptive prejudice, self-ordered either way, the more

---

[1]  A phrase used by the poet, Philip Larkin (Introduction, note 15), pondering 'small dramas of human frustration'.

mutual, is only the more stubborn. Can we expect it to give way or heed things exegetical in texts? Or these will it claim as exclusively its own?

Even so, the themes we have explored refuse to be ignored. The wide dispersion of Muslims today outside their *Dar al-Islam* is squarely caught in them. Their presence in 'foreign (non-Islamic) parts' might be potentially subversive and thus suspicion-drawing. Yet, disowning it so spells a duty for honest citizens about Shari'ah reading. Coping means wrestling with the very nature of Islam, discerning a valid history to disown an invalid one. Doing so entails the who? and where? and what? of all religious authority.

How minded, in temper or in tuition, is the West for the onus it has in that mutual situation? It cannot be adequate without patient attention to the case-making here outlined. The fond insistence: 'We have no enmity to Islam' on Western lips intends an honesty but no honesty is heard in the self-defending, self-absorbent mind-set of an Islam it has failed to register. For it has ignored the crisis in the very definition of Islam in history and in life. While it is a crisis of identity only Muslims can resolve, it is not one that non-Muslims can refrain from understanding. It has to be served with a deep and critical sympathy where-ever occasion may allow.

Occasion will least allow, while Western political relation to the world of Islam is seen there as deeply inimical. The explicit charge is clear and with few signs that its substance is being seriously addressed. The invasion of Iraq, if not of Afghanistan, is seen as intentional aggression based on—it must seem—wilfully elaborated 'evidence' of some reciprocal intention of aggression now proved mistaken. That attack was not properly made as a genuinely international concern for world order, acting against conspiratorial international crime. It was perceived to come with the veiled interests of super-power ready to assert itself, pre-emptively, as beyond the due constraints of genuine internationalism. Its significance, so read, played into the hands of a long Quranic rubric that incursion made demands retaliation given. 'To be against us has us forthwith against you.' There is a *lex talionis* requiring that peace can only be if it be reciprocal. Furthermore, the war opened up a frontier, hitherto adequately sealed from them, for the inroads and the motives of a dark-minded Islam. The overthrow of Saddam Hussein may have appealed on valid moral grounds to the Western mind amply flexed militarily to act, but it played readily into the hands of radical distrust of the USA and was taken to confirm its deep animosity toward Islam. Actions of such order are rarely read by victims in the terms that moved the victors, still less so when the latter are caught in their own ambiguity. For the answer as to what victory can ever be is very far to seek.

This aggravated distrust in the good faith of broadly Western, crucially American, relation with the Islamic world in its experience is confirmed by the inner reckoning of that experience with the negative achievement of Zionism. For, in terms of the Palestinian story it has meant the immolation of a would-be nation. The roots of its malignity go back to the ambivalence of the Balfour Declaration of 1917.[2] Emotions bedevil and distort the telling of the story but that the auspices, from Balfour, through the League of Nations and the UNO vote of 1947 and long beyond these, were 'Western' and, by consequence injurious to Arabism, is not in doubt. That Arab/Palestinian ineptness contributed to the impasse is evident but does not allay its tragic pain nor exonerate its Zionist origins and agency.

There is no doubt that this century-long issue generates an intensifying passion of alienation from the image it frames of a West unforgivably at odds with what matters to Islam and, it would seem, ever more incorrigibly so. Yet a solution, indispensable to sound Islam/Western relations, seems ever more intractable while American policy stays set

---

[2] The perennial problem of 'two nationalisms' was always there and was lucidly detected by the American King/Crane enquiry early in the nineteen-twenties, the one determined on growing physical presence under some (until its own) political power and the other already physically present, in numbers that would surely grow, keenly aspiring and suffering for its own power-control. What was inherently duplicitous in the Balfour Declaration has effectively remained so in the unavailing efforts of successive international auspices to resolve it. The League effectively handed it back to the British in the form of 'Mandate' (which the USA declined). Balfour's ambivalence bedevilled the Mandatory power which finally made the fledging UN heir to its dilemma. It turned to the long pondered 'solution' of 'Partition' and—in the earliest version of itself—the United Nations enjoined it on the parties. The new State of Israel accepted it on pragmatic terms. On idealist terms the Palestinians did not. Their nationalism was not pragmatic. Israel, however, did not accept the map which partition set and has ever since regarded it as open to deferment while settlements were creating irreversible facts and, by interminably inconclusive 'negotiation', calculated to defer the locating of a frontier, hoping that at length it might come to be the river Jordan. Unless we concede some 'right by conquest' (which Zionist ideology would scout as libellous) it remains true that the only juridical basis for the State of Israel is that never implemented UNO Resolution of November 1947. The inherent ambiguity of Balfour has endured a near ninety years with its reservations about a 'home in' and its ironical solicitude for an 'existing population'.

to refuse some better wiser mind. Enmity therefore rankles the more, symbolised by the brutal erection of barbed and blighting 'Wall' bisecting supposedly 'beloved land'.[3]

Rightly or wrongly, the 'war against the terrorists' diverted to Iraq fits—or is fitted into—this scenario of American commitment to Israel in the misguided self-interests of either. If the case against Iraq, as 'dossiered' by intelligence agencies was not owed in part to the Israeli ones, it certainly emerged as one eminently suited to the needs of Israel. Iraq was the only remaining Arab neighbour-power potential of military relevance to Israel.[4] Its disarming and humiliation in its Saddam form was a highly desirable result to seek by proxy. The Arab/Muslim sense of being the more vulnerable, even if wildly judged, was utterly convincing. If the now defunct Iraqi regime had been pretentious, it had had a nuclear neighbour on its doorstep.

Zionism has to reach its own moral and spiritual reckoning with what it has occasioned and continues to occasion in the despair and anguish of another people—a reckoning which could take its clue from its own ardour for a fulfilling nationhood and allow its urgency in the heart of the 'other people' no less authentically 'enlanded' in their midst.[5] In present context, the point at stake is the degree to which 'Islam and

---

[3] The initial *Hibbet Zion* movement in the eighteen-seventies cherished the native soil as somehow their 'sacrament of hand'. They were in the sweet tradition of Hosea when relationship was almost 'marital' and 'husbandry' meant love. Repellent and repelling, the 'Wall' may implement the 'geography' of settlements in creeping acquisition and also disqualify Palestinian resources of all viability. It fastens a divorcing apartheid on the other population and gives the lie to the finest traditions of the Zionist dream itself.

[4] Egypt under Sadat had contrived to recover 'his' Sinai by concerting peace with Israel, if only by—as he believed—effectively linking it with Begin's pledge of 'movement' also on a Palestinian 'peace'—thus to obviate Arab charges of betrayal, for having thus assured Israel of no southern menace. Of other neighbours, neither Jordan nor Syria was able for significant anxiety to Israel, encamped on the Golan Heights within easy range of Damascus. The hostile potential—and perhaps mood—of the more distant Iraq were more relevant. Aware of Israel's own nuclear equipment, Iraq alone might be moved and minded to seek to counter it. Any Palestinian nexus could also be a concern in Israel.

[5] How 'equally enlanded' is perpetually in tension or distortion. That 'occupancy' matters is evident in the Zionist drive to gain it and enlarge it in *Aliyahs*. Land-love and folk-identity, being no unique nexus, are comparably joined at least in sheer human terms of fearing exile and resenting alienation. Palestinianism has only its own tenacity to counter the Judaic mystique of Abraham and 'promise' and 'Covenant'. By the lights of both peoples, conscience should surely have some writ over the confusions of politics underwritten by the sanctions of sanctity.

the West' are so tragically estranged by bland American connivance with the frustration of that reckoning.[6]

What of the European factor in this burdened equation? Is it hamstrung by a sense of armed inferiority to a trans-Atlantic 'partner' with whom it must meekly 'go along', in some strategy of hopefully retaining influence? It could surely be more robust in not deferring to only one dimension of the American identity.[7] Europe, in the two World Wars had its own moral implicity, appositive and iniquitous, in the necessity for Zionism. There are resources of sanity and legacy on which it might more resolutely draw in fostering the inner springs of peace in Israel and in aiding the politics of a Palestinian justice, alert ever to the tangled politics of Palestinian violence and despair.

In his kindly Judaic wisdom, Marc Chagall, the eminent painter of the Shoah, explained his non-residence in Israel by saying: 'only that land is mine that lies within my soul.'[8] He meant 'lies' in no pejorative sense. He takes this 'Afterword' where it belongs—to the sincerity of religion. What ever attends on all the foregoing, the associations of 'the holy Mount', Al-Quds al-Sharif, the Via Dolorosa en route to 'Holy Sepulchre' will ever cling, both to sober and embitter, to rankle or perhaps redeem. None of the parties are 'innocents abroad' but the 'compromised at home'. The West should forbid itself a 'tourist' style politics, presuming to endow others with the nobler arts of democracy. All are violating the authority of their most cherished religious symbols. The desperate tangles of a religious sanction of attitudes, whether angrily to assert or urgently to escape, return us to the themes these chapters have explored. Forlorn their case may seem. Its making is only therefore the more urgent.

---

[6]   Observers often stand perplexed at the way in which the USA and Israel can contrive such political identity between them, and at how manipulable the former is by the other. Reasons can be detected in domestic American politics, if less in the Israeli mind to be the 'client' unless on her own terms. The measure of American aid, remittance, cancellings of loans, settlement funding, debt-deferring, arms supplying, wall erecting and UNO frustrating in this field are all phenomenal and unprecedented in any other direction. They also contravene George Washington's prescript about 'foreign relations' of 'no passionate attachment'.

[7]   For (see George Washington and previous note) there is another America—the USA of the 'Founding Fathers', of Jefferson and John Quincy Adams, and the sense of genuine 'self-interest', as well as conscience, in an alert internationalism as exemplified in Woodrow Wilson, F D Roosevelt, Adlai Stevenson and of George Marshall and his memorable 'plan'. Perhaps we should read the business of world peace as a hope for the saner mind of America.

[8]   Though he visited Israel several times to fulfil art commissions, whether Jewish, Christian or 'secular', he pointedly refrained from forsaking his beloved abode in Saint-Paul-de-Vence. The line comes in a poem he wrote—as he often did—to accompany a painting, i.e. 'The Soul in the City' (1945).

This long-running and vexing impasse between Arabism and Islam on the one hand and the West with Zionism on the other rankles in a much wider context of mutual suspicion. All is caught in a strange paradox, as if of 'love and hate'. In the East there is envy wed to emulation of the West. The sophistication of techniques is at once admired and coveted. Muslim violence learns and employs the skills of science in a strategy of subtle politics, well versed also in the manipulation of highly technical finance. Things phenomenally 'Western' reproduce themselves, as remarkably in Dubai, where a skyscraper capitalism is thoroughly at home.

Despite areas of desperate poverty in segments of Muslim society in Asia and Africa, Arab Islam is well aware of the vulnerable dependence on its oil of the Western economy and thus of its culture of incessant mobility. Hence the American urge to diminish that dependence and, in turn, to resist measures against 'global warming' that jeopardise both the culture and the calculations of the economy. The conservation—if we may so speak—of super-power is vital to its ongoing relevance and deployment. If its self-sufficiency is thus at risk from factors that turn crucially on attitudes elsewhere, then its equanimity is the more distressed.

Did the old English word 'machinations' have its sinister relevance from theatrical devices—trapdoors, screens, hidden artifices—which could engineer sudden denouement, create havoc or abort all rational action by sheer contrivances and conspiracy? Such a *Deus ex machina* might intrigue the audience but could hardly commend the plot to their intelligence or meaning for their decision. Nor would they be 'seeing their own image'—as Hamlet required of his players—unless perhaps of their innate duplicity, a rascality they might acknowledge as their own.

There is much that is currently apt for West and East in this analogy. 'Machinations', if not present, are everywhere suspected. Islam, many Westerners would want to say, is 'not to be trusted'—suspect, wayward, irascible and dubious. From some Islam westward the distrust is reciprocated. There is 'bad faith' in Washington. The West presents a sinister face of which we must beware.

The crippling presence of this malaise we have seen in earlier chapters as it clusters—even festers—around Muslim presence in diasporas. Indian Hindus must suspect Indian Muslims (depending on which is noun and which is adjective) since Islam created its Pakistan on the proposition that Muslims could never be authentic outside Islamic statehood. If majority Hindu rule, therefore, de-Islamises them how can they be loyal subjects? That latent matter apart, what of Muslims in Chicago, London or Madrid? How far are they *bona fide* in Marseilles or Amsterdam? The question is no mere matter of goodwill. For, as some interpretations stand—and the Qur'an in part might sustain—the holy Shari'ah ordains that resident Muslims inside *Dar al-Harb* ought either to leave it forthwith or work inside it to Islamise its power structure.

We see on every hand and have earlier noted, how the issue is double-edged. Tolerance by a generous good-will that welcomes the 'other' may be exploited by that which decries and flouts it. If attitudes, so fearing, harden towards rejection or isolation, the *bona fide* sort are the more betrayed, while the enmity-carriers and plotters are the more motivated for their conspiracy against their setting as exiles.

The cycle can only not be 'vicious' if the tolerance can take up the Islamic crux and go beyond openness of heart into mental appreciation of the challenge to Islam as, in measure, its own. That challenge is no less than a repeal of the Shari'ah or an 'abrogation' of the *Dar al-Harb* idea so that Islam passes back to the ethos of its Meccan definition.[9] The issue goes that deep. Thus it is idle—or worse—to opine: 'We have no problem with immigrants as residents. Our tolerance is axiomatic.' It must also be perceptive and—as may be within its power—co-operative with the 'good, the sound' Muslim's inner struggle over the very heritage of the Prophet's bifurcated story.

This 'good faith' issue between two parties plainly extends world-wide in something of the same terms as in diasporas. For both faiths—and all—are in diasporas within each other in many multi-racial nationhoods, however disparate in number and incidence.

In truth what is the theme of Muslim diasporas is worldwide across the continents. Is *Dar al-Islam* within this global world an aggressive entity set to politicise that world in its own terms? Or is it a religio-ethical, social expression of humanity co-existing and co-activating the public scene, the global economies, the ecumenical reality? *Dar al-Islam* could truly be either of these, but decision must turn on a present

---

[9] That point at issue between the ethos of Mecca and the armed thrust of Medina is present throughout. Any *Dar al-Islam* in the first existed only as the aegis of a preached truth prior to the Hijrah, which—some would say—alone brought any *Dar al-Islam* into being based on physical success. Of course, what should obtain with Islam in minority status did not then exist, except as fortitude under Quraishi persecution. It is the physical-territorial concept of *Dar al-Islam* (and its anti-thesis *Dar al-Harb* as not Islam, even though witness is there) which sets the current problem.

assessment of those two founding cities, Mecca and Medina, as to whether Islam is a message or a regime, and its Muhammad a preacher with *balagh* or a presiding leader with an army. Comparably, is *Jihad*, that much interpreted 'endeavour for Allah', an inward struggle for personal integrity as the only commendation of Islam, or a martial enterprise of empire and control?

We have seen aspects of this duality throughout. It is an either/or which may not be baulked, one which a present Islam must resolve, one which Western relations must recognise for what it is in urgency and radical character. Western misgivings will not be honestly laid to rest if its terms are not read in their true guise, either by a Western scholarship that might clarify and heal, or by an Islamic honesty that knows and faces its own dilemma. The point was fully argued in Chapter 11 as to how a religious faith might renounce all power-complex and physical militancy without abandoning inherently political duties. We noted at the end of Chapter 12 how deeply runs the issue of an Islamic tolerance, given and received, offered and enjoyed. There can be no mistaking how deeply it reaches into concepts of religious authority, its due custodians, their 'lay' bearings and their organs of decision. All here is much more than some eager exporting of Western democracy, if such takes no intelligent account of how apt Islamic norms for it might be, how viable in its real world, albeit 'the world of all of us'.

But the 'good faith' of Islam in itself and with this present world is not the only arena of legitimate disquiet. The West has its own 'bad faith' image discernibly presented, all malice aforethought apart—to the 'Easts' of the world. There is no need to recite the familiar catalogue—pre-emptive thoughts, invasive war, faulty dossiers of suspect plots elsewhere, manipulation of interest, rogue-ising of states, and multiple economic imbalance or exploitation.

The scenario is not helped by obfuscation and attempts to condone or deny its incidence. The 'oil factor' in the terms we noted besets all reckonings and mars their estimating. What does the USA signify by its military presence in Iraq? Policy two decades ago or more used Iraq as a potential shield against Khomeini-style revolution from Iran. Now the dice are differently loaded. The debate, currently, about Iran's intentions around nuclear power would be more appropriate if the Middle East was a nuclear-free zone, whereas Israel at its heart is a foremost nuclear power in competence if not in size.

Western power is ostensibly in Iraq until its presence succeeds in achieving the emergence of an Iraqi democracy in adequate national control. How attainable is that objective, the less so while American presence itself impedes the process? Even after ostensible withdrawal, will the USA factor remain to moderate the tensions between disparate elements in the Iraqi scene, whether 'federal' or 'unitary'. Such a continuity may well persist in the form of a highly inflated embassy-presence and the occupancy of permanent military bases. Any future seems likely to be loaded with ambiguities, tending to Western guile and Iraqi disquiet and suspicion.

Still deeper mystification abides in the controls the American 'Consul', Paul Bremer, decreed over Iraq's agronomy or agriculture. Those multi-national purveyors of seed or other monopolies—Monsanto and Synegia—with their suspiciously close liaison with the highest levels of American government, virtually control Iraq's productivity. Other large companies, like Bechtel and Halliburton, promise to dominate sundry other aspects of the local economy, so that Iraqis, whatever their political democracy, will hardly be masters of their own economies. US companies have taken over with effect for years ahead. Over a hundred 'orders' have been promulgated to provide legality(?) for American exploitation of the domestic economy of a 'liberated' Iraq. Trade unions are no less affected than the Central Bank. It is hard for a watching world, unless kept oblivious of these things, to take assurances of American 'good faith' with other than deep scepticism.

Thus the suspicions across the grim divide accentuate its mutual forfeiture of the healing factors. These become the harder to seek, while the more obvious to identify. Meanwhile, an acute shape of the menace in Islam has come home with fresh alarm to Londoners. There is an exasperating cunning in attack on public transport, as Madrid learned earlier. It poses F D Roosevelt's 'fear of fear' formula, leaving a nation sharing the trauma of 'not fearing fear', with sufficient resolve to defeat the strategy, that strategy meanwhile kindling anew the abiding problem of 'containing' the inward Islamic elements.[10]

---

[10] 'Containing' here in an obvious double sense of having them present in their citizen integrity as a thing of trust both ways, and dealing with the danger from such 'domestic' sources of subversion, 'nationals' travelling with British passports to visit Al-Qa'idah elements and the 'human right' to do so and freely to return. The American 'privatisation' of Iraqi resources was outlined in The (London) Times, 12 August 2005.

How far can any society remain a 'host community' in a positive, non-inferiorising sense of a doubtful term, when it finds to its horror that the perpetrators are 'home grown'.[11] There is then likely to be a paralysing gloom about the policy of peaceful integration, a fear of the failure of the 'multi-cultural' ambition, and perplexity about what the 'text' of Islam really is. Thus the problem we have analysed is the more embedded.

In this situation, long range advocacy of 'a new reformation in Islam', by would-be mentors like the novelist Salman Rushdie, seem impossibly futurist, or vitiated by his earlier, trivially malevolent, sallies against the Qur'an and its devotees.[12] When popular appeals multiply, in the wake of the attacks, for 'moderate' Muslims to condemn them, there is the damaging implication that they do not already do so or that their compliance ought to be unnecessary. There is unhappy innuendo either way. Yet the popular reaction has its deep psychic anxieties from Islam in action.

Something of the same complex attends governmental efforts to bring Muslims into constructive debate about a civic role. Unless all sides are alert to the whole nature of the current crisis in the very definition of Islam, Muslim participants will, somehow, be participating as if that crisis were 'not on the table'. Their allegiance to Britain has at sometime to resolve it, or their dual allegiance—Muslim and civic—is equivocal.[13] Meanwhile, there are the wounds, the griefs, the anxieties, the lurking intimidation, of private citizens in the daily scene.

But is all a 'clash of civilisations,' in that either has its means of guidance, its transcendent reference, obscure at times, or faltering, as these may be? Is it not rather a 'clash of wrongs'? 'It was their own selves they wronged' is a frequent Quranic comment on the pagans, which could by extension, be charged against Muslims via the root concept

---

[11] 'Host community'—though true story-wise—may be a usage to avoid, lest 'guest status' be somehow 'belonging less validly'.

[12] He writes in this vein from time to time, despite having alienated even those most likely to take his 'reformist' insights. There is an academic remoteness around some of them, quite different from the earlier pointedness of his bitter satire. See also p. 186, note 21.

[13] Its being 'dual' is aptly caught in the debate about descriptives, e.g. 'British Muslims' or 'Muslim/British'. Or, in other terms, can Islam be also 'civic religion', in sharing itself in citizenry with any other faith-people and the 'non-religious'?

of *zulm al-nafs*.[14] There is a deep wrongdoing of the self against the self, the violation of its own proper mind, as a 'tyranny' upon its legitimate conscience, the self-liability we studied as 'the whole point of the secular'. Whatever the religious shape of liturgy or law, this is the fundamental violation of their meaning, the travesty of their authority.

What, then—if we may so speak—is the current *Zulm al-Gharb*, 'the wrong in the West', and what the *Zulm al-Islam*, 'the wronging of Islam'? Positively, in either case, the one clue to *zulm's* defeat is the quest for integrity. It is the search for that 'sincerity' which, as noted elsewhere, came in presidential warning about America being a 'traitor to her own spirit'. A tradition has a vigilance for its own betrayal. It needs to be in play against all the blandishments of that 'evil whisperer' of Chapter 4, the cunning manipulator of the seductive pre-possessions of power, of power that thinks itself unlimited. The New England poetess, Emily Dickinson, captured this temptation to forego integrity when she wrote, mockingly:

> 'Tell the Truth, but tell it slant—
> Success in circuit lies ...'[15]

We have seen amply circuitous 'foreign policy' on Western part in recent years and Muslims have not been re-assured. But should they expect to be, when so much on their part—or on the part of the violent some of them—has had the venomous, enmity-breeding character dramatised on September 11 2001?

We have studied the full shape of the inner crisis in the liability of Islam, not only for its image, but for the criteria by which it must come clean about itself. That the question, in practice, though not in essence, is wide open is not in doubt.

---

[14] The *zulm* root, verb, noun, derivatives is very frequent and denotes every kind of violation of the good, the honest and the just, e.g. tyranny, exploitation, extortion, bribery, injustice. 'It was their own selves they wronged' is a refrain whether about idolators, miscreants, the envious or the liars. It is perhaps the closest the Qur'an comes to the sense of 'wrong' as what I am, more deeply than what I do.

[15] No. 1129 in *The Poems of Emily Dickinson*, ed. T H Johnson, Cambridge, Mass., 1951. She was not, in context, referring to media manipulation or the craft of 'spin' and 'economy with the truth', but to truth's own sunlight being too much for human eyes unless 'shadowed'. Re 'presidential warning', see Introduction, p. 7, note 6.

There is one concept, rooted in the Qur'an to which hope may still appeal and Muslim counsels invoke. It is the religious virtue of *ikhlas*. The phrases *mukhlisin lahu al-din* or *'ibada Allah al-mukhlisin* occur some sixteen times—'Sincere before Him', 'God's sincere servants'. Sincerity is the attribute that belongs essentially to relation with Allah ever the 'seer of the unseen'. The root meaning is of what is 'pure', 'unadulterated', and therefore, 'genuine'. The noun, which does not occur in the Qur'an (the concrete practice of the participle has the stress) describes a 'loyal attachment', 'a frank devotion', that is free from subterfuge and given only to candour and honesty. Notably Surah 12.54 in the story of Joseph in Egypt, Pharaoh uses the derivative verb *astakhlishu*. He wants Joseph to be summoned to his presence 'that he may enlist' Joseph to become the trustee of his Pharaonic will.

As a concept of divine relation on our human part, this *ikhlas* is a very far cry from the deceit, the subversive conspiracy, in Allah's Name, that move the bombers, unless by a perverse esteem of Allah as never 'exalted above all they associate.'

Whether Islamic *ikhlas* comes to its salvation in and through the present *zulm al-nafs al-Islami* turns on the issue with which we have laboured throughout in reading its own genius.

But, as with the integrity tradition of the West, all rests with the will to be 'sincere before God'. 'Clash of Civilisations' can take us only to futility and gloom. A 'Concern over Wrongs' might bring us to know the truth of ourselves and turn that truth to our deliverance by its very telling of the shame.

# GLOSSARY

### NOTE

The ' [open quote mark] and ' [closing quote mark] characters denote the *'ain* and *hamza* consonants. Heavy/velarised consonants and vowel lengths are not distinguished. 'Qur'an' is acceptable spelling. (Koran should have gone the way of such ill-usings like 'Mahomet' long ago.)

The final, though silent, *h* in words like *sirah* and *ghaflah* is retained to prevent confusion with words like *ikraha* or *dhikra* which lack it.

The use of italicised *islam* (small initial *i*) is vital for distinction from the structured, institutional Islam of history and culture. It denotes a long preceding inward quality of faith which can still be discerned differently from the 'established' religion with its contrasted *Dars* of true regime and *harb*. The same deep distinction extends into *muslim* and Muslim for the same reason.

| | |
|---|---|
| *'abd* | servant, responsive to the Rabb or 'sovereign' reality of Allah. Hence its frequency, 'possessed by' the divine Names, as in 'Abd al-Latif. |
| *akbar* | grammatically the comparative from the root 'to be great' and operatively the superlative. Yet it is neither, since Allah can come into no such likening. Leaves open the vital question: In what does 'greatness' consists, since no 'reading' can surpass it? |
| *asbab* | with *al-nuzul*, the points in time with which incidence of passages in the Qur'an coincided, hence called 'occasions', but only such in that temporal, never 'causative', sense |
| *Asma'* | the Names of Allah by which He is denoted, not described. Many of the traditional 99 are Quranic. |

*ayah,*

(pl. *ayat*)  denote the 'verses' of the Qur'an but more, the tokens or indices
in nature, in time and place, by which the attention of the alert
is drawn to the evidences—and invitations—of divine purpose,
evoking and enabling the trusteeship with them of humankind.
The basis both of science and, potentially, a sacramental world.

*balagh*  the original 'message' or 'preaching' of Islam in Mecca to which
Muhammad was explicitly and strictly confined, until the Hijrah
brought a different *jihad*. Islam as essentially a persuasive, non-
coercive, faith.

*Bismillah*  the inclusive confession that invokes Allah as ever, as its sequence
*Al-Rahman al-Rahim* runs.

*Dar al-Islam*

The realm, or rule, of Islamic faith and power in contrast to *Dar
al-Harb*, the realm of not-yet-Islam due—whether by word or
otherwise—to be brought into it.

*Da'wah*  the 'call' or invitation to Islam. Hence its missionary propagation
world-wide.

*dhikr* and

*dhikra*  denote the Qur'an as the supreme 'reminder' to humans from
God, thus exciting and requiring their responsive 'minding'
of its meaning and claim. Also denote the Sufi-discipline of
recollection.

*dhimmi*  denotes the status of tolerated minorities inside *Dar al-Islam*,
allowed personal law and religious liturgies under strict
conditions of political non-entity. A precarious and revocable
status but acknowledging a measure of 'culture diversity'.

*Al-Fatihah*  the opening Surah of the Qur'an with its seven verses for ever
recitable and enshrining the deep plea—and temper—of Islam
at prayer.

*fatwa*  a legal opinion, delivered by a competent legist on whose status
or repute its writ or obligatoriness will depend, where sources
or warrant are in dispute.

*fitnah*  what tries and, therefore, tests the mettle of believers. In the
Qur'an the term undergoes a very significant evolution. Under
persecution in Mecca it denotes the 'testing' of a minority.
When conflict ensued *fitnah* lay in any reluctance to fight out of
fear to die or leave orphans and widows. Finally, when Islam is

triumphant, *fitnah* is the subversive conspiracy of opponent and 'hypocrites'.

*Al-Ghaib*   Allah as the Knower of 'the hidden', impenetrable transcendence *per se*, the mystery of things unknown and what they hold of judgement.

*ghaflah*   that negligence and culpable unconcern which the damned woefully acknowledge in deploring the guilt it has drawn upon them.

*Haram*   an inviolate shrine within which things which it renders 'obscene' are banned. Mecca and Medina are the *Haramain*, the two hallowed enclosures of supreme sanctity.

*hasbuna Allah*
Allah as 'sufficient,' or 'adequate.' A cry or trust and confidence in the enabling reality of God.

*hisab*   the reckoning of the Last Day, the ultimate 'accounting', the verdict on one's mortal span.

*hudud*   the limits, not to be crossed or defied, explicit in Islam's 'enjoining the good and forbidding the evil', in a moral structure able to rely on precept and prohibition.

*Ijma'*   the concept of community consensus by which Islamic things may be moulded by collective mind as a source of law and guidance so long as 'not repugnant' to the Qur'an. Based on a tradition in which Muhammad was sure 'his people would never converge on an error.' Can it sustain the dictum: '*islam* is what Muslims say it is'?

*Ijtihad*   the necessary initiatives by which, in any collective, any consensus comes to birth by pioneers. There is much debate around who are qualified to be these. Vital questions about authority, its sources and its practice makes *Ijtihad* a crucial theme between 'conservers' who suspect it and 'changers' who invoke it as their right.

*ikhlas*   sincerity, the vital quality of the honest believer, the quality of 'good faith' in a context where *nifaq* or hypocrisy menaces both faith and society.

*ikraha*   the making 'over-riding' of religious claim, so that its presence or its preaching exert a 'detestable' pressure. According to Surah

2.256 there is (ought not to be?) such in *Din*, or 'religion.' Usually translated 'compulsion', it could be the safeguard of a genuine religious tolerance but the wiles of authority and dogma conspire to erode, if not cancel, the precept.

*Jihad*      root meaning 'endeavour' or 'exertion in a calling'. If 'inner' it could be a personal discipline of religious devotion and self-control. Otherwise it readily develops into the concept of vigorous—even militant—faith-propagation, quite nullifying the preceding entry here, as invoked by so-called 'terrorists'.

*Jahannam*    the most frequent of the several terms in the Qur'an for the place of eternal damnation, the abode of the lost after the verdict of the 'scales'.

*Jahiliyyah*   the state of 'ignorance' the Qur'an sees as descriptive of Arabian society before the advent of Islam. It denotes not merely lack of truth, but a wild uncouthness accompanying it in 'pagan' behaviour and practices, like infanticide. The condition the coming of Islam terminated, though some still read it in cotemporary Muslim living.

*Ka'bah*    the cube-shaped structure at the heart of the Haram at Mecca, around which is the pilgrimage ritual of circumambulation, as at the very navel of the earth. The hub of the universal axis of Islamic *Salat* and *Hajj*.

*khaliqah*   the human as the creature-custodian of the created cosmos, with the all-important creaturehood that makes our dignity as addressees of the prophet-messengers that dignity directs. Differs in its *q* from the same word with an *f*, i.e. *khalifah* as earth-trustee.

*khilafah*   the 'name of the doing' for which *khalifah* (above) is 'the name of the doer'. Identical with the Biblical 'dominion', it denotes the all important theme of the human vocation ever 'over nature' because—in that very warrant—always 'under Allah'. Our crucial sub-sovereignty in the intelligence-responsive order of this world. The crux alike of current technology and moral meaning.

*kufr*    from the root to 'cover' and so 'disavow', *kufr* is the total 'denial' of Allah, an 'atheism' both of disbelief and conduct. Significantly, it is the antonym of *shukr* or 'gratitude'. *Kufr* both defies and disdains divine reality.

*la 'alla*     the very frequent particle in the Qur'an, what Thomas Carlyle called 'the grand perhaps', governing numerous verbs about 'caring', 'seeing', 'appreciating', 'musing on' things in phenomena around us . Responsive to *ayat*, and the ever open question of human percipience, scientific, economic, social and spiritual.

*libas*     a term in Surah 2.187 where, in the context of sexual intercourse, limbs of either party are said to be a 'covering' for each other. Does it point to almost a sacramental experience in which the physical enshrines—in modesty and tenderness (also enjoined here)—the spiritual intimacy?

*marad*     a not infrequent analogy—as 'sickness' or 'disease'—of the condition of 'unbelievers'. Does it derive from a note of the Biblical Jeremiah (17.9)? It might point to a less judgemental, more gentle, attitude to human sin and wrong, while abating nothing of their 'seriousness'.

*Malik*     one of the three words for Allah in Surah 114, divine sovereignty, however measured.

*masir*     the becoming or destiny which persons are steadily accumulating by what they 'send on' into final reckoning.

*mansak*     the ritual, or liturgical form, of religious devotion. Such ceremonial may be diversified as peoples are.

*millah*     a community, like that of Abraham, by which faith is attested in conduct and loyalty, linked closely with *dhimmi* status of 'tolerated' folk-identity.

*minbar*     the mosque pulpit with all its awesome prestige.

*muhajir*     an emigrant, one who made the Hijrah from Mecca to Medina in 622, year 1 AH, adapted more recently to denote a violent militant in that type *jihad*

*mushrik*     a perpetrator of *shirk*, i.e. one who 'associates' idols, demons, powers etc., with Allah, whether by act, or claim, or credence, or implication, so as to violate the divine Oneness.

*mutashabihah* (sing.)
    a resemblance implied or borrowed, a metaphor or similitude, to be distinguished in the Qur'an from a *muhkamah*, a categorical statement that avoids all allusive allegory.

*naskh*     abrogation, whereby an earlier verse or ruling in the Qur'an is said to be over-ridden by a later one. Hence *nasikh*, the abrogator, and *mansukh*, the abrogated. It is now sometimes proposed that there can be 'abrogation' of later by earlier, in the interest of an exclusively Meccan, i.e. a de-militarised Islam.

*nifaq*  the 'hypocrisy', or merely feigned allegiance which some adopted in subterfuge when Islam was victorious, whether out of prudence or malice. Hence *munafiqun*.

*niyyah*  'intention', or focus of mind as a prelude to ritual acts in Islam.

*Qiblah*  the point, in and as Mecca, to which all Muslim prayer and piety are directed, as marked by the *mihrab*, or niche in the mosque. Also the way-taking of pilgrimage thither. Islam's original, when only in Mecca, was Jerusalem.

*Qiyas*  a source of Islamic law, whereby the duly qualified may argue the extension of an existing provision or ruling, to include also—by analogy—another instance of its intention, even if the detail of that instance was not explicitly included before.

*Rabb al-'Alamin*
Allah, as 'Lord of the worlds' (pl.)—these being the numerous 'items' within the universe of time and place, the heavens and the earth, cultures, events, phenomena and meanings.

*Al-Rahim*  the second divine Name in the *Bismillah*, allied with the first, i.e.

*Al-Rahman*
both from the root of *Rahmah*, or 'mercy' as attribute of Allah, the quality He has 'prescribed' upon Himself. There is a clear progression of meaning in the pair, so that first denotes 'mercy' as a divine dimension irrespective of its immediate exercise: the second that quality in actual occasion and employ (cf. abstract justice as a concept and justice done in court). There is a deep theology in this partnering of the twain.

*Rasul*  the defining title of Muhammad as essentially 'apostle' 'the-sent-with-a-message-one'. He is not otherwise denoted in the Qur'an except by synonyms to this one. He has the *risalah*, i.e., what the *Rasul* tells. This in Mecca was strictly his sole vocation.

*Salat*  Islamic ritual prayer as 'performed', never merely 'said'. The first of the 'Pillars' after *Shahadah*.

*Shahadah*  The saying with intention of *la ilaha illa Allah: Muhammadun Rasul-Allah*, the divine Unity and His Apostle.

| | |
|---|---|
| *Shahid* | One sincerely making that *Shahadah*, but also one who is alert and observant of the *ayat* of Allah. Thence derivately a 'martyr' who confesses with life-forfeiture—but where the question is open whether contrived self-forfeiture is authentic martyrdom. |
| *Shekinah* | A term of Hebrew origin but used in the Qur'an to denote the divine covering of protection guarding Muhammad and Abu Bakr during their Hijrah to Medina. |
| *Sibghah* | lit. 'baptism', but when conjoined with Allah would seem to denote those cultically defined as Allah's devotees. |
| *Sirah* | the life-course, or personal career of Muhammad especially during the years of *Tanzil* of the Book. The synchroning of biography and text-incidence is important for exegesis, via *Asbab al-nuzul*. |

*Al-Sirat al-mustaqim*
the 'straight, non-deviating path' of faith and conduct on which *Al-Fatihah* prays to be always led.

| | |
|---|---|
| *shuhh* | gross forms of selfish passion engrossing human souls. |
| *shukr* | the prized virtue of thankfulness and, as such, the antonym of *kufr*, or divine denial. Most humans are thankless folk, callous Allah-ignorers, no less heinous than His deniers. |
| *shura* | the 'counsel' Muslims take with one another, towards some collective mind, whether—initially—tribal or truly communal, understood as 'practice among themselves'. Much is problematic around its actual working, or association with *Ijma'*. |
| *sujud* | the movements of the body at prayer into complete prostration in token of submission before Allah. To such, in respect of the creature human the angels were summoned, in Surah 2.30f. |
| *tadabbur* | that alertness both to nature and the text of the Qur'an to which all mortals are summoned, as opposed to a 'locked' mind or heart. For this the book pleads repeatedly. |
| *Tanzil* | the serial process of 'sending down' of the Qur'an to (or upon) Muhammad in recipience of the accumulating Book during the years of his *Sirah*. |
| *ta'widh* | the seeking of refuge with Allah from the wiles and snares of evil and wrong. |
| *taqiyyah* | a much fraught term in Shi'ah Islam as a 'piety' which |

'conforms' under a Muslim regime of whose Islam it nevertheless inwardly disapproves—a posture nursing the ultimate hope—and duty—of displacing that regime. Hence it acquires, perhaps improperly, the notion of 'dissimulation'. An acquiescence differs from a capitulation.

*taqlid*  the attitude of 'hide-boundness' which appeals to the past and resists 'innovation'—so dubbed reprovingly.

*taqwa*  a definitive Quranic concept of total devotion to faith and conduct, the inner *islam* of reverent fidelity.

*tashbih*  language usage that draws on analogy and metaphor to the potential risk of absolute meanings.

*Tasliyah*  the salutation or celebration of Muhammad in his stature, enjoined on Muslims in the Qur'an in line with such, as Allah's own 'greeting' of the Prophet. Hence the recital at every mention of his name: *Salla Allahu 'alaihi was sallam.*

*Tawhid*  the affirmation of the Unity of Allah, the 'making' of Him One in the singularity of worship and relation.

*Ummah*  the entire community of Islam in *Dar al-Islam*; a modern Arabic term for 'nation' which can be pluralised but the other sense, never. The issue between the two meanings runs deep in contemporary ideology.

*Umm al-Kitab*
lit. 'the Mother of the Book', the eternal Qur'an in heaven, mediated into the Arabic text on earth, via *Tanzil.*

*wahy*  Muhammad's experience of 'inspiration/revelation' in one, by which the Arabic Qur'an was vouchsafed to him and whereby its 'recital' became possible: at once cognisance and utterance, neither without the other.

*Al-Yaqin*  'the certain', the impending reality of final judgement. Hence also the sure incidence of death.

*zaigh*  the deviance of the deviant (and devious) from 'the straight path: the guilt of 'those who go astray' which breathes in the first Surah.

*zann*  the suspicion that corrupts relationships and distorts the truth of things.

*zain*  the 'beautifying' of faith whereby it is 'attractive' to the self and soul of true believers, leading to 'endearment'.

*zawiya*    the corner, or nook, or angle of a mosque in which students gather round a shaikh.

*zulm*    inclusive wrong/wrong-doing, whether political tyranny, social injustice, bribery, corruption—whatever violates truth and good.

*zulm al-nafs*

    'self-wronging' the Qur'an attributes to wrong-doers, flouting and degrading their *khilafah*-status under God. Takes wrong beyond deed and action into inward character.

# QUR'AN CITATIONS

| | | | |
|---|---|---|---|
| Surah 1 | 167 | 4.165 | 175f., 181, |
| Surah 2.2 | 40, 79 | | 183 |
| 2.10 | 101 | 4.172 | 145f., 149 |
| 2.30-31 | 29, 34, 36, 47, | | |
| | 70, 75 | Surah 5.3 | 164 |
| 2.97 | 98 | 5 45 | 155f, 170 |
| 2.107 | 23 | 5.52 | 52 |
| 2.115 | 82 | 5.82 | 172 |
| 2.118 | 101 | 5.105 | 38f., 55 |
| 2.138 | 34f. | 5.112-114 | 122f. |
| 2.140 | 35 | | |
| 2 143 | 82 | Surah 6.5. | 175 |
| 2 148 | 167, 188 | 6.25 | 101 |
| 2:156 | 175 | 6.91 | 99, 151 |
| 2.186 | 99, 152, 153 | 6.107 | 75 |
| 2.187 | 33 | 6.125 | 51 |
| 2.256 | 91, 190 | | |
| | | Surah 7.29-31 | 48, 114, 120 |
| Surah 3.7 | 82f., 101, 103, | 7.172 | 36 |
| | 104 | 7.180 | 84 |
| 3.19 | 112 | 7.200 | 16 |
| 3.33 | 32 | | |
| 3.36 | 23 | Surah 8.53 | 163 |
| 3.85 | 112 | | |
| 3.173 | 183 | Surah 9.59 | 183 |
| | | 9.129 | 148 |
| Surah 4.5 | 33 | | |
| 4.2 | 32 | Surah 10.99 | 164 |
| 4.59 | 155f. | | |
| 4.82 | 95 | Surah 11.12 | 51 |
| 4.128 | 165 | | |

| | | | | | |
|---|---|---|---|---|---|
| Surah | 11.18 | 168 | | 27.40 | 40 |
| | 11.47 | 16 | | 27.73 | 40 |
| | 11.53–54 | 102, 203 | | | |
| | 11.61 | 28, 29 | Surah | 28.88 | 82 |
| Surah, | 12.53–54 | 102, 203 | Surah | 30.31 | 32 |
| Surah | 13.11 | 163 | Surah | 31.112 | 40 |
| | 13.28 | 102 | | | |
| | | | Surah | 33 5 | 101 |
| Surah | 16.93 | 168, 188 | | 33.36 | 23 |
| | | | | 33.40 | 33 |
| Surah | 17 1 | 114, 139f., | | 33.56 | 147 |
| | | 151 | | 33.60 | 103 |
| | 17 37 | 26 | | | |
| | | | Surah | 35.18 | 45 |
| Surah | 19.18 | 16 | | | |
| | | | Surah | 36.9 | 156 |
| Surah | 20.5 | 152 | | | |
| | | | Surah | 37.5 | 5 |
| Surah | 21.16 | 190 | | 37.94–95, 96 | 66–68, 69 |
| | 21.34 | 169 | | | |
| | 21.87 | 17 | Surah | 38.27 | 156 |
| | 21.105 | 162 | | | |
| | | | Surah | 39.7 | 182 |
| Surah | 22.29–30 | 107, 108 | | 39.22 | 51 |
| | 22.34 | 30 | | 39.67 | 99, 151 |
| | 22.46 | 102, 105 | | | |
| | 22.67 | 30 | Surah | 40.56 | 16 |
| | 22.74 | 99, 151 | | | |
| | | | Surah | 42 8 | 168 |
| Surah | 23.97 | 16 | | 42.10 | 157 |
| | | | | 42.16 | 176 |
| Surah | 24.41 | 49 | | 42.38 | 170, 171 |
| | 24.50 | 103 | | | |
| | 24.116 | 23 | Surah | 44.38 | 190 |
| | 25.60 | 152 | | | |
| | 25.62 | 174 | Surah | 46.14 | 40 |
| | | | | 49.1 | 23, 96, 101 |
| Surah | 26.194 | 98 | | 49.3 | 101 |
| | | | | 49.7 | 120 |
| Surah | 27.4 | 120 | | 49.13–14 | 33, 10l |

| | | | |
|---|---|---|---|
| Surah 50.37 | 94f., 102, 105 | 73.10 | 156 |
| 50.39 | 5 | | |
| | | Surah 75.2 | 102 |
| Surah 55.17 | 5 | 75.31–37 | 66, 67, 68 |
| Surah 56.58 | 33 | Surah 76.9 | 174 |
| 56.60 | 11 | 76.24 | 75 |
| Surah 57.16 | 101 | Surah 77 whole | 83 |
| 57.25 | 170 | | |
| 57.27 | 72 | Surah 81.24 | 74 |
| Surah 58.22 | 101 | Surah 85.9 | 23 |
| Surah 59.16 | 40 | Surah 89.27 | 102 |
| 59.23 | 23 | | |
| | | Surah 90 | 110 |
| Surah 64.12 | 12 | | |
| 64.18 | 76 | Surah 94.1 | 51 |
| Surah 70.11 | 11 | Surah 106.2 | 105, 141 |
| 70.40 | 5 | | |
| | | Surah 107.5 | 48 |
| Surah 72.18 | 114 | | |
| 72.23 | 23 | Surah 112.1–4 | 146 |
| Surah 73.5 | 78 | Surah 113whole | 16 |

# BIBLICAL REFERENCES

| OLD TESTAMENT | | | NEW TESTAMENT | | |
|---|---|---|---|---|---|
| Genesis | 2.19–20 | 36 | Matthew | 11.9 | 181 |
| | 3.8–9 | 191 | | 27.36 | 130 |
| Exodus | 3.10. | 128 | | 28.31 | 135 |
| | 3.14 | 181 | Luke | 9.31 | 129 |
| Numbers | 6.25–26 | 83 | | 12.56 | 35 |
| Psalms | 2.7 | 147 | | 22.15 | 130 |
| | 24.4 | 171 | | 24.17 | 132 |
| | 32.1 | 108 | John | 1.1 | 80 |
| | 37.29 | 162 | | 6.32f. | 127 |
| | 40.1 | 54 | | 21.16–17 | 122 |
| | 73.25 | 17 | Acts | 17.16–33 | 153 |
| | 76.1 | 181 | | 20.28 | 122 |
| | 80.1 | 122 | Romans | 5.8 | 90 |
| | 103.1 | 50 | | 7.24 | 54 |
| | 115.4–8 | 70 | | 15.5 | 15 |
| Proverbs | 23.25 | 96 | | 15.13 | 15 |
| Isaiah | 17.9 | 88 | 1 Corinthians | 2.16 | 157 |
| | 181.71 | .128 | | 10.11 | 131 |
| | 44.9–17 | 70 | 2 Corinthians | 4.5 | 60 |
| | 52.6–7 | 181 | | 9.8 | 183 |
| | 53.1–6 | 11, 131, 147 | Philippians | 2.5–8 | 144f., |
| | 60.13 | 128 | | | 149, 151 |
| Jeremiah | 17.9 | 103 | 1 Timothy | 1.15 | 15 |
| Amos | 2.4f. | 60 | Hebrews | 5.8 | 149 |
| | 9.7 | 18 | 1 Peter | 1.3 | 15 |
| Micah | 4.1–4 | 188 | 2 Peter | 1.5–7 | 56 |
| Malachi | 1.11 | 128 | 1 John | 3.19 | 102 |
| | | | Revelation | 3.20 | 133 |

# INDEX OF THEMES

## A

abeyance of the human, in *Tanzil* 97
abnegation 60
abrogation 164
—in reverse? 164f.
absence, divine 74
absolutism 75, 90
absurdity 165
accountability, human   180
acculturation 112
activism 60, 72, 92
addressees of God 17, 29, 30, 182
adequacy 116, 131, 137, 181, 183, 184
—of the New Testament 149
Adoptionism 146
advertising 46, 64, 70
agency with words 143, 147
aggression, Western 193, 194
agnosticism 40, 46, 95, 158
—religious cause of 42
agronomy 126
alienation, mutual 19, 58, 60, 65, 84, 90,
    105, 167, 194
aliens, making of 84, 85, 112, 166
Almighty, the 71 (see also: omnipotence)
anathemas 92, 93, 122, 123, 139
analogy 15, 67, 77, 81, 82, 84, 103, 112,
    113, 148, 189
—of clay 70
—of Mecca for today 160
—of feudal system 178f.
analysis, linguistic 41, 74, 86, 89
angels and humans 55
anger 3, 92, 105

—divine 185
animal sacrifice 108f.
anointing of Jesus 143 (see also:
    Messiahship)
answerable God, an 177 (see also: liability
    divine)
anti-criminal action 6f., 199
antipathy 6, 135, 186, 194
anti-Semitism 59
apostolicity, in Muhammad, theory of
    96, 97
architecture 119, 120
argument against God 176f., 183
armed conflict. Post-Hijrah 60 (see also:
    *Jihad*)
arrogance, alleged Western 92
art 56, 107f., 111, 113, 118, 119, 120
assessments of Islam 188, 189
asceticism 60, 71, 72
astigmatism, re , servant, and , son, 165,
    166
atheisms 30, 55, 166, 180, 182
—an 'atheism' in Christianity 182
—and 'atheism' in Islam 182
—as ingratitude 39, 40 (see also: *kufr* and
    *shukr*)
authority, religious 21, 22, 23, 42, 58, 79,
    117, 118, 155, 168
—practitioners of 161, 162, 169
autonomy, human 90, 183 (see also:
    *khilafah*)
avarice 165
aversion 152
awareness, of generations 93, 94

awe, religious 29, 44, 56, 88, 101, 190

## B

baptism 125

baptism of God, , the 34f.

becoming, our 45, 60 (see also: *masir*)

begotten, , meaning of 146, 147, 148

being-in-doing 34, 45, 48, 61, 71, 72

—divinely 186

believing in belief 55, 86, 153 (see also: unbelievers)

—via ritual 108, 111

beliefs, plural 189, 190 (see also Wilfred Smith)

belligerence 7, 9, 10, 11, 44, 90, 91 (see also: power)

beloved, , the 150 (see also: Christology)

bigotries 9, 58

birth, no option situation 35, 45, 48, 52, 68

blasphemy 66, 84

body, the —as a mosque 48

bond with humans, the divine 152

boredom 42, 43, 45, 46, 95

bosoms of men, 49, 50f., 62, 77, 96 (see also: whisperer)

bounds, setting of 53 (see also: *hudud*)

burden-bearing 9, 78 (see also: vicarious)

burden of faith, the 78, 89, 91, 100, 177

## C

caliphate, the human 19, 29, 35, 41, 45, 48, 52, 53, 68, 70, 71, 104, 117, 138, 156, 162, 175, 176 (see also: *khilafah*)

—inclusive of faith issues? 117

calligraphy 89, 100, 114

capacity in revelation 99, 100

caravans of Mecca 141

case-making against Allah 176, 177, 179

Catholicism 166,

celebration, , the table, 126, 127

certainty, right, wrong kind 84, 85, 86, 87, 89

Christ event, the 129, 130, 131, 134

Christianity 32, 34, 48, 49, 65, 74, 89, 90, 124, 135, 147, 155, 157, 185, 189

—in contrast to Islam 74 (see also: two theisms)

—and Islamic relation 122f.

Christology 86, 144 (see also: Messiahship)

Church, dimension of 132, 133

—role of 58, 134 (see also: ministry)

citizenry, a moral 168f.

clash of civilizations 5, 26, 118, 161, 162, 185, 201, 203

clash of wrongs 201, 203

coercion, post-Meccan 90f.

co-existence 6, 15, 170, 187, 188, 189, 190, 198

commendation 90, 163

commission, to mission 135

commodity 70

common good. the 165

commonweal, an Islamic? 187

community, human 17, 18, 120, 129

compassion 25, 104, 157

comprehension, of Qur, an 12, 26, 79

compulsion, to belief 11, 75, 90, 91, 92, 190

conceptions 147, 148

confrontation 19, 162 (see also: enmity-making)

conscience 25, 26, 42, 60, 67, 76, 102, 163, 168

consumerism 26, 92, 138, 161, 186, 188

contemporary, being 5, 11, 16, 24, 25, 41, 162, 163

controversy 11, 67, 124, 135f., 143, 144, 151

—over word-significance 79f., 87f.

cosmos, the, as sign-laden 28, 104, 105

courage 55, 103, 109

counsel, of people 170 (see also: *shura*)

covenant theme 33, 35, 126, 195

—as ethnic 142

creation 20, 29, 32, 69, 88, 104, 123, 124, 137, 162, 179, 182, 184, 185

creaturehood. human 11, 13, 17, 27f., 35, 37, 68, 105, 137, 176, 184, 185

—and the, secular 64, 67, 71, 88
—sexuality in 33, 35, 68
crisis, in the West from Islam 20, 21, 193f.
—in Islam 193
Cross, the 129, 143, 149, 147 (see also: redemption)
—for all here and now 134, 140
—sacramentally recalled 130
—theological significance of 130
culture, human via nature 32
cup his Father gave, the 143
cursings, mutual 58, 97
custodians of faith 117, 118
cynicism 171

### D

death 44, 76, 145
—of belief 43
—reward beyond 9 (see also: suicide)
deconstruction 57
delegacy, human 28f., 47, 48
denigration. mutual 46
de-politicising of Islam? 159, 160, 188
deputies, under God 29~47
desire and desirous 52, 53
despair 178, 195
destiny 66, 67 (see also: forwarding)
dialogue 12, 41, 96, 167, 192
—ultimates in 183
diaspora, Islamic 5, 11, 19, 91, 158, 159, 160, 169, 187, 193, 197, 198
dilemma of Husain at Karbala' 59, 172
discipline, pastoral 90, 114
discipline, of ritual acts 108f.
discriminatory Qur'an 90, 91, 92 (see also: unbelievers)
disease, of soul 101, 102, 103 (see also: marad)
disesteem, of Allah 151
distrust, radical 193, 194
distinctiveness, growth of in Islam 142f.
diversity, of peoples and creeds 15, 17, 18, 30, 168, 174, 188, 191
divine and human, open to each other 174f.

doctrine, necessity of 190
dominion, human 12, 24, 69, 70, 73, 75 (see also: khilafah)
doubt over language 78f.
doxology, Quranic 31
drama/dramatist, analogy 148f.
duplicity 197
duty, environmental 183, 191

### E

Earth, the, as habitat 27f., 35, 36, 37, 77, 124, 148, 156, 192
—our table 123f.
ecological crisis 48 (see also: global reality)
education, via messengers 69, 105, 143, 151, 181
egoism, moral 32, 52, 57, 60, 61
egoism, physical 32, 52, 60, 61
elections, vagaries of 171
emotion, in Muhammad 98, 99, 100
emulation, mutual 167, 188
endearment, to faith 96, 120 (see also: zain)
enigmas 30, 89, 153, 179
enmity 16, 159, 89, 104 112, 117, 124, 163, 185, 194, 203
—conflict generated 60, 163, 190
enterprise 69
envy 8, 165
eternity and time 144f., 149
ethics 30, 48, 62, 63, 69, 103, 165, 166
—and eschatology 84, 103
—and politics 155f., 165
—and threshold of religion 41, 56, 165
ethicism apolitical? 168
evil, devious 42, 103, 155
—prohibiting 164, 165 (see also: zulm)
exclusion of God, , the 40, 70, 75
exclusion of human agency in Islam 97
exegesis 69, 83, 100, 101, 132, 133, 140, 148, 149, 152, 193
exhortation 151
exilic Muslims 91, 92, 158, 159, 169
existence, as a gift 35, 46, 68, 105
expectancy about God 131, 146, 150

—how large? 150, 157
experience, Christian 132, 133, 136
experience, human 67f., 77, 194

# F

face of God, the 82
factors in early Islam 9 (see also: *balagh* and Mecca)
faith 40, 42, 56, 113, 177
—itself a new fact 131
—and ritual expression 107f., 111, 120
—and , works, 78f.
fallibility of democracy 22, 171
—of religions 55
fanaticism 9, 62, 91, 115
fascination, deceptive 120, 174
fatalism 66
Fatherhood, divine 137, 141f., 149, 186
—how Sonship reciprocal 143f., 186
fear 14, 58, 200
feeding event in Gospels 126, 127 (see also: *Al-Ma' idah*)
feminism 46, 47
fidelity, issue of 101
finality, a question 11, 116, 142, 144, 169
—of Shari'ah? 170
final truth, proprietors of 185
folk Islam 105
forgiveness-seeking 34
form and spirit 110, 111
forwarding 30, 43, 44, 45
freedom, academic and other 21, 25, 26, 66, 69
frontiers 48
frontiered cultures 174
fundamentalism, 42, 75, 89

# G

gentle faith 190
geography, sacrament of 126, 128, 129 (see also: land)
geometry in Islamic art 119
global reality 18, 25, 48, 93, 95, 112, 137, 163, 174, 185, 189
Glory be! 140, 151

God, as humanly liable 11 (see also: liability and *hujjah , 'ala*)
—as incomparable 85
—never in construct, 15f.
goodwill, quest for 166, 167
government 163, 167, 170, 171
—moral resources of 164f,
grace 40, 52, 56, 71, 145, 191
—self a place for 52
gratitude 29, 39, 40, 42, 99, 182, 183 (see also: *shukr*)
grammar, points of 15, 17, 79, 100, 113
gravitas 92, 191
gravity, centres of in faiths 183f.
greatness, divine—how defined? 137, 175, 184, 185
—in love capacity 180
greed 165
guarantee, no—only trust 182
guidance 46, 49, 53, 71, 137, 151, 178, 184, 186
guilt 56, 57, 71
—Western 192f. (see also: indictment)

# H

habituation, in Islam 112, 113
hardness of heart 55, 101, 103
hate, mutual 9, 14, 20
head-scarf 47
heart in faith, the 80, 81 (see also: *qalb*)
—and its reasonings 94f.
hegemony, religious, issue of 20, 162f.
hereditary Imamate 172
heritage of the righteous 162
history, human 11, 12, 30, 100, 185
—onus of 72, 95, 131, 136, 178, 185
—sacrament of 126, 128, 129, 140
Holy Spirit, the 137
honesty 56, 62, 104, 139, 193, 199, 203
—in case for faith 177, 178
—in education 53
—in history 179
—religious 53
hope, instincts of 15, 77, 109, 203
—of God 15

—the Messianic 130, 131
hospitality of God 129, 130, 139
— of nature 124
host community 201
human nature, crisis in 150
—and Islam 34, 68, 150
humanism in theism 13, 17, 27, 39, 40, 68f., 88, 89, 104, 105, 124
humiliation, in what consists? 143f., 147 (see also: *kenosis*)
humility, proper in man 36, 41, 62, 88
—factors against 90
humour 190, 192
hypocrisy 15, 55, 102, 151

### I

iconoclasm 68, 69
iconography 114
identity, confusion in 42, 44, 193
—and ritual 107, 112
idolatry 67, 68, 69, 70, 99, 158
ignorance 53, 79, 151, 176, 178 (see also: *Jahiliyyah*)
—of clergy 59
illiteracy, Muhammad's? 80, 81, 97
imagery 67, 82, 95, 103, 114, 122, 143 (see also: Surah 3.7)
—of *Jahannam* 83, 84
immaculate Qur'an, the 97
imperialism 161
*imperium*, the human 28, 179
impercipience, in-the West 19
Incarnation 79, 80, 122, 143, 150
—as truth through personality 148
indictment, of the West 25, 26, 46, 62, 92, 178, 179, 193f., 197, 199
individuation, our 52f., 199 (see also: selfhood)
inclusion of Jew/'Gentile' 133
infanticide 70
insanities, religious 8
integration 201
integrity 56, 58, 73, 79, 89, 109, 131, 165, 203
intensity, in ritual 110

intention in religion 48, 51 (see also: *niyyah*)
intercourse, sexual 68
interests, bias of 20
inter-faith discourse 47, 123, 168, 170
inter-humanity? 169, 171
international order 7f., 193
invested with authority, those 155, 161, 169, 170
invocation, of God 36 (see also: *Bismillah*)
—of nature 83
irony 55, 59, 60, 104, 182
—in sacrament 134
—in US history 72, 86
irreligion, fact of 190
*islam*, point in 49, 70, 71, 89, 100 112, 161, 162, 163, 167 169, 170
Islam, as first powerless 10, 90, 198
—in mission 90, 91, 190
—and natural order 71
—peace-seeking? 185
—present crisis in 9, 10, 19, 75, 162, 198, 199
—self-sufficiency of 35, 89, 142
Islam in danger, cry of 92

### J

jealousy, divine? 54, 55, 74
—human 161
jesting Allah, a 40, 190
judgement at the house of God 167
judging by revelation sent 155, 168, 170
—rule, or , wisdom? 188
just—a-religion, formula 158
justice 56, 69, 157
—a critical 170
—social 22, 25

### L

laity and laicisation 21, 118, 122
land factor, the 12, 42, 57, 77, 78f., 95, 103, 113, 144f., 150, 152, 170.
landscape 123, 124, 191
language in faiths 12, 42, 57, 77, 78f., 95,

103, 113, 144f., 150, 152, 170
—common dilemma in 88, 89
— games, in? 41
—heavy Islamic reliance on 80f., 88
—sanity of 41
laughter, lack in Qur'an 190
law 53f., 63, 103, 163, 184
—dilemma of 52, 53, 54, 167
leadership, religious 117, 118
lending our minds out 118
lessons in stones 83 (see also: ruins)
letting God be God 76
liability of God, the human 11, 40, 49, 54, 55, 137, 138, 173, 174, 175
—inclusive, not selective 173, 179, 180
liability, human to God 67f., 153, 154f., 165, 166, 168, 169, 171, 172, 174, 175, 180
liberation 128, 181
liberty, political 160, 169
—dream of 179
life expectancy of Hajj for a Hajji 110
liturgy, forms of 58, 72, 87
living sacrifice, call to 44
locks on hearts, 102, 113
loss of self 39, 41, 43, 45
love 180, 181, 186
—answer to Murdoch 62
—and knowledge 88, 120
—that reconciles 52, 60, 62
—and self-expenditure 52, 60, 62, 137

### M

machinations 197
majorities, duty of 161
man , on the loose 67f.
marriage 32, 33, 47
martyrdom 44
—and suicide? 61, 76
masses, God of the 1, 22 (see also: 'Ali Shari'ati)
mass media 42, 75
—and sexuality 47
meaning 79, 84, 89, 109, 132, 149, 150, 176

—elusiveness of 67
—forfeiture of 67f.
—zeal for 43, 46
measure, of Allah 99, 131, 148f., 151
memory 28, 122f., 131, 133, 140 (see also: *anamnesis*)
—theme in 132
mercy, divine 31, 82
—self-prescribed by Allah 175, 176
—to the worlds 110, 189
Messiahship 11, 132, 133, 143f., 150, 178, 181
—and the Cross 147
Messianic dignity—the issue 144f.
metaphor 67, 81f., 84, 95, 105, 113, 148, 149, 150
mind, a taker-in of things 95f.
minding the Qur, an 94f., 176
ministry, of faith in society 9, 133, 167, 168
—Christian pastoral 122
minorities 21, 159, 160, 161, 164, 198 (see also: *dhimmi*)
miscarriage, human 70 (see also: perversity)
monitoring one' s faith 21, 167
months of truce 187
moral challenge 70
moral theism 181
mortality 13, 45, 134, 135
mosque, role of 111, 113, 114
motion by nexus, analogy 149, 150
music/musician analogy 148, 149, 150
mystery 74, 88, 95
—of evil 177
mysticism 72

### N

Names of Allah, the 82, 84, 85, 86, 152, 181
—casting a spell by 130
nationhoods Palestinian/Israeli 195
nations 17, 18, 92
nation under God, this 157
Nation states 160

nature, as neutral 30, 41, 73 (see also: earth, land, cosmos)
—signs in 31, 83 (see also *ayah* and signs)
nearness, divine 153
negation of God 182 (see also: atheisms)
negative capabilitiy 40
negligence 95 (see also: *ghaflah*)
nomadism 35
nuclear power 163
numinous, the l89, 190
number, no theological category 135, 136, 188

### O

oath-taking 56
obduracy, human 177
—against Muhammad 9, 102
obedience 10, 86, 100, 147, 156
—to Allah and the Prophet 155, 156
oblivion, not the issue in Eucharist 134
obscurantism 9, 58
occasions of the Qur'an 99 (see also: *Asbab al-nuzul*)
—Muhammad's role in 99, 100
omnipotence of God 66, 69, 71, 73, 104
—nearness of 150
—obligation in 175, 176
oneness beyond number 136f.
Oneness of God 116, 182
on-our-own, humans as 180
original love 150 (see also: creation)
original sin, 50f., 65
orphans, in the Qur'an 33

### P

paganism 90, 151, 152, 158, 164, 184
paradise 182
paradox 39, 65, 68, 74, 77, 85, 109,110, 119, 142, 187, 197
—in secular, religion 76
parenthood 33, 35
Passion of Jesus 122, 131, 132, 139, 140
pathos 68, 95, 134, 135
patience, nature of 12, 89, 104, 109, 120

—of God 15, 89
peace, between faiths and cultures 76, 77, 106
—original peace of Islam 10 (see also: Hijrah)
peace, road to in Israel? 196
peace, stability of 7, 34
penitence, pride in 57
peoplehood 27, 31, 89, 142, 174
—in tenancy 27, 34
perception, alert 94, 100, 102, 117, 151 (see also: *tadabbur*)
perjury 56
perplexity 132, 152, 177
personhood 24f., 68, 96, 143, 145
perspective, on humankind 151
persuasion 90, 92, 93
perversity, human 11, 73, 101, 137, 155, 165, 171, 203
—in suicide 76
—in text-reading 82, 101
'pleasure of the Lord' 145, 147, 149
poetry 43, 55, 68, 72, 77, 79, 80, 89, 125
polemic, obtuse 123
political order, the 11, 23, 24, 25, 58, 60, 63, 64, 65, 73, 75, 141, 153, 154, 155f., 164, 167, 171, 199
political non-entities 158 (see also: *dhimmi*)
positive overcoming negative 84, 85, 87, 89, 93
poverty 25, 70, 115, 197
power, role of 73, 90, 91, 153, 154f., 163, 164, 167, 199
—as divinely liable 155f., 164, 170
—Muhammad's role with 10, 60, 90, 91, 163, 171
praise, divine 39, 69
prayer, asking or querying? 152, 153
—postures in 111
preaching, Muhammad's original task 9, 10, 12, 24, 31, 75
prejudice 25, 42, 67, 95, 105, 113, 192
pre-emptive concept, the 198
presence, divine 89

privilege, the human 11, 13, 28f., 35, 45, 46, 48, 49, 104, 140, 171
procreation 30, 32, 33, 35, 46, 69
prophethood 11, 29, 34, 71, 93, 98, 99, 100, 105, 149, 176, 181
—finalised in Muhammad 19, 24
—innocent of power Biblical 168
—*qua* an Amos 59, 60
—sealed, 156 164, 182
—suffering and 129, 130
pulpit, the mosque 115, 116, 117 (see also: *minbar*)
purity, of the heavens 120
purity of heart 51f., 171

### Q
quarrel with Islam? 158
Qur'an, the issues in 9, 74, 81
—exegesis and reader's problems 12, 21, 100
—Muhammad's active role in 98, 99
—a theme between parties see: Quraish
—repugnancy to 116

### R
readership of the Qur'an 99, 100, 101, 105, 113
realism 151
recital of the Qur'an 89, 115, 146 (see also: *tajwid*)
redemption 74, 122.124, 130, 137, 139, 151, 182, 191
—drama of 134
—need for 53, 54
refuge-seeking 16, 17, 26, 94, 185 (see also: *ta'widh*)
reminder 71, 176, 184
repentance 28
relationship of faiths 99, 110 (see also: dialogue)
religion and power 24, 58, 59, 63, 64, 90, 91, 155f., 165, 168
—and rituals 108f.
religions, dismay over 42f., 178
—in original intent 11

—sins of 55, 56
religious studies 118
renewers 167
repoliticising of Islam 161f.
repugnance to the Qur'an, principle of 11, 89, 116, 119, 169
Resurrection faith 132, 144
retaliation 6, 75, 76, 156, 193
retribution 53, 100
revelation 62, 140, 148, 164, 182
—concept of in Qur'an 96, 97, 116
—divergence in 74, 80
— judging by, 155f.
—occasions of 163
—scripted 137
rhetoric of the Qur'an 83, 88, 89, 90
risk-taking in faith and witness 89, 91
ritual, role of 107
ruins 100, 105

### S
sacramental, the 13, 28f., 32, 33, 47, 74, 124f., 130, 135, 162, 186
—marriage as 32
sacred, the 40, 185
—and the secular 66f., 70, 71
salutation of Muhammad 150 (see also: *Tasliyah*)
sanity of mind 8, 51, 162
scepticism 15, 46, 55, 167
sciences 25, 41, 73, 77, 118, 170
—and jinn 51
scruples over words 70f.
secular, the—right measures of 11, 29, 30, 31, 40, 66f., 77, 125, 155, 203
secularisation, outright 70, 73, 74, 109, 190
—living with 157, 158
secular statehood 65
security 3, 14, 15, 18
self-approval, tangle of 62, 63
self-criticism of religions 166, 167
self-definition of Islam 19
self-doubt, need for 117
selfishness 38f.

selfhood 38f., 44, 48, 51f., 57, 61, 67f., 165
—in suicide 44, 76
—forfeiture of 46, 52
self-obsession 26, 465113
self-reproach 102
self-responsibility 39f., 48, 51
self-sufficiency of Islam 117, 167
sense experience 79
separation of faith from power 65, 168, 169
separatism 110, 111, 169
servant to God 11, 58, 151
sexuality, human 32, 33, 46, 64
—abstinence during Hajj 108
—the Qur'an and 32, 46
shepherd, the Christian imagery 114, 122
ships and harbours 112
sickness of heart 102, 103, 104
significance of words, in Qur'an 81f., 89
signifiers 86
signs *(ayat)* 28f., 30, 32, 39, 49, 79, 83, 88, 98, 124, 151
—Qur'an and verses as 99, 100
—sex as 32
similitude 83, 85, 103
simplicity as elusive 156
sin, issue of 48
—awareness of 54
sincerity 55, 56, 101, 114, 123 (see also: *Ikhlas*)
—quest for 203
sociology 64, 118
solidarity, human 17
—Islamic 110f., 114
Sonship, divine 137, 143, 144, 146, 147, 149, 186
—love origin of 150
souls are our own 39f.
sovereignty divine 16, 20, 23, 89, 136, 151, 152, 157, 161, 164, 182
—awaiting recognition 174
—and human dominion 27f., 31, 49
—and the political order 23

sperm 68
Spirit, the faithful, 99
Statehood, Islamic 11, 91, 157, 158, 168, 169, 197
subversion of Islam by the West? 158, 160, 192f.
subversion of the West by Islam? 158, 160, 192f.
suffering servant, the 143, 150
—and Sonship 145
sufficiency, of the New Testament 148, 149
suicide 61, 76
suiciding bombers 44, 45, 47, 61, 191
superstition 109
suspicion, mutual 6, 96, 195, 196, 197
—of God 54 (see also: *zann*)
sympathy, as mental duty 86
synagogue sermon, the 132

### T

table from heaven 121, 122f., 130, 132
—nature as 123, 124
technology 7, 25, 35, 42, 73, 75, 106, 118, 162, 185
—and terror 197
temper of mission 89
terrorism, a confused theme 6f.
tether, and the 'secular' in the Qur'an 67f., 73
text and textile 78, 80, 89 (see also: exegesis)
text with biography 99, 100 (see also: *Sirah*)
thanklessness 182
theocracy, never was 23
theology, criteria of 11, 17, 40, 74, 83, 85, 118, 123, 124, 140, 150, 153, 177, 180, 184
—equivocation in 85, 86, 89, 146, 147
things allegorical/categorical, in Qur'an 81f., 103
things reciprocal between God and man 17
time 44, 45, 46, 72

—extemporised 43
— and place factor in Qur'an 101, 126
  (see also: *Asbab al-nuzul*)
—time–world of Qur'an 176
tolerance 158, 160, 198
trade 69, 70
tradition 42, 116, 118
traditionalism 109
tragedy 75, 119, 184
—Shi 'ah at Karbala' 172
transcendence 31, 66, 74, 89.105, 122,
  189, 190
—via the Cross 150
—and the secular 66f.
treachery, fear of 161
tribalism 186, 187
Trinity, the doctrine of 17, 135, 144
—as inter-relation divine 136
trust of the earth as cosmos 35, 39, 68, 70,
  74, 156, 165, 170
truth, sanctions of 9, 119
—age of lost ..., 43
—implanted in Muhammad 142 (see
  also: *mi'raj*)
—and language 78, 81, 82, 83
—through personality 148, 151, 181 (see
  also: Incarnation)
—victim of custodians 58, 59, 62
two realms of Islam 63, 65, 155
two theisms 151f., 186
tyranny 161, 165, 170
—of dogma 161

U

unbelievers 161
—as rejectionist principle 185
understanding, failure in 153, 192, 193
unification under Islam 187
unilateral dominance 91
unitarian issue, the 135f.
unitive state, the 102
unity of God 17, 90, 135, 186
unreality, doses of 42, 43
unselfishness, issue in 38f., 45, 52 (see
  also: egoisms)

usurpers of God 75

V

vehemence religious 75, 89
vested interest against Meccan Islam 90
vicarious suffering 181
victory, Islam's 158, 194
vigilance 51, 58, 62, 157, 177, 203
vindication, divine 184
violence 170, 171, 172, 203
virtue 56
vocabulary, Quranic 90, 144, 152, 153,
  170
vocation, human 29, 45, 93, 105, 170
—and the Ego 61
—of Islam 20, 22, 140
—of Muhammad 140, 141
—of Muslim minority experience 161,
  164
—of prophethood 78, 143, 145, 150
volition, arena of the secular 71
vulnerability 158, 183

W

war. enmity-creating 60, 61, 76, 194
'warden', Muhammad as not 75 (see also:
  Surah 6.107)
warming, global 197
warning 176
wealth in our weal, God' s 182
weapons of mass destruction 14
well-being via ritual 109
wilfulness, human 52, 61, 62, 102, 179
will, divine 63, 73, 88
will to good in persons 165, 166
wills in congruence 149, 150, 161
wisdom 9, 40, 75, 153, 161, 170
witness 89, 137
womanhood, east and west 47
womb, the 68, 82
wonder 41, 42, 83, 88, 190
words, the art of 77, 88
—neglect; of 95
—sense of 78f., 81f., 86
worship, rationale of 11, 16, 25, 30, 34,

67, 70, 71, 83, 87, 88, 116, 152, 162, 182, 184
—and language 85
—prostration in 111, 112
—recession in 157
—shapes of 107f. 122
written-ness, in Islam 115
wrong, nature of 48, 52, 53, 70, 103, 151, 181, 182, 202
—in character beyond deed 54 (see also: *zulm al-nafs*)
—righting of 184

## Z

zeal, mistaken 75
zealotry 168

# INDEX OF NAMES AND TERMS

## A

Aaron 127
'abd 23
'Abd al-Nasir 92
'Abd al-Raziq, 'Ali 22
'Abd al-Sabur, Salah 43
Abraham 33, 34, 35, 68, 69, 70, 112, 114, 128, 142, 195
Abu Bakr 24, 156
Abu-l-Kalam Azad 91
Acton, Lord 63
Adam 36
Adams, John Quincy 7, 196
adoption 146
Adoptionism 146
Afghanistan 193
Africa 25, 47, 173, 197
akbar 89, 184, 185
—how construed? 185'
'Ali 59, 117
alihat (pl.) 15, 18
aliyahs 195
Allah 6, 9, passim
—grammar and 15, 16
—not overtaken 11f. (see also: 'theology')
almsgiving 53 (see also: Zakat)
America 5, 7, 19, 22, 27, 36, 72, 157, 173, 174, 192f., 196, 202
—Episcopal Church in 47
Amerindians 27
Ammon 59
Amos 59, 176
anamnesis 134, 139 (see also: 'Eucharist')

Andrewes, Lancelot 124, 141
apartheid, Judaic 185
apartheid, Islamic 185
Aquinas, Thomas 12
Arabia 51, 64, 66, 85, 110, 127, 141, 158, 163, 175
Arabic 6, 12, 15, 17, 28, 31, 46, 50, 71, 80, 81, 83, 96, 98, 102, 115
—Letters heading Surahs 94
Arabism 26, 169, 186
Asbab al-nuzul 98, 163
Ascension in New Testament 132
—of Muhammad 142 (see also: mi'raj)
Asia 25, 38, 47, 52, 60, 78, 80, 197
Al-'Ashmawi, Muhammad 22
Al-Asma al-Husna 84, 85
Atlantic Ocean 175, 179
ayah (sing.), ayat (pl.) 31, 32, 40, 49, 79, 85, 86, 133, 151 (see also: 'signs')

## B

Ba'ath Regime 8, 19
Badawi, Dr Zaki 91
Baghdad 19
balagh 22, 24, 60, 90, 102, 164, 199
Balfour Declaration, the 94
Bashier, Zakaria 159
Baudelaire. Charles 50, 55
Beatitudes, the 130, 134, 162
Becket, Archbishop Thomas 55, 61
Bechtel 200
Beersheba 174
Beethoven 148
Bible, enmities in 163

*bila kaif* formula 85, 86, 87
Al–Biruni 136
*Bismillah* 63, 84, 152
Black Islam, USA 110
Black Stone, the 111
'bless' and 'blessing', double sense of 174
'the body of Christ' 133
Book of Common Prayer 71
Boorstin, D J 179
Bradley, F H 68
'bread and wine' 87, 116, 122f., 132, 134, 139, 173
Bremer, Paul 199, 200
Britain, Muslims in 201
British Mandate in Palestine 194
Browning, Robert 58, 118, 119, 180, 181
Buber, Martin 129
Buddhism 38, 52, 71, 78
Bush, G W President 14

## C

Cairo 22, 92
California 107
Caliphate, the political 19, 22, 24, 117, 156, 158, 169, 170, 178
Camus, Albert 22, 54, 158
Canaan 187
Capetown 123
Capitulations 20
Caxton, William 173, 174, 175
Central Bank, the 200
Chadwick, Owen 157
Chagall, Marc 196
Christendom 59, 89, 155
'Christ in God, the' 131, 181
Churchill, Winston 136
Constantine 10
Copperfield, David 45
Cuba 45

## D

Damascus 59, 98, 101, 117, 141, 172, 195
Dan 174

*Dar al–Gharb* 21
*Dar al–Harb* 18, 20, 158, 187, 198
*Dar al–Islam* 5, 18, 21, 158, 159, 160, 187, 193, 197
*Dar al–Sulh* 20
David 115, 142, 156, 181
*Da'wah* 84, 190
*Dawlah* 160, 168
Decalogue, the 70, 151, 156
democracy 73, 166, 171, 196, 199
*Demos* 22
Derrida, Jacques 86, 87
*dhikr* 18, 94, 102, 133
*dhikra* 94f., 133
*dhimmi* status 91, 158, 164
Dickens, Charles 45
Dickinson, Emily 32, 57, 202
*Din al-Islam* 158, 159, 168
Donne, John 93
Doughty, C M 15, 51
Dryden, John 22
Dubai 197

## E

East, the 5, 42, 104, 197, 199
Edom 59
Egypt 17, 21, 44, 91, 115, 128, 187, 195
Eightfold Path, the 38, 71
Elisha 101
Eliot, George 134
Eliot, T S 16, 43, 50, 54, 61, 125, 153
—*The Wasteland* 158
Emmaus 132
Ephesus 122
Ethiopia 189
Eucharist, the Christian 114, 122f., 134, 139
Europeans 20, 27, 157, 179, 192, 196
Exodus, the 127, 128, 129, 131, 173, 181
Ezekiel 174, 188

## F

'face of God', the 82, 83, 141
Fanon, Frantz 22
Al–Faruqi, Isma'il 64

'Father, Son and Holy Spirit' 122, 135
Fathers, the founding 157
*Al-Fatihah* 167, 185
*fatwa* 117
Fazlur Rahman 84, 91, 97
Fire, the 23, 83
First World War, the 43
*fitnah* 92, 103
*Foreign Affairs* 5
Foucault, Michel 41
France 86
Frost, Robert 16, 27, 36, 72, 125

### G

Galilee 127
Gaza 44, 59, 141
Genesis 29
'Gentiles' 18, 89, 133, 183, 185
Gethsemane 139, 143, 145, 149, 181, 191
*Al-Ghaib* 74
*ghaflah* 95
'God in Christ' 129, 131, 146, 181, 183
Golan Heights, the 145
Golden Calf, the 177
Gospels, the 126, 127, 132, 134, 149
*Grapes of Wrath, The* 107, 108
Griffiths, Bede 72

### H

Hajj, the 107f.
Hallelujah 17
Halliburton 199, 200
Hammarksjöld, Dag 180
*Haram* 141
Hardy, Thomas 31, 68, 179
*harpagmos* 144
Hasan 117
*hasbuna Allah* 148, 183f., 191
*Hibbet Zion* 195
Hijaz 188
Hijrah 10, 31, 82, 90, 126, 155, 197
Hinduism 52, 113, 120
Hippocratic Oath 104
*hisab* 24

Hodgson, Marshall 74
Holy Sepulchre 196
*homo erectus* 111
Hopkins, Gerard Manley 36
Hosea 173, 195
*hudud* 76
*hujjah* 175f.
Hume, David 63
Huntington, Samuel 5, 20
Husain 59, 117, 172 (see also: Karbala')
Husain, Saddam 19, 193

### I

Ibn Maryam 143
*ihram* 107
*Ijma'* 21, 116, 118, 162
*Ijtihad* 21, 116, 118, 162
*ikhlas* 15, 35, 205
*ikraha* 91
*Ilah al-nas* 15f., 20, 21, 22, 25, 40, 90, 105, 185, 186
—'god of the masses' 21
*imperium* (human) 29 (see also: *khilafah*)
Imran 32
India 91, 169, 197
infanticide 70
International Crime 7
Iqbal, Muhammad 167
Iran 19, 21, 97, 199
Iraq War 8, 193, 195, 199
Ireland 14
Iron (Surah of) 170
'Isa 114, 143
Isaac 142
Isaiah 68, 70, 143
'Islam and the West' formula 5f., 14f., 18, 26, 46, 192f.
*islam* 49, 51, 70, 71 89, 100, 160, 162, 169
Islamic Foundation, Leicester 159
Islamicization of Knowledge 64
*Isra'* 40f., 151
Israel (people) 26, 127
Israel (State) 194, 195
—as nuclear 199

isti'mar 28, 31
itmi'nan 102

## J

Jacob 128
Jahannam 23
Jahiliyyah 53, 60, 79, 175, 178, 184, 186
Jami'ah (mosque as 'gatherer') 111
Jefferson, Thomas 157, 196
Jeffersonians 179
Jerusalem 10, 114, 128, 132, 138, 140, 149, 153, 181, 187
—as first qiblah 82, 132
—Night Journey to 140f.
'Jesting Creator' a? 190
Jesus 17, 54, 57, 60, 107, 140, 177, 184, 182
—in Christhood 80, 86, 143f., 148, 151 (see also; Christology)
Jewry 26, 34, 59, 133, 142, 163, 187
—defined in Ex6dus 128
Jihad 18, 26, 164, 165, 199
jinn 51
Jinnah, Muhammad 'Ali 158
John, Letters of 149
John of Patmos 17
Jordan, State of 195
Joseph 128, 203
Joshua 162, 188
Judaism 166, 185
—and apartheid 185

## K

Ka'bah 10, 111
Kafka, Franz 43, 84, 158
Kant, Immanuel 79, 87, 166
Karbala' 59, 117, 172
Keats, John 40, 51
Kedar, tents of 141
kenosis 144f.
Kenyatta, Jomo 173
Khadijah 141
khalifah 24, 29 (see also: creaturehood and entrustment)
khaliqah 47 (see also: creation)

Khawarij, the 169
Al-Khannas 50f. 55, 61
khilafah 24, 29, 44, 47, 66, 75, 90, 155, 161, 162, 168, 170, 185
Khomeini, Ayatollah 199
King/Crane Enquiry 194
King Lear 124
Kipling, Rudyard 5, 61
kufr 39
Kurios 17

## L

la'alla 31, 99
La ilaha illa Allah 15, 148
Lane, Edward 31, 67
—Arabic Lexicon 67
Larkin, Philip 13, 43, 192
Last Day, the 53, 83, 90, 95
Latin 59
laughter, lack of, in Islam 190
Lawrence, T E 15
League of Nations, the 194
Lennon, John 125
Lewis, C S
lex talionis 6, 187
libas 33, 34
Lincoln, Abraham 18, 157, 171, 173
Lord's Supper 132 (see also: Eucharist)
Luke the evangelist 132
Luqman 40

## M

Mahfuz, Najib 137, 186
—Awlad Hawratina 186
Al-Ma'idah 122f., 138.
Malik al-nas 17, 25
Malachi 117
mansak 30, 169
marad 53, 101, 102, 103
Marshall, George 196
Martha 107
Mary 107 (sister of Martha)
Mary 32 (sister of Aaron)
Marx, Karl 64, 72
Al-Masih 143, 145

*al-masir* 45
Al-Masjid al-Aqsa 114, 140f.
Massachusetts 27, 179
Mecca 10, 12, 24, 26, 35, 60, 80, 96, 107,
  114, 126, 134.141, 142, 149, 152, 160,
  162, 164, 175, 185, 187, 197, 199
Medina 10, 12, 19, 23, 24, 80, 114, 126,
  142, 152, 158, 160, 162, 164, 169, 186,
  197, 199
—Al-Haramain, 'the two sacred sanctuaries
  26
Mediterranean Sea 176, 188
Melville, Herman 173
Messiah 11, 35, 126, 129, 143f., 181
—'a suffering' 143, 144, 178
Meynell, Alice 14, 124, 125
Micah 188
*mihrab* 113
*millah* 34
Milton, John 61
*minbar* 44
'mind of Christ, the' 151
*Mi'raj* 142
Moab 59
monasticism 72
More, Thomas 59
Moriah, Mount 142
Morocco 67
Moses 155, 177
'Mother Church' 59
Mu'awiya 172
Muhammad 5, 9, 12, 15, 21, 53, 72, 75, 97,
  101, 105, 115, 151, 152, 158, 162, 164,
  175, 177, 199
—Biblical associations of 127f.
—as his own 'Constantine' 10
—illiteracy of? 80
—messenger role (see also: *balagh*)
—as orphan 33
—Night Journey of 138, 139f.
—vital role in the Qur'an  97, 98, 99,
  100
*muhqam* 90
*mulhid* 30
*mulk* 23, 36

*munafiqun* 55
Murdoch, Iris 62
—Sovereignty of Good, The  62, 63

**N**

Naaman  101
Nabakov, Vladimir 46
Nabateans 28
Names of Allah 82, 84, 85f.
Napoleon 61, 64, 179
*naskh* 188
Nehemiah, Book of 163
New England 202
Newman, J H 15, 166.
New Testament, The 6, 10, 54, 74, 80, 86,
  89, 122, 129, 133, 134, 135, 140, 142,
  148, 151, 174, 178, 181, 182, 191
—as 'sufficient' 80
New York 107
Nicodemus 127
Niebuhr, Reinhold 179
Nigeria 21, 169
Night Journey, the 140f., 149
*niyyah* 48
Noah 29, 175
Noahid covenant 86, 142

**O**

'Only begotten', meaning of 147, 148,
  149
Ottoman Caliphate 20

**P**

Padwick, C E 16, 150
Pakistan 92, 97, 158, 168.197
Palestinians 59, 194, 195, 196
Papacy, the 20
Paradise 83
Passover 126, 129, 130
Patmos 17
Paul 15, 54, 57, 90, 122, 129, 131, 144,
  145, 151, 153
Pentagon, the 8
Peter 15
—Second Letter of 56

Pharisee 57
Philistines, the 61
Pilgrimage 26, 53, 107f., 134, 160, 185
Pillars of Islam, the 48, 53, 112
'Place of the Name', the 128, 129, 181
Proust, Marcel 19, 43
Psalms, Book of 162

## Q

*Al-Qa'idah* 8, 19, 21, 76, 192, 199
*qalb* 50, 94f.
*Qiblah* 129, 134, 141, 175
Quraish 15, 60, 84, 152, 158, 159, 190, 197
*qutb* 172
Qutb, Sa'id 19, 92

## R

*Rabb al-'Alamin* 89
*Rabb al-nas* 17, 25, 110, 152
Rahbar, Da'ud 69
*Al-Rahim* 84, 152
*Rahmah* 175f.
*Al-Rahman* 8, 152
Ramadan 35, 110, 112
*Rasul* 99, 100f., 149, 156
Reagan, President 8
Red Sea, the 189
refuge-seeking 16
*Risalah* 100
Rome 166
Roosevelt, President F D 14, 196, 200
Rushdie, Salman 42, 189, 201
Russell, Bertrand 166, 167
Russia 169, 173
—as 'evil empire' 8

## S

*sabr* 50
*sadr* 96f.
Said, Edward 20
Sale, George 34
*Salih* 28, 34
*Samad* 146
Samson 44, 61, 163

—*Agonistes* 61
Sartre, Jean-Paul 158
Sayigh, Tawfiq 43
Scripture, Islamic 9, 11, 29, 42, 65, 77, 80, 96, 98, 100, 119, 148, 156
seal of prophethood 116, 164, 182
September 11th 2001 8, 14, 77, 202
Settlements, Israeli policy of 194
*Shahadah* 93, 134, 166, 171, 182
*Shahid* 96f., 101
Shakespeare, William 92, 166
*Al-Shakur* 174
*Shari'ah* 21, 22, 115, 116, 118, 119, 160, 161, 162, 170, 193, 197
Shari'ati, 'Ali 21, 24, 167
*Shekinah* 156
shepherd analogy 22
Shi'ah, the 59, 117, 169, 171, 172, 178
*shirk* 71
Shoah, the 196
*shuhh* 165
*shukr* 39, 182
*shura* 22, 170
*sibghat Allah* 34f.
Sinai 36, 142, 177
*Sirah* 12, 23, 104, 114, 116, 152, 156, 163, 178
—Night Journey in 139f., 142
—significance for the Qur'an 101
*Al-Sirat al-mustaqim* 167
Smith, Wilfred C 189f.
*sobornost* 169
Socrates 12, 17
Solomon 40, 127, 142
Steinbeck, John 107, 108, 111
Stevenson, Adlai 18, 196
Stock Exchange, the 71
Sufism 59, 117
Sunnis 59, 117
Synegia 200
Syria 88

## T

*tadabbur* 12, 79, 95
*Tafsir* 92, 98, 102, 118

*tajwid* 116
Taj Mahal 119
*takbir* 90
*takfir* 90
*Tanzil* 97, 98, 102, 107, 152, 156, 168, 170
*Taqwa* 101, 114
*Taqiyyah* 100, 147, 149
*tashbih*— 83, 85
*Tasliyah* 100, 147, 149
*Tawhid* 72, 90, 135
*Ta'widh* 16
*Te Deum Laudamus* .157
Temple, the 128, 181
Thamud 28
Thomas, Dylan 14, 77
Torah 105
Turkism 159
Twain, Mark 192
Tyndale, William 59, 173
Tyre 174, 188

### U

*Ummah* 19, 26, 58, 91, 158, 160, 169, 185, 187
*Umm al-Kitab* 80, 97, 98
Umayyad Caliphate 59, 172, 178
United Nations 194, 196
United States 8, 18, 22, 73, 86, 157, 193, 199
—and Israel 194, 195, 196
Updike, John 46
Upper Room, the 139
Usamah bin Laden 19, 26, 159

### V

'very God of very God' 131
Via Dolorosa, the 196
Virginia 27, 179
Voltaire 63, 91

### W

*wahy* 98, 99, 128, 164, 170
Wall, the, in Israel 195
'War on Terror' 18, 76, 195
Washington, George 18, 196
The West 5, 18, 27f., 41, 46, 137, 159, 162, 163, 196, 199
—indictment of 70f., 92, 138, 159, 161, 171, 178, 179, 190, 194
—and the Qur'an 104, 105, 156, 157, 158
'whisperer', the 50f., 77, 178
Wilson, Woodrow 196
Wilde, Oscar 103
'Word made flesh', the 89, 115, 122, 148, 151
World Order, a 6
World Trade Center 6, 8, 119
Wordsworth, William 78, 79, 125

### Y

Yahweh 18, 128, 129, 142, 155, 181, 187, 191
*Al-Yaqin* 84
Yathrib 12, 96
Yazid 172
Yemen, the 141

### Z

*zain* 120
*Zakat* 35, 48, 53, 92
*zann* 15, 54
*zawiya* 157
Zion 35, 147
Zionism 59, 194, 195
*zulm* 170, 202
*zulm al-Gharb* 202
*zulm al-Islam* 202
*zulm al-nafs* 203